*Surviving Terror
and Betrayal Through
Courage and Hope*

KEEPING
MOTHER'S
Secrets

TRACY MAY

Bounceback Press

Contents

Dedication

This book is dedicated to the following people:

Jonathan H. Cable, my dad, who gave his all to fight for me, to love me and to care for me. He became the first father in the State of California who was granted sole custody of a young daughter while the mother was considered a "fit person." In doing so, he saved me from a terrible fate.
I love you Dad.

Mary Jane Knudson, even though she had five kids of her own, she took me into her home and then into her heart. She gave me practical and realistic guidance on a daily basis. She became my surrogate mom and treated me as if I were one of her kids. She never hesitated to stand up for what she believed was in my best interest. She was also very helpful and supportive during the process of writing this book. I wasn't the child of her body, but she is, and forever will be, the mother of my heart.

Elsa L. Gordon, M.D., who diligently worked with me and helped me to recover from the early years of severe abuse that I had suffered as a child. She stood up for me by giving my voice credence and by fighting for my rights and well-being in court.

Joseph F. Di Maria, ESQ, a.k.a. Indian Joe, who, against his better judgment, took on my father's case. Thank you for all of your wonderful stories, for fighting for my rights as a child to be safe and for making it possible for my dad to gain custody of me. Thank you for being my friend.

I dedicate this book to the four of you. Your efforts and sacrifices helped save my life. In every conceivable way, I would have been lost forever without your help and support. I deeply appreciate all you have done.

Acknowledgments

To Jeff, Janie, Rich, Brian and Barry Knudson: my heartfelt appreciation for accepting me into your family and allowing me to be "one of the kids." Thank you for sharing your laughter, friendship, adventures, understanding and love on a daily basis. But, most of all, thank you for sharing your mom.

I am thankful to my Uncle Les, Aunt Nita and their daughters: Linda, Gwen, Leslie and Jean for coming back into my life after so many years of being apart.

I am grateful to the Gibson family for their friendship, kinship and all of the Thanksgiving holidays Dad and I spent with them. Their family and country home in the hills held wonderful adventures and was always a delight to visit.

My thanks to my twenty-eight beta readers. Your comments, feedback, critiques and ideas have been so helpful. Thank you for your interest, support and encouragement.

My special thanks to my family and friends who have taken time from their busy schedules to help me edit all or part of the book, throughout the almost five-year writing process:

Mary Jane Knudson
Linda Malnassy
Harriet Gibson
Rodney May
Sam Pesner
Ed Parecki
Sue Alford
Cary Davis
Trevor May
Lou Malnassy
Gwen Malnassy
Janie (Knudson) Ham

Thank you for your kindness, ideas, advice
and *all* those corrections!

I thank my mother, Kathryn Cable, for giving me her blessing and approval to share our story in the hope that it will help others.

My thanks to each person whose care, assistance, friendship and/or guidance helped me to find my way in life.

Author's Notes

Because of certain content,
Keeping Mother's Secrets is intended for adult readers only.

Keeping Mother's Secrets is the story of my childhood fight to survive the four types of child abuse, including the steps I took to heal, to find happiness and, ultimately, to thrive as an adult.

I wrote *Keeping Mother's Secrets* from my memories. If I couldn't fully remember a situation, I didn't write about it. As a child, I purposely worked diligently to keep my earliest memories vivid, because my memories and experiences were under attack by one of my parents for twisted reasons. I replayed my memories over and over in my mind and used my stuffed animals to reenact some of them. Without my memories, I would have been lost. They were all I had to validate my situation and, at some point during my childhood, I realized that I was holding on to my memories to save my sanity.

After I had written *Keeping Mother's Secrets*, I researched and added legal documents of my family's court records to the story. I also added some of the memories of others who were involved. Part of the story is written as a child would speak, depending on the age and situation.

It is *not* my intention to make anyone look good or bad, or to embellish the story to add to its interest or suspense. It is told as truthfully as humanly possible.

In certain parts of the story, I have added my thoughts. To distinguish my words from others, I put my words in [square brackets]. In a few areas, I have also used square brackets to describe what was happening when others were speaking.

Keeping Mother's Secrets includes an explanation and understanding of the four types of child abuse: physical, mental, neglect and sexual. At times, it is graphic.

I have written *Keeping Mother's Secrets* with the sincere hope that it will interest, engage and enlighten the public. It is also written to give hope to those who have suffered child abuse, while providing insights for the professionals whose job it is to help.

This book is a memoir and is based on my life experiences. However, the name that I use today is not the same name by which I was known during childhood. Also, I have used fictional names to identify my mother and father, who are called Kathryn Cable and Jonathan Cable in this book, and to identify all of the following people: Tom Padmore, Dr. Alan Foster, Dr. Cooley, Dr. Justin Perkins, Dr. James Marshall, Dr. John Archer, Dr. Don Lynwood, Dr. Helen Rothenberg, Dr. Edward Stern, Dr. Daniel Hanson, Mr. Peter Molino, Mr. Rush, Mrs. Hayes, Judge Riley, Judge Rizzo, Dr. Ruth Brown, and Dr. David Mathews. Any similarity between these fictional names and any real people is strictly coincidental.

This book quotes from various legal proceedings in which my family and I were involved. All such material is quoted from court records. However, I have omitted the case numbers and used the fictional names of my parents to identify the parties in these proceedings.

The profits from Keeping Mother's Secrets will be donated to Child Help to help abused children.

1

Living in Terror

A Fight to Survive

San Jose, California

Fear gripped my five-year-old body like a vise. The angry pounding of my mother's spiked heels on the hardwood floor intensified as she walked towards my bedroom.

Through the small opening of my door, I had just witnessed a terrifying fight between my parents. Dad was outside our open front door and Mother was just inside. From my room I could see them both clearly. She was beating him with a pot in one hand and a large frying pan in the other. He raised his hands to ward off the powerful blows. They came with intense rage and great accuracy, confirmed by the blood trickling down the front and left side of his head. His yells and pleas for her to stop were almost drowned out by her high-pitched wild screaming. Bolts of fear shot through my small body as the front door slammed shut and Dad disappeared. Now she was coming for me.

At first, fear glued my feet to the floor as horrible thoughts of what Mother would do to me raced through my mind. The will to live overpowered the grip of fear, which had temporarily paralyzed me. Quickly, I shut my bedroom door and dove under the bed for cover. My door flew open with such force that I thought it would take the wall out with it as the pot and pan, today's weapon of choice, slammed to the floor. Her face came into view as she looked under the bed. It was contorted in anger as she screamed and snarled her intentions to kill me. She could not fit under the bed, so she rolled it one way and then the other as she frantically reached for me. I slid on my belly and managed to keep my distance from her long, clawing red nails that reached out to engulf me in their steel-like grip.

"Help! Daddy, help me!" I screamed.

Mother was livid that I was screaming for Dad and resisting her efforts, which fueled her rage to a level I had never experienced.

"Your daddy is gone! He's not here to save you and I am going to *kill* you!" she shrieked.

Mother shoved the bed to the middle of the room attempting to reach me from all angles, as I continued to scream for help.

"There is no escape. No one is going to save you, Tracy. This is the last day of your life and one day I will kill your father too!"

Scratched, scraped and bleeding from Mother's gouging claws, I managed several times to escape her grasp. Finally, after what felt like an eternity, she gave up and left me alone, slamming the door shut on her way out. I remained under the bed, wide-eyed and gasping for breath, too terrified to move or even make a sound. Then, the house went deadly silent.

Hours passed. Then Mother called to me saying dinner was ready and she wasn't angry anymore. I was still under my bed in the same position where she had left me hours earlier: on my belly, motionless and quiet. I didn't trust that it was safe to come out and remained glued to the floor. I saw her shoes softly approach. She looked under the bed and tried to convince me that it was okay to come out. I didn't speak or move. For a moment, our eyes locked and then she left the room. She returned with a plate of food and a glass of milk, which she left on the floor next to my bed. I didn't touch it. She wanted to kill me, so I thought that perhaps it was poisoned. I stared at the plate, as she walked away. I remained motionless, trying not to breathe. I wished that I could turn invisible, that my mom could be like other kids' moms and that my dad would stay home more often so I could feel a little safer. These wishes would never come true.

The events that led to this particular fight had begun earlier in the day, after Dad had left for work.

That morning Mother told me to collect my beloved cat, "Cinders," and her two kittens as she handed me a box to put them in. I asked why. She explained that they had to go to the vet's office because they were diseased and covered in germs. I had had Cinders since I was three years old and she looked fine to me; so did her kittens. Mother said I was too young to be able to see, as she could, the multitude of germs, which she said covered my pets. So, I put them in the box and climbed into the back of our red and white Ford Fairlane, and we were on our way.

We drove to several vets' offices. Mother would go inside, then quickly return and we would drive on to the next, where the same thing would happen again. Finally, she settled on one. I brought my pets in, terribly concerned that they were sick. The vet came in with the shots, which I assumed would make them better. He grimly looked at my mother and never said a word; then he injected Cinders first. I felt something was wrong and tried to stop him. However, Mother held me back firmly. So, I started asking questions, none of which were answered. Then, I started to panic.

Cinders looked a little woozy after her shot. Neither Mother nor the vet spoke. The vet quickly gave the kittens their injections and left the room. One by one, I watched my most cherished and beloved pets fall over, lie still and quiet. They looked like they were sleeping. They were supposed to be made well again, so I was confused.

"They had to be 'put to sleep' because they had too many germs," Mother announced.

"What does 'put to sleep' mean?"

"It means put to death."

I burst into tears, trying to wake my pets, screaming for the vet to come back and make them alive again.

Mother grabbed me and hauled me out to the car. She threw me into the back seat and we drove away. I kneeled on the backseat looking out the rear window, begging her to go back, as I watched the vet's office slowly disappear from view. Mother had stopped at many vets' offices before she found one that would do what she wanted.

I cried on and off all day thinking of my three lovely kitties lying dead on the vet's table. Mother made me a lunch, which I refused to eat. I thought to myself, *If my kitties had germs and I touched them, maybe I would have germs too. Then maybe she would want me dead too.*

When Dad came home from work, I was waiting for him on the front porch.

"Hi, Baby!" Dad said cheerfully. Then he noticed I was crying and his smile quickly faded.

With tears running down my cheeks, I told Dad what Mother had done to Cinders and her kittens. I saw the emotions on his face change as I told him every detail. He had given Cinders to me two years ago. He knew that Cinders and her kittens were healthy and should not have been put down. When I finished telling him how I watched my precious kitties die, he was furious.

Dad brushed past me and I followed him into the house. He turned toward me and told me to go to my room and play my hi-fi as loud as it would go. I had been told to do this same thing, many times before. I was frightened because I knew my parents were going to fight. However, this was the first, and only time, I was ever brave enough to peek down the hall at them. Nothing could have prepared me for what I saw. I had never seen Mother beat Dad over the head with pots and pans before. Unfortunately, it would not be the last time.

When Life Was New

I was an only child and Dad loved to take pictures of me. Throughout my life, he told me that I was a happy baby and toddler with bright eyes and an easy smile. This was apparent in the multitude of photos he took of me during this time.

Years before I was born, my parents, Kathryn and Jonathan Cable, were having lots of marital difficulties. My mother was also having many physical complaints. However, the army of doctors whom she saw continually could not diagnose anything physically wrong with her. At times, she would say odd things and act unpredictably. My dad told me that shortly after they were married she had told him she "hated men." She would often turn her odd statements into jokes right after she said them.

My parents lived in a small cottage in Los Altos, California. Dad owned a sports store. He had to work long hours, six and sometimes seven days a week. Mother, like most married women in the 1950s and 1960s, was a full-time homemaker. On the day Dad was going to tell Mother that he wanted a divorce, my mother had learned that she was pregnant and told him about her news first. He then felt he could not leave her and did not bring up the subject.

To Dad's surprise, Mother's demeanor seemed to improve almost immediately. Her odd statements and constant need to see doctors declined. She seemed to be happier and more predictable. She busied herself crocheting baby blankets, looking through catalogs for baby-related items and reading everything available about having a healthy pregnancy. She was also starting to receive a lot of attention from family and friends over her long awaited and assumed impossible pregnancy. Dad was happy with the change of events, both with my mother and their marriage. They were both looking forward to my birth.

When I was born, Mother was forty-two and Dad was forty-one. Their marriage was much improved and my dad was thrilled to have a healthy baby girl. He named me Tracy. My mother was happy, but she had her heart set on having a boy whom she would have named Mark. Both my parents told me, or wrote in my baby book, that I was a confident, gentle, curious and engaging toddler who loved to giggle. I also met most of my developmental milestones early.

Mother wrote that my first words, at eleven months, were "Hi!" and "Hi there!" I started talking in full sentences at a very young age. When I was eighteen months old, we moved to San Jose, California. Mother taught me a short prayer, months before I turned two years old: "God is good. Bless our food. Amen." She also wrote that I was happy and had a "sunny disposition." My dad, certain family members and old family friends have told me that I received a wonderful start in life. They all said that I was a happy and normal baby and toddler.

When I started talking and walking, all the attention Mother had been enjoying for some time now started to shift towards me. Dad said that she didn't deal well with this loss and that she began competing with me for attention from others. Soon afterwards, she began another mental decline. He said that she returned to her old unpredictable ways. Now she was even more out of touch with reality, becoming hysterical over certain issues and saying things that were inappropriate or offbeat. Time did not improve things. She continued to deteriorate more severely than at any previous time he had known her. As a result, their marriage began to suffer again.

I have few memories of that early time in my life. Mainly, I remember general feelings or sensations that I later identified as security, love, happiness and having my needs met. Until now, my world was soft, kind, loving and caring. Unfortunately, this was not going to last. As my mother's mind began losing stability, so did my little world.

Memories

The memories of my mother run like old black and white movies in my mind. Some contain daily routines and events like walking to the library twice a day: once to borrow a pile of books and once to return them. She was brilliant and had an IQ of 198. As quickly as she could flip the pages, she had a book read and memorized verbatim. I wondered whether I would be able to read that fast when I grew up.

Mother spent hours playing the piano, filling our house with beautiful music. Sometimes her fingers would move over the keys so quickly they would be a blur. At other times, she would play from songbooks and my parents and I would sing together. *"Home on The Range"* was our favorite song. This song's lyrics were about living in harmony, happiness and peace. This was interesting, as it was completely opposite to my parents' form of communication and lifestyle. Music was a great equalizer in our house. It was the only happy or fun thing that we all enjoyed doing together.

When Mother didn't play the piano, she played records. She played *"The Cry of The Wild Goose"* song so often that I could sing it, in its entirety, at two-and-a-half years of age. She was so proud of this achievement that she had me sing the song for family and friends. I remember this, and I still know all the words. Mother was a great reader, but she didn't read to me, as she couldn't stand the content of children's books. Occasionally, if she was in the mood, she sang bedtime songs to me instead. *"You Are My Sunshine"* was her favorite and she would sing it repeatedly. She would always repeat and emphasize the part of the song about not taking *her* sunshine away, as if fearful that this might happen someday.

Mother always wore bright red lipstick and nail polish. She often made chocolate pudding. I remember watching her pour it into small glass bowls to cool as I waited patiently to lick the spoon. Every Halloween I would help her make popcorn balls for the Trick-or-Treaters. When they were done, we wrapped them in pastel colored saran wrap tied together with matching curly ribbon on top. She loved to cook and when she baked, the house filled with mouth-watering aromas so delicious I could almost taste them. Unfortunately, most memories of Mother were not so pleasant.

I have some fragmented memories from age two-and-a-half, when Mother and I flew to Tampa, Florida to see her parents. This was my only visit with them during my childhood. At my grandparents' house, I remember feeling happy and carefree. Looking back, I recall my grandmother taking care of everything and everyone. I recall floating on a lake in an inner tube and watering the garden with my grandfather. I loved him very much and always wanted to be with him. We stayed with them for six weeks. This trip was a Mother's Day present from my dad.

When Mother and I arrived home, Dad wasn't there. He was in Hawaii visiting his father and stepmother. We flew there to join him. I have a few fragmented memories and feelings about this trip, too. Mother told me it was going to be a big surprise for my dad and he would be so happy to see us. I was excited to surprise him and happy to go. However, when we arrived he was not happy at all. Instead, he was very angry. I remember being confused and terribly disappointed. I wondered why he wasn't happy to see us. My parents began fighting and I was afraid.

Later, as an adult, I learned that money had been tight and Dad had not planned for our trip. To pay for our tickets and accommodations, Mother had used all of the money in our family emergency fund. He was furious about this and arguments ensued. Money wasn't my dad's only issue. Grandfather was in the process of negotiating a deal with Dad to join him in his very lucrative and long-standing Honolulu-based business. Dad knew that the presence of Mother, with her behavior issues, would be detrimental to these negotiations.

Grandfather had developed Bright's disease and his doctor told him he was terminal. He wanted to travel more and enjoy what time he had left. This is why he wanted Dad to become a partner with him and eventually take over his business. My parents and I would then live half the year in California and the other half in Hawaii.

When Mother and I showed up unexpectedly, Grandfather changed his mind about the partnership.

"If you can't control your wife and family matters, how can I ever trust that you will be able to control my business? Forget it, John, the deal is off." Just like that, the offer was terminated. This quote was not from my childhood memories, but from my dad. He told me this story and quotation many times, when I was an adult.

The entire trip was very unpleasant. My grandparents were irritated and my parents were always fighting. It was clear to me that Mother and I were not welcome. I felt unwanted by Dad. He treated me as if I had done something wrong. I remember feeling very sad, ashamed and guilty when I was around him. However, I didn't have a choice in the matter. He left for home a few days earlier than he had planned. I wanted to go home with him, but he told me I had to stay with Mother. I cried and begged but the answer was still "No." Mother and I stayed a while longer. Knowing something was terribly wrong, I felt uneasy and more frightened.

Doctors, Germs and Reality

Most of my early, vivid and connected memories of Mother began around age three. I learned the hard way never to challenge or deny my mother's reality.

One day, I was on Mother's lap and we were having fun playing by touching each other's face. All of a sudden the mood changed.

"Ouch! You poked me in the eye!" Mother accused.

I shook my head no.

All the fun came crashing to a halt. I was touching Mother's face but my hands were nowhere near her eyes. She was angry with me and kept accusing me of hurting her eye. When I denied it, she became furious. She spanked me and threw me crying into the back seat of the car. As she drove us to an eye doctor's office, she told me she would *prove* that I poked her in the eye.

The doctor took Mother into his exam room and I stayed in the waiting room with her stern orders to sit and be quiet. I did what I was told. After quite some time, the doctor finally brought her out to the waiting room. She was smiling and seemed happy. He asked me to come into his exam room, while she waited in the waiting room. I sat down on the examination chair and looked at all the testing equipment. He showed me how it worked and even let me play with some of it as he told me how he used it to help people improve their vision. His hair was as white as his lab coat and his eyes were deep blue. I also remember that he was very kind.

After the doctor and I played and talked for a while, he said that my mother told him that I had poked my finger into her eye. I started to feel anxious and denied it. He calmed me by telling me that there was nothing wrong with her eye. I remember feeling relieved that he believed me. However, a few minutes later the doctor said he wanted me to run up to her saying that I was sorry for poking her in the eye and then give her a big hug! I didn't understand. Why should I be sorry when I hadn't done anything wrong? He wanted me to *act* as if I had poked her and that I was very sorry. I told him I wouldn't do it. He explained that it was very important because he wanted to see how she would react to me. It took him a while to convince me to deliver my lines like a little actress, but he was a nice man -- so I finally agreed.

We went to the waiting room and I ran to Mother. Saying that I was sorry, I leapt into her arms. She said that she forgave me and, after all, I was just a small child; accidents like that could understandably happen. I looked up at the doctor, who was looking at us. Looking back, I realize that he was studying us intently. He saw me looking at him and gave me a warm smile. I smiled back. He opened the door for us and I waved as she carried me out to the car. It was a great act and it worked. It made my mother happy again.

Mother seemed to be addicted to doctors. We went to see them often. She frequently told me that she could see germs everywhere. According to her, my germs were "very potent." She taught me not to share food I had partly eaten or any glass from which I'd been drinking. She told me my germs were strong enough to kill other people. Because of this, I was not allowed to kiss anyone on the lips, as they would be made seriously ill from direct mouth-to-mouth contact with me. It was my first lesson that part of me was "bad."

The germ lesson hit home when I became seriously ill, just a month before my fourth birthday. When I was an adult, Dad told me that I had high fevers, headaches and swelling in my brain, which caused me to go completely blind. During this time, I lived in the Stanford Hospital's ICU/ Isolation Ward. He told me that I was in and out of comas, lasting up to five days.

The doctors ordered an encephalogram and repeated the test when the doctors thought they saw a tumor. To perform this test they drilled holes into my skull and x-rayed my brain. This was before MRIs or CAT scans! The test results were normal, but some of the doctors were convinced I had a tumor and wanted to operate immediately.

Dad told me that Mother had hired many doctors to make a diagnosis and a treatment plan. There was a 50% chance of surviving the operation. Dad was against this surgery for a "phantom" brain tumor. He also didn't like the survival odds, not to mention the question of my ability to function after major brain surgery, if I survived. In the 1960s, the man of the house was the legal "head of household." Dad interviewed these doctors and dismissed all but one, David Mathews, a neurosurgeon who was against performing surgery for a brain tumor they couldn't find. Mother went ballistic. She wanted the surgery and believed my dad was denying me a "lifesaving operation." I had just turned four years old.

I remember being terribly sick and completely blind. People were constantly holding me down for painful and intrusive tests, which deepened my confusion and fear. Anytime I heard someone enter the room, talk to me or try to touch me, I became terrified. I went to the furthest corner of my cage-like crib and prepared to defend myself against whatever horrors that were going to happen next.

Dr. Mathews did not believe the brain tumor theory. He believed I had an unknown disease, which he called "Virus X." He wanted to take a conservative approach. However, my health continued to decline. Virus X was killing me. The doctors could not slow it down, stop it or cure it. He prepared my parents for the worst, telling them that I could die at any time.

A frequent customer of Dad's came in the store one day and asked how I was doing. Dad told him that the doctors said I was not expected to live. Days later, the man returned with a small wind up music box in the shape of a house, which he had made for me. When the music played, the top of the house opened and there was a girl dancing inside. I played the music box all the time, but could only feel the figure of the dancing girl. Then, one day I told my dad that I could see that the girl was wearing a red dress! As the swelling in my brain slowly decreased, my sight returned, as did my health. It was wonderful just to be able to see again! I must have dropped that music box a hundred times, but Dad always fixed it and it still works today.

The sight I regained was evaluated at 20/20, but I had many small blind spots in both eyes. These blind spots made near-vision tasks like learning to read and seeing things below chest level (like uneven pavement or stair steps) a real challenge. However, my distance vision was much less affected. I was left with slightly less coordination and was physically slower than before. My eyes, which shone brightly in younger photos, looked dimmer, and mentally I was a little slower. Despite these issues, I made a good recovery, which amazed everyone.

Before the age of four, I knew what it was like to be seriously ill. Mother used this disease to further her lessons of how potent my germs were, as she literally pounded this point into me repeatedly. In doing so, she made me hyper-aware that my saliva had the power to make others just as ill as I had been or worse. In reality, my mouth wasn't the problem. What was coming out of my mother's mouth was pure poison.

Crazy Making

Mother often heard voices in the kitchen and master bedroom walls. When she told Dad about this, he thought that maybe she was hearing the refrigerator in the kitchen. However, it wasn't the refrigerator or any other household noise. She insisted that she could clearly hear someone talking in the walls. Dad told her it simply was not so. She didn't believe him and they argued about it. From then on, every time she would say someone was in the wall talking, he would deny it. He would often laugh at her, saying she should get her ears checked and other things to make fun of her. All these approaches ended in disaster, as she would become completely unglued and lose it on him, screaming and often becoming violent.

One day, after Dad left for work, Mother called for me from the master bedroom. I was three or four years old and powerless to refuse her. She looked up and saw me standing in the doorway.

"Come in here, Tracy; Daddy is in the wall talking."

This was a dangerous subject and I was afraid. My parents had fought many times about this issue. As I entered, Mother pointed to a spot on the wall. I put my little ear against it and listened. Hearing no sounds, I looked up at Mother, keeping my ear pressed firmly to the wall and my mouth shut. My brain was racing and my heart was keeping pace. I thought to myself, *If I say that I can't hear Daddy's voice, then maybe she will get mad and hurt me.*

"I can hear Daddy talking," I replied eagerly.

She immediately dropped to her knees and hugged me for a long time.

"I knew you would be able to hear him! I knew it!" Mother cried. "After all, you're *my* baby! I love you so much, Tracy!"

It was as if my validation saved Mother from something awful, yet completely unknown to me. In that rare moment, she was completely relieved and happy -- and so was I!

Somewhere between this experience and the experience with the eye doctor, I began to understand that telling my mother what she wanted to hear was often safer than telling her the truth.

Even at this young age, I thought that the walls would be too thin for people to be inside them, but I wasn't completely certain of this. Later, when Mother was busy elsewhere, I went back to the same wall. There was a section of the wall, which extended into the closet. I put my hands on each side of the wall to measure its width. The space between the walls was small and my dad was big; I knew there was no way he could fit in there. Of course, I never told my mother.

When Mother went on a tirade with Dad, I learned to hide under my bed for protection. Many of these tirades took place after I was put to bed for the evening. Sometimes, I would hear her screaming threats that she would stab him with a knife as he slept. Whenever I heard her screaming at him, I would quickly grab my pillow and blanket and dive under my bed for cover. I hid there all night hoping and praying that I would be safe. As time went on and years passed, I spent many more nights under my bed than I did on top of it.

Mother told me that she could *see* germs in the tap water. Then, a man came to the house and took a sample to test it. This happened on many occasions. Of course, he never found any germs.

When we were out driving, Mother would claim that people were following us. She had me watch the traffic behind us for cars that she thought looked suspicious. She said that the drivers were sneaky and changed cars and drivers often, so I had to watch very carefully. She took down the license plate numbers and told my dad about it. When I was able to identify numbers and letters, I would relay the plate info to her as she drove and she would write it down. She was happy that I was helping her and would often praise me for doing so. In this moment, I was happy too; because I felt safe.

Mother would occasionally smell odd odors in the house and I would try to help her sniff them out. I was at a disadvantage though, because I couldn't smell them to begin with; but I didn't let her know that. I just tried to help her find them. When Dad came home, he tried to find the source of the smells, too. It was funny, as all three of us were running around the house sniffing here and there.

Sniffing for smells, which Dad and I could never smell to begin with, and checking for all those cars, which were supposed to be following us, was all fun and games to me. However, these were not games to Mother -- they were her reality. Between three and four years old, I started to realize that she could hear, see and smell things that Dad and I could not. Secretly, in my own mind, I started to wonder why.

After a while, the cars and odd smells went the same way as the people talking in the walls. Dad denied their existence. He teased Mother about them or told her that it was all "crazy thinking." Fights ensued and the war between the two of them raged on. When the war became violent, I would "hide in the trenches" (under my bed) covering my ears tightly.

Some mornings, I was jolted awake by Mother yelling, "Tracy, get back in bed right now!"

I was of course already in bed and told this to Mother.

"I can hear you running around the house. *You woke me up!* Now get back in bed this instance!"

"Mommy, I am in bed, honest!" I replied.

"YOU ARE *LYING!* GET BACK IN BED *NOW* OR I WILL SPANK YOU!" she screamed back.

"I *am* in bed; not running around the house. Mommy, you woke *me* up, yelling!"

Mother was unconvinced and continued screaming at me. I started crying, wishing I could turn invisible. Sometimes my dad would come in my room to check on me and report to her that I was actually in bed. By the time he finally came in, I was often confused and inconsolable. However, when Dad wasn't home, she would get up and go to the kitchen to get her wooden spoon. As I heard her returning down the hall towards my room, I knew what was going to happen.

Mother walked into my room and found me in bed, as

long. She grabbed me, despite my pleas and
, turned me over and angrily spanked me for
ˉhis seemed to run in cycles. It would hap-
 μ·ıı every day for a while. Then, for no reason, she would
stop doing it for an indeterminate amount of time. Later, she
would reintroduce it, forcing the cycle to repeat itself again
and again.

This type of abuse happened from the time of my earliest memories. It hurt me mentally and emotionally, as well as
physically. In between the ages of three and six years old, I
started to doubt myself. I wondered whether I was truly in bed
or not, and questioned whether I was lying or telling the truth
about this. I became uncertain and confused. I thought I knew
the truth, but my mother said I didn't. I thought I was in bed,
but my mother said I wasn't.

This was all going on as I was learning language and
concepts, distinguishing what was real from make believe,
right from wrong and truth from untruth. I was confused
and, at times, did not know how to think correctly. Mother
was teaching me to doubt my own reality, which was *crazy
making*.

Where Mother was concerned, I never knew what to expect
next. She could be having a good day, but the smallest thing
could send her immediately spinning out of control. I believe,
looking back, that she was distressed and overwhelmed with
her own issues and personal problems. Life with Mother was a
wild rollercoaster ride with sunny skies one moment and F-5
category tornados the next. Unfortunately, I was in the direct
path of her rage. I was an easy target, a whipping post, used to
vent her vicious outbursts in the form of painful physical and
emotional punishment that often led to torture.

Punishments and Tortures

Mother excelled at inventing creative tortures and pun-ishments for me. Some even became ritualistic. Most were brought on because she was angry or upset about things that I had nothing to do with, didn't understand and were beyond my control. Looking back, I believe she used me in this capac-ity to momentarily relieve her rage and, at times, to have me witness how miserable she felt by making me just as miserable.

As time went on, some of these punishments and tortures became common practice. Mother took advantage of the fact that I was available, defenseless, vulnerable, impressionable and frightened. If I did something wrong she would usually com-pletely lose it with me, often leaving me fearing for my life. From my earliest memories until six-and-a-half years of age, I was forced to endure these punishments and tortures.

The easiest punishment for me to endure was when Moth-er decided to invite my neighborhood friends over for so-called "parties." She would bake delicious treats to eat and have fun games to play. However, I was not allowed to join in or enjoy any of it. I was made to sit on a chair in the corner of the room and watch in silence for the entire duration. She warned me that if I got up or engaged in any way, I would be severely pun-ished in front of all of my friends. When my friends arrived, my mother told them that I was upset or simply not feeling well to explain my sitting alone. All of the kids always had a wonderful time, as I sat and watched. After everyone had left, she forced me to clean up the mess in silence. God help me if I uttered a sound!

Mother's favorite and most frequently used punishment and torture was to hold my hand over a candle flame or some-times a hot stove burner. There were times that she would use my arm for this purpose as well. However, she favored using a candle flame and my hand. She always had a butcher knife next to her, within easy reach. She told me if I resisted in any way that she would "stab me to death" or "slit my throat." I don't know when she started this type of punishment and torture, but I can remember it back to my earliest memories.

Mother was usually calm and methodical while administering this particular form of abuse, which was out of character for her and very eerie. If she spoke, her voice was flat and lifeless. I think when she was calm and quiet she was more depressed than angry. In a trance-like state, she would hold the palm of my hand firmly at different levels above a candle's flame or the hot stove burner. High above the flame, she would move my hand slowly back and forth heating my flesh gradually. When she lowered my hand closer to the flame, she would move it back and forth more quickly. At times, she would move my hand away from the intense heat altogether, only to return it after my flesh had cooled. She would take her time doing this abuse. Sometimes she would set a timer, for up to an hour. As always, I had to remain still and endure this torture, not knowing whether I would catch on fire or be seriously burned.

Looking back, I think Mother's intention was more to terrorize me, as this type of abuse had a lot more to do with mental torture. She rarely did serious physical harm to me and usually only burned me slightly. She occasionally burned me enough to raise blisters, but took great care not to permanently scar me. My skin was usually bright pink or red when she was finished.

To a little child, a candle flame looks much bigger than it actually is and I would watch in wide-eyed fear, as Mother slowly roasted me. At times, it was very painful. I was rarely brave enough to look at her face. When I did, I was horrified by her twisted smile. Many years later, I realized she was looking at me sadistically.

If I cried or pleaded with Mother to stop, I was often slapped or spanked. Sometimes she would hold the blade of the butcher knife to my throat, threatening to kill me if I didn't "shut up." When I fell silent, she would simply go back to torturing me again. There were also the rare times that she allowed me to cry and beg for mercy. When she was upset, she was extremely unpredictable and, at times, very dangerous. These situations were terrifying for me. I never knew how far she would go or whether, at any moment, she would fly into a rage and kill me.

Then, one horrible day, I spilled my milk during lunch. Mother flipped out and screamed her intentions to burn me alive as she collected and lit the candle. Her face contorted as her rage grew. She grabbed my hand and yanked me over to the burning candle, holding my palm close to the flame. I was so terrified that I accidentally wet myself, which formed a puddle on the kitchen floor. It was like throwing gasoline on a roaring fire. She blew up, shrieking her threats at me as she went to the drawer where she kept her wooden spoon.

Words tumbled out of my mouth, as I pleaded with Mother, saying that I was sorry and hadn't done it on purpose. I begged her not to hurt me. All of a sudden, she grabbed me and threw me towards the kitchen table. She bent me over and with the wooden spoon gave me a horrifying bare bottom spanking. When she finished with that, I was crying hysterically. She pulled me back to the candle and slowly forced the palm of my hand down onto the flame, extinguishing it and rubbing my hand into the candle's hot wick, torturously searing my flesh. I screamed. She threw me down on the floor in the puddle of cold urine and left me there crying, burnt and blistered.

As the years passed, the regular "burn sessions" became less frightening because the frequency and regularity of these events became commonplace. Mother was usually calm, flat and devoid of emotion. The sequence of events became more predictable. By the time I was six, I had become emotionally numb to the "burn sessions" and sometimes went into a trance-like state. I often focused on the oven clock, watching the minutes tick by and wondering when it would be over.

Whenever I bore the marks of Mother's abuse, she would keep me home until my wounds had healed. She would inform Pre-school, Kindergarten, first grade and friends that I was "sick." Dad didn't notice these injuries because I was often asleep by the time he came home, if he came home. Mother kept me away from others until my wounds had healed. Most of the time I couldn't identify the triggers which inspired her actions. Looking back as an adult, I realized that often there were no triggers.

Mother also used needles, pins, forks, combs and knives as weapons of punishment and torture. She would usually take me to the sofa with a needle or pin and poke my tender flesh. Sometimes she would make me bleed and sometimes not. I was scared to death of needles and once she started this form of torture, it seemed to go on forever. Again, this was used more to terrorize me than to do severe physical harm.

When using forks, Mother would hold the prongs to my skin and press them in to hurt me. Sometimes this would cause little bruises. She would take her time doing this and, if I cried, she would scratch my inner arms with the prongs to punish me for my tears. This caused me more pain and, at times, made me bleed.

Sometimes Mother would hold a sharp butcher knife against my skin and act as if she was going to use it. Sometimes she would do this to my arms and legs. Most of the time she would hold the knife with the point touching my chest, as if she were going to stab me. She also placed the blade across my throat and threatened to slit me ear to ear. Once, I remember her piercing my skin with the sharp tip and leaving a small cut where the blade had been placed against my throat. The latter, I was told, was my fault for moving.

Sometimes, after I was completely terrified, crying and begging for my life, Mother would release me. However, there were times when she would keep on going and ignore me.

During some of these punishments and tortures, Mother was silent. When she did talk, she would often tell me that I was being punished for being born a girl. Sometimes she said I was being punished for simply being born.

When Mother's hair was tangled, as it often was, she would call me to her and slap my inner arms with the comb or score them with its teeth, so I could "feel her pain." If I moved or re-sisted in any way, I would be slapped, hit, pinched or spanked. Then, as always, she would start the original abuse over again, as if she hadn't done enough. Sometimes she would just sit and cry which made me fearful and sad. Then I would cry too.

After the punishment and torture sessions, Mother always warned me that if I told my dad or anyone else, she would kill us as we slept. At times, she went into detail as to how she would kill us. She told me, repeatedly, that she would wait for my dad and me to go to sleep and then she would stab us to death or slit our throats. Knives seemed to be her favorite weapon choice for this particular atrocity. Sometimes she would say that instead of using the knife, which would be too messy, she might strangle my dad and me or suffocate us as we slept. However, death by stabbing us was definitely her preference. These warnings were given after most every episode of her abuse.

I completely believed that my mother would follow through with her threats. Therefore, I kept my mouth tightly shut. All of these events caused severe emotional and mental anguish, which I experienced in many ways. Some included the following thoughts and feelings: that Mother didn't love me, so therefore I must be unlovable; that all these bad things happened because of me; that I was just plain bad and should never have been born. My life was a mess. I was a very sad, hurt and empty little girl. I lived in a state of high anxiety, terrified about what would happen to me next.

As time went by, Mother would check in with me and ask if I was still keeping "our little secrets?" The answer was always yes.

The Knife

In my fourth year, I learned certain techniques to calm Mother down when she was enraged. I also learned how to distract her when she was on a dangerous decline. Sometimes it worked and sometimes it didn't. I learned to do exactly what I was told, and to respond to Mother instantly. Not to do so would risk the unleashing of frightening consequences.

These new survival skills helped me to be safer, although the ritualistic "burning sessions" with my hands and arms continued.

One day, I found a big knife under Mother's pillow. I took it out and looked at it. I had heard her tell Dad, during their many fights, that she would kill him one night as he slept. I remembered the many warnings she had given me with a knifepoint pushed against my chest or with the blade across my throat. I thought of her many warnings not to tell Dad or anyone else about the abuse I had suffered or she would slit both Dad's and my throat as we slept. My young mind wondered if the knife was under her pillow to be within easy reach for that purpose. Holding and looking at the knife, I became extremely frightened of what she planned to do with it.

Terrified that Mother would catch me with it, I quickly put the knife back under her pillow. After that, I avoided my parents' room like "the Plague." When Dad was home, I could run and hide behind him when I was frightened of Mother. Unfortunately, he was seldom home during my waking hours -- except on Sunday and sometimes in the morning before he left for work.

When Dad was home, he often sharpened all of the knives in the house. He would use a knife stone to accomplish this task. Knowing the plan my mother had for some of those knives and watching him sharpen them sent chills down my spine. Sometimes he would notice me watching him. He would smile at me and I remember running away from him. I was very frightened as I wondered if Dad knew he was sharpening knives that might be used to slit our throats.

Whenever Dad would play with me, hold me or let me sit on his lap Mother would turn it into a shameful event. She would accuse him of getting "sexual pleasure." He would, of course, deny it and tell her that she was "nuts" to think such a thing. This would bring on yet another fight. I was too young to know what sexual pleasure meant, but I knew from the fights I witnessed that it was something to feel shameful about. Days after these events, Mother couldn't let this go. She told me that I was dirty and bad to play with my dad and I should never let him touch me. I remember feeling so guilty and ashamed of myself. He no longer wanted to interact with me, which further reinforced these feelings. Then my dad stopped playing with me altogether. It got to a point where he only touched me when absolutely necessary. He often gave me "special treats" like M&M's and popsicles.

Unfortunately, I witnessed most of my parents' fights. Sometimes they would end by Dad packing his clothes and leaving the house. He had a makeshift bedroom in the back room of his store where he slept when he didn't stay at a motel. He stayed away for days, weeks and sometimes longer.

One day, without warning, Mother packed my bags and took me to her friend's house. She told me that she had to go visit someone for a week. She stated that I would have more fun if I stayed with her friends, because they had three kids around my age. I knew them and liked playing with them. It was fun and a little wild at their house. No one was yelling or hurting anyone and the rules all made sense. She left me there for longer than a week, with no contact. Finally, she came back for me. I never knew what she did or where she went.

When I turned five years old, my world took a turn for the worse. Mother severely restricted opportunities for me to play with other children. We became more and more isolated from friends, family and neighbors. She became increasingly unstable, unpredictable and violent. She had my beloved Cinders and her kittens killed, while I was made to watch and then I witnessed the terrible fight that followed. Dad stayed away from the house for many weeks at a time, leaving me even less protected than ever before.

The tortures and punishments increased. For my own survival, I became very quiet and hyper-alert to any event, any slight change of mood or tonality that might signal my mother becoming enraged. Inside I was speeding up and becoming hyperactive. Also, at five and throughout most of my sixth year, I resigned myself to Mother's new daily routine of taking me into my room in the afternoon and giving me a terrible bare bottom spanking with a wooden spoon. Often stripping me naked before she began, she told me repeatedly what a terrible disappointment I was to her and that this was my punishment for being born a girl. I blamed myself and felt completely ashamed. I thought, *I must be very bad to deserve all these punishments.* I felt completely unlovable.

My cousins Linda and Gwen came to visit us for a week. Gwen was seven and Linda was nine.

When we were adults, Gwen told me, "Every afternoon around three o'clock your mother would take you into your bedroom and spank you really hard. Linda and I couldn't figure out what you did to deserve this, because you hadn't done anything wrong. I was always afraid and worried that your mother might start hitting Linda and me, too."

My cousins had no idea what the spankings were all about.

Soon after my cousins went home, Mother taught me to do sexual things to her. This included fondling her breasts and kissing them, inserting things into her vagina and bringing her to an orgasm. She also taught me to pull my nipples and fondle my breasts. These sessions were very frightening, and the knife was always within easy reach. She would become very fixated that I should have been born a boy. Some of the punishments took on a bizarre sexual content and I became terrified to see anybody naked, especially my mother. I became very ashamed of my body. She taught me that my "privates" were "bad parts" and, to further her lesson, she would hurt them. I felt so bad about my body; I couldn't even look at myself in the bathroom mirror without clothes on. I also felt terribly guilty for being a girl.

Through this type of abuse, I became somewhat sexually confused as to whether I should feel and think like a boy or a girl. Mother would dress me in dresses to keep up appearances. However, she praised me for acting boyish and the punishments were less if I did. All of this was very confusing, as I remember being made to feel very guilty about who I was.

As an adult I wondered whether Mother wanted me to be born a boy to replace the five-month-old male fetus she had

had aborted during a back-room procedure, before she had met my dad. I also wondered if she had created these bizarre sexual punishments to punish me for that child's death.

When Dad was home, he showed me little to no affection. Mother warned him to "keep his filthy hands off me." Then she would take her anger toward him out on me. On two occasions, he tried to take me for a ride in the car -- once around the block, so I could have an opportunity to ride in the front seat and once to go out for an ice cream cone. On both occasions, Mother grabbed a chair and sat behind the car so he couldn't back out of the driveway.

Dad had become a stranger to me, who sometimes lived with us.

One day, when I thought Mother was busy in the kitchen, I ventured to peak under her pillow to see if the knife was still there, and it was! Before I could put the pillow back in place she walked into the bedroom and caught me! I thought she would be angry and hurt me with another punishment. However, she remained calm.

"Does the knife scare you?" Mother asked.

"Yes," I replied, fearfully.

"I keep the knife under my pillow just in case someone breaks in at night, so I can defend us."

I had enough experience with Mother and knives to know this wasn't true, but said nothing. She wanted me not to be afraid, but I was. She also warned me not to tell my dad or anyone else and, as always, I promised to keep her secret.

Putting an End to Me

At five years of age, Mother started giving me iron in large quantities. I remember the liquid filled dropper coming towards me and being ordered to open my mouth to receive it. She often gave it to me several times a day. It's a wonder that I didn't die from iron poisoning. Perhaps the thing that saved me was that I was always on the anemic side. Unfortunately, my baby teeth were not as lucky. I had eighteen cavities at one dental visit! When the dentist inquired about any liquid supplements that I might be taking, Mother told him about the liquid iron. However, she was evasive as to the amount involved. The dentist told her that liquid iron could be responsible for the cavities because it was mixed with sugary syrup. However, not knowing the amount she administered, he blamed the cavities on drinking juice or milk before bedtime. When Dad found out about the cavities he hit the roof and he and my mother got into a verbal confrontation. I hid under my bed, feeling guilty. I knew it was all my fault.

Mother discontinued the liquid iron and started to give me iron pills. She forced me to swallow three to five iron pills each day. In the beginning, she inspected my mouth to be certain I was actually swallowing them. I decided to pretend to look forward to the pills every day, to win her trust. Soon she was satisfied that I was swallowing and no longer made her inspections. I hid the pills in my closed mouth. After I drank some water and made a big gulping sound, as if I had swallowed, she told me to go play. I would go to the bathroom to flush them down the toilet or to the backyard behind the hedge lining the fence to spit them out. However, if she seemed to be suspicious of me, punitive or acting more unpredictable than usual, I would simply swallow them.

One evening Dad came home and looked at the iron pill bottle he had just purchased days before. It was almost half-empty. He asked Mother about it and she said she had just caught me with the bottle, "Eating the iron pills as if they were candy!" (She didn't mention that she was the one forcing them down my throat!) She then flew into a rage ranting about how angry she was with me that I was *stealing* pills! He tried to calm her down, but she went to the kitchen drawer to get her wooden spoon. I begged Dad to stop her, telling him that I didn't take the pills, but he ignored me as he stared at the bottle. She gave me a horrible spanking, in front of him, and then sent me to bed without dinner.

Later that night, after Mother was asleep, Dad came to my room and sat on my bed.

"Did you take those iron pills?" he asked softly.

"No," I whispered.

After some discussion, Dad believed me. I didn't tell him I was spitting them out, because I didn't want another spanking for wasting them! When Mother wasn't around to notice, Dad started checking the iron pill bottle, daily. He was concerned that she was feeding me too many iron pills, but he did nothing about it. After this, she tried to convince him, my doctor and anyone else who would listen that I had a compulsion to take pills and often stole them when no one was looking.

Along with the iron pills, Mother started to force me to take other pills. I was suspicious of this because we hadn't been to the doctor and the pills came from a big box where she kept all of her prescription drugs. Ever since I was very little, I always had the fear that she would poison me. When she gave me these pills and the water to wash them down, they were small enough that I could hide them under my tongue. As when I first started the iron pills, after I swallowed the water she would inspect my mouth to be sure they were gone. Thankfully, she never thought of looking under my tongue! When she was done with me, I disposed of the pills.

One summer morning, after I had recovered from a

torturous burn session where my mother deliberately blistered my arm with the stove burner, she abruptly announced that we were going to spend the rest of the day at the coast. I was eager to go and jumped into the backseat of our car. However, an eerie feeling came over me as we drove in silence.

It took forever to get to the coast.

As the ocean came into view, my mother started talking to me. "We are not going to the beach. I'm taking us to the cliffs," she announced in a tense, flat tone.

I wondered why we were not going to the beach, but said nothing.

Mother drove down several side streets and finally chose one that was fairly flat and dead-ended at the top of a cliff. She pulled over, parked and then told me her intentions of pushing the car off the cliff, with me in it!

"You will die, Tracy, but since you believe in God you will probably go to heaven," Mother said in a calm, flat, lifeless tone completely devoid of emotion. Then she added, "I will make sure that it looks like an accident. It will appear that the car just rolled off the cliff. I will tell everyone how I tried to stop the car to save you, but couldn't."

I was stunned and couldn't believe my ears.

Mother pulled the car into the center of the street, facing the ocean. She put the car in neutral and jumped out. Dad always said she was "strong as an ox," but I didn't know how strong she was until that day. I started to panic and tried to get out. She blocked me and pushed me back into the car. The reality of my situation hit me. Panic overtook me as I continued to struggle to get out of the car. I kept pushing against Mother with all my might, trying to get past her. I was making a little headway until she became enraged at my efforts and started hitting and kicking me as she shoved me back into the car. I slid across the seat to the opposite door and quickly hopped out. Before I could run away, she was on top of me, grabbing me by the hair and shoulders as she threw me back into the car like a little rag doll. I jumped to my feet and tackled her with all my strength trying to break free of the car, which was to become my coffin. Again, I was thrown back in the car as Mother punched, kicked and hit me. I was cut, bruised and bleeding. I opened the door again and she punched me with all her might. I flew backwards, onto the backseat. I wasn't strong enough to escape.

I was crying hysterically as I kneeled on the backseat and watched Mother walk around to the back of the car. I begged and pleaded with her not to kill me. I yelled that I would be good and do whatever she wanted me to, if she would just stop and take me home. Her face was contorted in anger as she ignored my pleas. She struggled at first as she rocked the car back and forth to get it rolling towards the cliff. As it picked up a little speed, I looked over my shoulder in horror and could see that we were gaining on the ocean. I screamed and pleaded for her to stop as I pounded my fists on the rear window ledge, but she kept on pushing. I had been burned, beaten and kicked and was now in total meltdown. I knew I was going to die. I screamed a prayer to God to please make the car stop, but there didn't seem much chance that that would happen.

Then, I noticed the car was slowing down. There was a small incline in the road, before the cliff. The car slowed, and then came to a complete stop just a few feet from the edge. Mother was pushing with all her might to make it go forward again. Despite her efforts, the car slowly rolled backwards. She was still pushing against the retreating car, ending up walking backwards with it. The car finally came to a stop. She wasn't finished with her plan. Again, she pushed the car and it began to roll towards the cliff. The same thing happened again. I *knew* God was protecting me. I was still shaking and crying. As the car was rolling backwards, I watched her run around to the front of the car and pushed it backwards. I was confused as to why she was doing this. The car rolled quite some distance away from the cliff before it stopped.

My first thought was that Mother had changed her mind about killing me and that maybe this ordeal was finished. Those thoughts were soon shattered as I realized that she just wanted to get some more distance from the cliff for a running start! When the car stopped, I also realized I had an opportunity to try to save myself. As she ran to the back of the car to start pushing it toward the cliff again, I jumped out and ran as fast as I could. She wasn't expecting this and I ran right past her. She screamed at me to stop, but I didn't listen and was quickly putting distance between us. It was useless though. We were in a deserted area and there was nobody there to save me. I kept running until I felt my mother's hand gripping my shoulder. As she spun me around, I lost my footing and landed hard on the road, painfully scraping my hands and knees, which were bleeding. She grabbed me by my hair and yanked me to my feet as I screamed out my pain and rage.

Mother was livid and hit me repeatedly as she brutally yanked me back to the car. When she threw me into the back-seat, I was completely exhausted. She slammed the door behind me, went behind the car and started to push. The car moved forward and then picked up speed. It was going much faster than before. This time I knew she would be successful. Again, I screamed at her to stop, which had no effect. I was in a lot of pain and wondered how much more it would hurt when I died. I felt sad that I would never see Dad, my beloved Nan or any of my friends ever again. Mother was now running behind the car and it was going faster. When the car reached the incline, it began to slow, but kept moving forward.

All of a sudden, the front dropped as the car came to an abrupt stop. My body was thrown forward. Mother kept trying to push the car forward with all her might, but the car wouldn't budge. She exploded in anger, then jumped in and started the car. She tried to back it up, but couldn't. She turned around and slapped me hard across the face. The blow sent me reeling into the far reaches of the backseat. She told me to stay in the car, and what she would do to me if I disobeyed her. She said she needed to find a phone. I watched her walk away until she was out of sight. Then, I got out of the car and examined the front tires, which I was amazed to see had gone over the cliff! The body of the car was resting on the incline. Part of the incline was wedged between the back of the front tires and the car.

I stood there for a while looking out to sea. Suddenly I realized how slowly I was breathing as the salty sea air flowed in and out of my lungs. The day was gloomy with gray clouds. At some point, time seemed to stop. God had answered my prayer after all. My body hurt all over, but I felt very lucky to be alive!

Mother was gone for what seemed to be an eternity. At some point, I decided to get back into the car so she wouldn't come back and catch me outside. When she returned, she told me that she went to a house and used their phone to call a tow-truck. She warned me to keep my head down and not to say a word to the tow-truck man. She looked very tired. The tow-truck man finally came and pulled the car back onto the road. The car seemed to be unaffected by the experience.

The tow-truck guy tapped on the backseat window to get my attention. Remembering Mother's warning, I kept my head down and refused to look at him. He hung around in his truck after he was done. She nervously waited for him to leave. When it was obvious he wasn't going to leave anytime soon, she started the car and drove away from the cliff.

Looking back, I think the tow-truck driver probably saved my life. At first, I thought Mother was going to look for another place to kill me. I curled up in a ball on the floor of the backseat, wedging myself tightly behind the base of the driver's seat. I thought if she tried to push me off another cliff that this would be the safest place for me. I didn't make a sound as we drove. After a while, I realized we were going home, but I still didn't move. She warned me if I ever told anyone about today, she would slit my throat. I promised to keep it a secret.

When we arrived home, I ran inside the house and dove under my bed for protection, reopening the fresh scabs on my knees from the earlier scrapes. On my belly, I watched my bedroom door slam shut. I stayed under my bed afraid to move, breathe or make a sound. Later, Mother offered me food -- which I refused to eat. Like many times in the past, I was fearful that the food might be poisoned, especially after she had just tried to kill me. She tried to convince me that she wasn't angry anymore and attempted to assure me that it was safe to come out. I didn't believe her and remained still and quiet. She left the food on the floor by the bed. I didn't touch it.

Dad didn't come home. I woke cold and stiff during the night. I hadn't moved since I had dove under the bed. Some of my open wounds had adhered to the hardwood floor and it was painful pulling them free. I had to go to the bathroom, but was too afraid to leave my room, move or make a sound. There was an empty vase in my room, so I quietly slid out from underneath the bed and peed in it. Then I dove back under my bed, too frightened to take an extra second to grab my pillow or blanket. Thanks to the iron pills, I was often constipated. So, luckily, all I had to do was pee.

The next day I remained under my bed all day long, refusing all food and liquids my mother offered. I was hungry and very thirsty, but I was more scared than anything else. I was still dressed in the same clothes I wore the day before, too fearful to take the time to change. That night, after she was asleep, I tiptoed into the bathroom for some water and then tiptoed back to my room. I slept the rest of that second night under my bed. The following day I woke before she did. The sun was up. I tiptoed to the kitchen for some cereal and brought the box back to my bedroom. During most of her waking hours that day, I stayed in my bedroom with the door shut. When I needed to go, I looked down the hall both ways and then ran to the bathroom, quickly locking the door behind me.

When I heard Mother walking on the hardwood floor near my room, I dove under my bed for protection. At night, I would wait for her to fall asleep. Then I would tiptoe out to the kitchen for more food to bring back to my room. I would never choose anything that she had prepared. I mostly took things like bread, jam, peanut butter and cereal.

Mother visited me a couple of times a day. When she entered my room, she sat on top of my bed while I hid underneath, staring at her shoes. She talked to me softly, patiently trying to convince me that it was safe to come out and she wasn't going to hurt me. I didn't trust her. I was like a frightened caged animal and didn't respond to anything she said. I stayed quietly under my bed, barely breathing.

Then early one morning, about a week later, I was on my way back to my room from a food run when I saw Mother standing in the hall. I froze in fear. She extended a hand toward me and cocked her head to the side as she suggested that we have breakfast at the table together. I looked at her hand, but didn't take it as I slowly backed away from her towards the kitchen. She didn't look angry anymore, but I had learned that I could not trust her facial expressions. Keeping out of arms' reach, I cautiously agreed to eat my breakfast at the table.

I wondered what I did that made Mother hate me so much. I didn't understand why my dad was always gone, especially when I needed him the most. I blamed myself. I had to be the reason that Mother wanted me dead. Secretly I wished that one day I would wake up and learn that it had all been a nightmare -- that somehow my parents had been replaced by a mother who loved me for who I was and a father who was happy to come home to his family every night. The wish never came true. My life was a nightmare that never ended.

A Temporary Haven

I was almost six, when Mother accused Dad of having an affair with one of his employees. Now, my mother said both he *and* the employee were in the walls talking and spying on her. I was grateful when I started the first grade and could get away from her for several hours a day.

If Dad came home at night, Mother would flip out and call him a "filthy pig" or a "swine." This would quickly turn into a nasty fight. Mother often told me that Dad was dirty and that she was going to kill him for cheating on her. After many fights, again he packed and left.

Mother was convinced that Dad had hired people to follow her around in black cars. Now, when Mother was driving, she had me on the lookout for only black cars and their license plates. It was no longer a fun game, as she would angrily speed recklessly whenever there was a black car behind us so she could "lose them." When we returned home, she would go on a tirade yelling at the walls about these cars and what a horrible person my dad was to have her followed. As she screamed and carried on, she often ignored me as I slipped away and hid under my bed until she calmed down. Sometimes she used the candle to calm herself by roasting my flesh in one of her burn sessions.

One morning, at the beginning of Easter vacation, I walked into my room and was surprised to see that Mother was packing a large suitcase. I asked if we were going to take a trip and she said that she was going away for a couple of days and I was going to stay with the Knudson family, our neighbors who lived two doors down. I was very happy about this, as it was the home of my best friend, Janie. We were only six days apart in age and had been friends since we were about eighteen months old. She had four brothers, Jeff who was the oldest, Rich and Brian who were younger and a new baby brother, Barry. I loved this family and played there as much as I was allowed. Unlike our family, they always ate their meals together and there was always someone to play with. Their mom, Mary Jane, was affectionate and kind to her kids. She never did weird tortures or spun out of control with them.

None of the Knudson kids were fearful of their mom and no one slept under their beds for protection at night. Mary Jane was practical and had a common sense approach. Her rules were consistent and made sense. She was a homemaker, like my mother, who also cooked and baked a lot. Everything she made was delicious! Their dad, Darrell, always came home every night and there were no violent or frightening fights between them. The family's interactions were very different from mine. At their house, I could be a normal six-year-old kid in a normal happy family. For me, it was paradise.

I prayed to God every night that I could live with them forever and that Mother would never come back for me. It looked like God was going to grant my prayers, as my mother didn't come back -- not in two days, three, or four! Each day that passed, I felt more certain that this was going to be a permanent situation for me.

Mary Jane was concerned that my mother had not returned and called my dad at the store. He was staying at the store or a motel. Dad was completely unaware that Mother was gone and I was staying with the Knudson family. Neither he nor Mary Jane knew the whereabouts of my mother. He asked Mary Jane if she would be willing to care for me until school started and she agreed.

Dad tracked Mother down and found that she was a patient in Twin Pines Sanitarium, where she stayed for three weeks. When vacation was over, Dad and I moved back to our house. I was having such a good time at the Knudson's and was sad to leave. I cried into my pillow that first night back at our house, asking God over and over why He didn't answer my prayers. I didn't realize that God had answered, and the answer was "No."

Stronger Than My Dad

Dad had to work and asked his mother, my Nan, to move in with us, until my mother returned home. I loved Nan dearly and was very excited that she was going to stay with us for a while. Out of my five grandparents (which included my step-grandmother), Nan was my favorite -- just the sound of her English accent could make my day! Unlike my other grandparents, Nan only lived an hour away. She was the only relative that made my childhood special and, at times, even magical.

She was the only person in my life who gave me unconditional love. Dad was her only child and I was her only grandchild. In her eyes, I was "brilliant" and could do no wrong. What a change from my mother's views! Dad had a very different relationship with Nan. To say they tolerated each other would be almost generous.

Nan walked me to and from school. As we walked, she often shared her stories of growing up in China, England and India. She told me her father was an engineer who built the first railroad in China. Her grandfather invented the Sheppard Slide Rule. Stories of her childhood adventures in faraway countries intrigued me. She shared her great respect for the people of these countries and their customs. We talked and held hands together everywhere we went and we were always together. In the afternoon, she taught me how to prepare and enjoy a proper English tea. I had milk instead of tea. She was interested in my friends, school and anything I had to say. She always had time for me and was gentle and kind. At night she read children's stories to me. In the morning, she got me ready for school and lovingly brushed my hair. I would do anything for her. I was eager to help her prepare meals, clean the house and search for the house key she often misplaced.

When Mother returned, Nan went home. I felt so sad and made myself scarce. Dad moved out of the master bedroom and into the spare bedroom. The peace that Nan had brought to our home was soon shattered when my parents started fighting again.

One evening Dad was lying back in his recliner and I was on the floor playing, when Mother came in with a cup of coffee for him. As she approached him, she started making high-pitched screeching and cackling sounds like a witch. I stopped playing and looked up.

Mother was holding the coffee over the lower pa
stomach (the groin area). In a bizarre tone of voice,
that the coffee was boiling hot and she intended to p   ʋn
him. I could see steam rising from the cup. If he tried to get up
it would have spilled all over him.

Mother began to make sounds that I didn't know a human
could make. It sounded like shrieking and laughing all mixed
together. Then she started swaying back and forth, saying she
was going to scald Dad. I jumped to my feet and saw the fear
in his eyes. I wondered if I could stop her by grabbing her arm
and yanking it away. However, I realized that doing this would
cause the hot coffee to spill on him. Both Dad and I were in a
state of fear. I decided the best way to help was to stay where
I was and join him in pleading with her not to hurt him. She
purposely spilled some on him and he cried out in pain. She
seemed satisfied with his reaction. Mother slowly put the coffee cup down on his side table and returned to the kitchen. I
watched as Dad got up and left the room without a word.

Mother's violent behavior was increasing in frequency and
severity. I witnessed her doing such things as stepping on Dad's
bare feet with her spiked high heels and punching him in the
head and chest. These things happened when she was just casually walking past him. There were no words or other triggers
that I witnessed. She was not visibly angry. It seems that she
was hurting him just because he was there.

Mother was starting to randomly slap, spank and pinch me
in front of Dad; something she had never done before. It was
the first time he had witnessed her hurting me for no apparent
reason. When I was an adult, Dad told me that this was the
first time he had worried about my safety. Finally, after many
years, he saw some of the hostility in her attitude and actions
toward me. He thought that she only took her aggressions out

on him. I believe Dad became so wrapped up in his own problems that he turned a blind eye toward my situation and was in denial, thinking Mother would never hurt me. Unfortunately, his new level of awareness did little to protect me.

Dad continued to sleep in the spare room. Mother had a history of violent "night raids," so he locked and barricaded his bedroom door at night. He told me, many years later, that the only reason he stayed at the house was to try to protect me. I wondered how barricading *his* door was supposed to accomplish this. I never questioned him though, because I knew he did it to protect himself.

One night, during one of Mother's "night raids," she came into my room and started hitting me as I slept. I woke and somehow managed to break free from her. I ran to the spare room and pounded on the door with all my might, yelling for Dad to let me in. Unfortunately, it took some time for him to remove the barricade. She came at me, so I ran around the house with her hot on my heels. As I raced by Dad's room again, he reached out and snatched me. The next thing I knew I was flying through the air. I landed on his bed, as he slammed the door shut, locked it and re-established the barricade. Dad looked angry and I didn't know if I was safe with him or not. Mother banged on the door, screaming for him to let her in so she could "teach me a lesson." I prayed that the locked, barricaded door would be strong enough to keep her out. Dad told Mother to calm down and that he wouldn't open the door until he knew it was safe to do so.

Mother ranted and raved as she pounded on the door for some time. Then she finally gave up and went back to her room, slamming her door behind her.

"Daddy, please let me stay with you tonight so I'll be safe and she won't get me," I begged.

"No, you have to sleep in your own room," Dad grumbled. As an adult, I understood why he didn't let me stay. Since Mother believed he was getting sexual pleasure when I sat on his lap, I can only imagine what she would think if I slept with him in a locked and barricaded room! Of course as a child, I didn't understand his reasoning at all. Dad waited until the house was silent and then told me to go back into my room and go to sleep. Right! Like who could sleep after that?!

Defeated, I said nothing and obediently returned to my room. Hearing Dad lock his door and reestablish the barricade behind me, I felt that I wasn't worth the effort to save. Feeling terribly betrayed and abandoned by Dad, I gathered my pillow and blanket as I crawled under my bed for the little protection it provided.

At some point during that night, I realized I was much braver than Dad. After all, I slept across from Mother's room, the "witch's den," with my door wide open. I wasn't allowed to close it, let alone lock it and barricade it as he did. I felt not only braver than Dad was, but in many ways stronger, too. I didn't turn tail and run away every time Mother was mean to me. I had acquired some skills to calm her down, while Dad's words only seemed to infuriate her. Even though he was a big man standing (6'2" and was overweight) and I was only a small child of six, I viewed him as being weak and even, at times, needing *my* protection. I thought of him as a coward. He continued to sleep in the barricaded spare room for several more months.

When Everything Breaks

One evening, Dad had just made dinner for me and was bringing it to the table as Mother returned home from running some errands. She came into the kitchen and started to beat him with her bag. She knocked the plate of food out of his hands and it landed on the floor. She called him "a dirty pig" and started screaming that she knew he was having sex with his employee. She also ordered him to call off his "dogs" and stop having her followed.

Dad bent over to clean up the mess as he denied Mother's accusations. She quickly picked up a large iron frying pan and started to beat him on his head and shoulders. Blood went flying as he yelled for me to go to my room. I ran to the hall and froze in my tracks. She almost had him down on the floor as she continued hitting him and screaming wildly. I thought she might actually kill him. My mind raced wondering what I could do to help him.

Dad had his hands up to protect himself against Mother's powerful blows; but as always, he didn't hit back or get physical with her in any way. He just yelled at her to stop. He was struggling to get to his feet and saw me standing in the hallway. He yelled at me to go to my room again and close the door. His face was contorted in pain and anger. Fearfully, I ran to my room, slamming the door behind me as I dove under my bed, not daring to make a sound. I heard the fight intensify. Then I heard Dad leave the house, slamming the door on his way out. He never came back.

The mighty storm that tore through our house that night was terrifying. I heard closets fly open and then slam shut after the contents had been violently thrown against the walls and the hardwood floors. Mother was in the grip of an out-of-control rage and trashed our house as she screamed, howled and cried.

Glued to the floor, silent and afraid to breathe, I hid under my bed all night long. I knew that my door could fly open at any moment and I would probably not survive what would happen next. Silently I prayed to God for protection. I had learned about Passover when I watched the movie, *The Ten Command-ments*, and talked with Mother about it. I prayed that God would allow this horrible storm to pass over me this dreadful night. As her fit intensified, she made howling sounds, which were almost non-human. The crashing of dishes, things being thrown and broken against the walls, things ripping apart and doors slamming got worse and worse as time went on. I said a quick Amen to end my prayers and covered my ears tightly. The destruction and howling went on for hours.

When I woke in the morning, I was still under my bed fully dressed from the day before. The house was silent. My door was shut and my room was intact and, even better, so was I. God had answered my prayers and had granted me my own personal Passover, keeping me safe from the storm that was my mother. I was cold and very hungry, as I hadn't had dinner the night before. I was also thirsty and had to use the bathroom very badly. Finally, when I could hold it no longer, I quietly emerged from under my bed. Slowly opening the door, I was stunned to see the devastation from the night before. The floor was completely covered and piled high with debris.

I used the bathroom and on my way out saw Mother stand-ing down the hallway, fully dressed and facing me. She was quiet, with a faraway look on her face that was empty and de-void of emotion. I was scared to death that she would blame me for the mess, but she didn't. I quickly offered to help clean it up and she muttered okay using such a soft voice that I could barely hear her. She didn't move as I squeezed past her to get to the kitchen. The house was completely trashed and looked like a war zone.

In the hall lay ripped and broken pictures and other things that once decorated the walls. Every closet had been opened with the contents flung all over the floor. Dad's clothing littered the place and had been sliced up with a knife. I passed the spare room where he had been sleeping for months. It was completely upside down. The bed was slashed, including many pillows with their stuffing pulled out.

The kitchen was a complete disaster. All of the things that were kept in the cabinets and drawers now completely covered the floor. Many things had been broken. I peeked into the living room. The furniture had been overturned and our books were tossed everywhere. Some of the walls had been damaged as well. Shrapnel, that had once been our things, littered most every inch of floor space in our house. It was hard to walk without stepping on things and causing more breakage.

In the kitchen I found two unbroken bowls and a cereal box on the floor. I poured the cereal into the bowls. The contents of the refrigerator were untouched, so I added some milk. I was surprised to find Mother standing in the same position in which I had left her. Silently, I handed her a bowl of cereal, but she seemed not to notice as she continued to stare straight ahead like a statue. She didn't move or acknowledge me. So, I brought her bowl back to the kitchen and quickly ate my cereal. Then without a word, I got right to work. I didn't ask questions or make any more noise than I had to.

This was the first time I ever felt a lot older then I actually was. I felt more like a grown up than a six-year-old kid. On some level, I realized the only functioning person in my family was me. I knew that it would be up to me to bring order to all the chaos in our house by straightening, reorganizing and cleaning it up. I did not need help to accomplish this or an adult to tell me what to do, as I knew where most everything went. The task before me was simple: the items that littered the floor needed either to be put away or thrown out.

Later, Mother finally came out of her trance-like state and

joined me in cleaning the house. She didn't say a word and neither did I. It was intense and uneasy as I wondered if she would stay quiet and keep working or if, at any second, she might turn on me. She brought the garbage can inside and we threw away Dad's shredded clothing and things that were beyond repair. I found many ripped up pictures, which I threw away as well. If Mother was in a picture, she had sliced off her head! I saved the photos that had other people in them, even though her head was missing.

I don't remember which one of us made lunch, but I do remember eating with Mother in silence. We worked quickly and steadily all day and into the night until the house was clean and orderly. During the entire day, we never spoke and I tried not to look at her. I remember going to bed exhausted. I continued to sleep under my bed for the next week or so. It was very sad to see how many of our things had been destroyed, along with our family.

Lies, Abandonment and Shock

Not long after Mother trashed the house, she packed a large suitcase with my clothing. She said we were going to visit her brother, my Uncle Les and his wife, Aunt Nita. They had four daughters ranging in age from two to ten-and-a-half years old. Not long after Mother and I arrived, my aunt and older cousin, Linda, opened my suitcase. Linda still remembers her mother's astonishment to see that this suitcase was filled with filthy and clean clothes all jumbled together. Most of my clothes were way too small for me and some of them were shredded, including *all* of my panties.

"Kathryn, why are Tracy's clothes in this condition?" Aunt Nita asked.

"Because her father never allows me to buy new clothes for her," Mother replied in a flat tone.

Aunt Nita thought the statement was odd. It also didn't explain the dirty and shredded clothes.

I walked into the living room the next morning and saw that my mother was preparing to leave without me. I cried and pleaded with her not to leave me behind. She said she was going home to clean the house and would come back for me when she was finished. I panicked and offered to help her. She quickly gathered her things, ran to the car and drove away. Aunt Nita was crying as she restrained me. I screamed for Mother to come back and take me home. It was the third time she had physically abandoned me in my short lifetime.

The emotional damage my mother had done to me was enormous. Living with my aunt and uncle didn't improve things. At times, my aunt could be very tough and seemed determined to toughen up my cousins and me, too! The main way that my aunt accomplished this, was to turn some of our most joyful moments into unhappiness. Some of her punishments were severe and unpredictable. I didn't understand many of my aunt's and uncle's rules, nor their reasons for punishment. For no apparent reason, behaviors that were acceptable one day, were not the next, but then became acceptable later.

One Saturday morning I woke up and was afraid to get out of bed. I was also just as afraid to stay in bed. My older cousins, Linda and Gwen, came into the bedroom and tried to convince me to come out to the den and watch TV with them. They kept telling me I would get in trouble with their parents if I stayed in bed. I told them I would just pretend I was asleep. *Their parents couldn't be angry with me for being asleep*, I thought. Linda and Gwen told me that if I remained in bed I would be in big trouble. I refused to budge. Then they left the room but returned several times trying to convince me. I remember wishing I could just turn invisible. I was so frightened and didn't know the right thing to do. I didn't know if I could trust what my cousins were telling me and I was terrified of being punished.

Living with my aunt and uncle added to my anxieties. As a result, I became withdrawn and didn't talk very much.

After Mother left me, she didn't go home to clean the house. Instead, she checked into Agnews State Hospital. She told the doctors that her husband had questioned her mental status and that she had come to the hospital to be cleared by getting declared as *sane*. Her passionate view was that she was fine, but everyone else had problems. Many psychiatrists, both in and out of Agnews, agreed she was psychotic. Most believed she was a paranoid-schizophrenic, while others had diagnosed her as schizophrenic reaction, paranoid type. Mother was committed.

California Superior Court transcript of Cable v. Cable stated: "A panel of eight doctors had committed her as psychotic-schizophrenic-paranoid." The same court transcript stated that on May 5, 1965, Mother's attorney entered her Agnews State Hospital records into evidence, on her behalf, as "Plaintiff's Exhibit No.4."

Mother was born in Chicago, Illinois. From the court records, I learned that she believed that her parents were strict and the children were thrown together. They didn't live around other children and therefore she didn't have a lot of interaction with peers. She did a lot of reading in the library. Her father was away a lot on business so her mother acted as both parents. She had an "A" average in school; she was the editor of the school annual and enjoyed her teachers.

Mother felt her father was a good person; bright, happy-go-lucky and kind to his children. He was a real estate broker who was born in Hungary, as was her mother who was a teacher -- strict but quick to laugh. Her mother believed that children should be seen and not heard. Both of her parents had a good sense of humor. My mother was raised with European attitudes and was chaperoned on dates until she was eighteen years old. She felt her family relationships were good. She was the oldest child in a family of four children and the only girl. Before she turned twenty-one years old, she had lived in Hungary on two separate periods, totaling about ten years. Her father was very wealthy during World War I. However, he lost all of his money in the crash of 1929. During this time, her mother had an affair with another man who had maintained his wealth. My mother's father found out about the affair and kicked her mother out. The children pleaded with him, which softened his heart and saved the marriage. Mother was nineteen years old when this happened.

Mother had a similar experience during her first marriage. She fell in love with her employer and divorced her husband during World War II, while he was fighting in New Guinea. The plan was that her employer was to obtain a divorce and the two were to be married. She followed him to New Jersey to keep working with him and learned she was pregnant. In the end, the employer refused to get a divorce because of his Catholic beliefs, but offered to maintain her as his mistress. She had an illegal abortion and felt she couldn't return to her family, as she was certain her father would accuse her of being like her mother. For a brief period, she did move in with her family in Chicago. Dad met Mother through her first husband. After Dad learned about the divorce, he began to correspond with her. He sent her money for two trips to California and eventually they were married in 1949.

At Agnews, Mother acted differently and altered her personality depending on which doctor or staff member was interacting with her. Some of the staff and doctors considered Mother to be very pleasant and sweet. At times *overly* sweet. Others considered her a bit scatterbrained, with impaired judgment, was inappropriately flirtatious, evasive, and at times delusional. The doctors felt that when first meeting Mother that she was very good at hiding her mental issues, but she couldn't keep up this facade for long.

Mother told the Agnews staff that she had never harmed Dad or me. She told them about the black cars following her and that my dad secretly checked on all of her doctors. She had a long list of bizarre medical complaints that often had to do with infections in her rectum. The doctors couldn't find any infections or problems and felt these complaints represented some kind of somatic delusions. At times, she didn't seem to understand why she was in Agnews.

Dad told the Agnews staff that Mother's suspiciousness, temper outbursts and delusions, had become increasingly more serious and severe. He told them that she had physically attacked him, threatened him with a knife, and believed that he had people following her with phony license plates all the time. She had accused him of being involved with a female employee for some years. Dad thought Mother's mental situation was declining. He had made the mistake of telling her that the only reason he remained married to her was because of me. After this, Dad said he had to be very careful not to be too affectionate with me. He had witnessed my mother taking her hostility out on me. Anytime Dad went any place with me, upon returning, Mother questioned me intensively for long periods. Dad said that Mother had accused him of various misbehaviors, in front of me, and that he had made continual efforts to get me out of the house and out of earshot, so I would not be subjected to these scenes. Dad also told the Agnews staff that because he was so terrified of my mother, he had moved out of the house after having locked and barricaded himself in the spare bedroom for many months.

The Agnews staff didn't approve of Dad's choice not to visit Mother during her hospitalization. They were also unhappy that he only called once or twice during that time. He did send her the things she requested or needed, and weekly fruit baskets that she enjoyed. Some doctors thought it was unrealistic that Dad wanted Mother to remain in Agnews long term, and that he was rallying doctors, friends and family to back him up. A couple of the doctors wondered if my dad played a deeper role in my mother's mental problems. Some, before interviewing Dad, had only listened to Mother's explanations and were convinced that he caused Mother's problems. Others felt that Dad had little to nothing to do with Mother's mental issues. The doctors felt that Dad should seek psychiatric help as well, which he was already doing.

When Mother was committed, she was considered chronically and severely mentally ill. In regards to her improvement, the doctors believed that she was very hard to evaluate because she was quite intelligent, often able to hide her mental issues, evasive, watchful and circumstantial. None of them seemed to know how long she was going to need to be in Agnews.

Transformations

I had lived with Aunt Nita and Uncle Les for almost four months and couldn't understand why it took so long for Mother to clean the house. After the second month, Dad began visiting me on weekends. On his first visit, Gwen ran up and hugged him with tears rolling down her cheeks.

"Uncle John, I thought I would never see you again!" Gwen cried.

Uncle Les told her to go into the house and proceeded to talk with my dad in private.

I was polite, quiet and kept my distance during these early visits. As time went by, I started to feel more comfortable with Dad and he decided to bring me home. When we were almost there I remembered my forgotten pet cat that was given to me during my stay. We were less than two blocks from home and he immediately turned around to go back to get it. He had just driven over four hours there and back. Now we were on our way back again and I was certain he was going to abandon me there as my mother had done. Even though I loved the cat very much, I begged him *not* to go back. I knew he wasn't fond of cats and with every passing mile I became more fearful that the actual reason we were going back had nothing to do with the cat!

When Dad and I arrived, I refused to get out of the car. He went up to the door and requested the cat. He held the cat under its arms, as far away from his body as possible. The cat's legs were outstretched towards the car, with its ears back. I don't know who was more unhappy, my dad or the cat! He put it in the car and drove us home. When we arrived, I looked through all the rooms. Dad had repaired the damaged walls from Mother's last tirade and repainted the interior of the house. He thought that I was admiring his work, which I didn't really notice. I was anxiously looking for my mother.

A couple of weeks later, Dad and I met Aunt Nita, Uncle Les and my cousins for a camping trip in Yosemite National Park. Then we all went to Disneyland for a few days. During this trip, Dad saw me doing something with my chest, out of the corner of his eye. He was uncertain about what he saw, until he saw me do it again. He was shocked to see that I was pulling on my breasts!

"What *are* you doing?" Dad demanded in a booming voice.

I was scared and felt ashamed because of the way Dad was looking at me. I felt that I had been caught doing something *terribly* wrong.

"Daddy, it's okay. Mommy had me do it to her all the time and taught me to do it to myself. Mommy says it's okay. So it is okay Daddy. You can ask her if you want." I held my breath, waiting for his reply.

Dad walked away, without saying another word. As I watched him walk away, I felt very confused, embarrassed and ashamed. I never did it again and he never again brought it up.

In the fall, I went back to school. Dad asked Nan to move in with us. I was so happy that she was staying with us again. Unfortunately, Nan and my dad were not getting along, so she went home after a month or two.

I was a very frightened and withdrawn child. During times of severe stress, I created a secret fantasy world in my mind where I could temporarily escape. My hyperactivity and anxiety had become much worse. I had an attention span that was, at best, less than a minute. I felt that everything wrong with my family, including the negative things that had happened in my life, truly were my fault. Secretly, I knew I was no good and realized on some level that this was the reason I was rejected and unloved by my mother. I strongly believed that I should have *never* been born!

I didn't speak to adults unless it was absolutely necessary, and then did my best to give only one-word answers. I learned through many painful experiences that it was safer to keep my mouth shut around adults and not talk too much to kids either. My longest sentence was, "I don't know." I used that sentence with adults to avoid answering questions, engaging in conversations or as a defense mechanism. I shut down inside and was numb most of the time. When I wasn't numb, I was angry with Mother for the horrible things she had done to me. Being a quiet, fearful child of six, the only words I could use to express my feelings about Mother adequately were: *"I hate her guts!"*

Some adults and children told me it was wrong to feel this way, that I should love and respect my mother, no matter what! Even at the age of six, I knew these people didn't know what they were saying. They didn't have mothers like mine. I knew that the people judging my situation and me had no background or understanding of my life. Their judgment hurt me to my core; it also made me angry. They had no idea what my mother had done to me and how I had suffered. Over the years, being cognizant of these facts taught me that no one has a right to criticize another person's feelings. Life experiences shape our feelings: my mother did an exquisite job of shaping mine about her!

I was fearful of everything, especially at night. These fears included: gaps between my curtains, furniture in my room, toys on the floor, and sounds I could not immediately recognize. I suffered *constantly* with night terrors. I felt horribly abandoned and betrayed by both of my parents. I lived in a continual state of extreme anxiety. Even though I was now living with Dad and things were much more predictable and consistent, he was basically a stranger to me. I lived in a state of fear that Dad might leave me or at any moment turn me over to Mother. I was also afraid that he might start hurting me as she had done. I felt he was weak in comparison to my mother, but I still feared him. I couldn't trust him. I couldn't trust anyone, not even myself!

There had been big changes in my short life. I was no longer the happy and engaging baby and toddler I was born to be. When my life was new it was soft, kind and secure. That disintegrated into the utter chaos of physical and mental torture, resulting in a state of terror and severe anxiety. I believe that this changed the course of the person I was meant to become. When a child lives for years in an environment of family violence, abandonment and terror mixed in with the unpredictability of a volatile, abusive mother who has little or no sense of reality, it alters the child greatly. Just trying to survive on a daily basis feels like an insurmountable task for a child living under these conditions. It was certainly true for me. I believe that some of the changes in me were last ditch attempts to try to hold my fragile world together as it was rapidly falling apart.

Afraid to Tell

Living alone with Dad was a very different experience for me. I was still only six years old and by that age I had lived under four different roofs with four different families who all had different sets of rules, discipline techniques, personalities, schedules, routines and their own unique views and ways of dealing with life in general. Every new living environment meant being uprooted and thrust into another uncertain situation. These transitions were hard for me. Living alone with Dad was now the fifth new living environment that I had to learn to fit into. All these transitions occurred between just before I turned five to a few months before I turned seven.

At first, living with Dad was difficult. I had never lived without a woman in the home and frankly that was a challenge in itself. He didn't know how to interact with me and I didn't know how to feel about living with him. I had no idea what to expect. I felt it was a temporary situation as he had left me *so* many times before. We were virtually strangers starting from scratch. He never really had the opportunity to parent me. It wasn't an easy situation for either of us. On top of that, I had suffered many different modalities of severe abuse, abandonment and displacement. It all took an enormous toll on me mentally, emotionally and physically. I was left very disturbed. Now, back home again, nothing felt real.

One day, shortly after I began living with Dad, he took me to lunch. We went to a "mom and pop" restaurant. I ordered a cheeseburger. When they delivered our order, the burger was huge and I couldn't finish it. Dad was still hungry and decided to eat the rest of it. I was terrified that my germs would kill him.

"Daddy, please *don't* eat my burger."

"Why?"

"Because I don't want you to die," I cried.

"That's not going to happen," Dad replied.

However, I was well brainwashed by my mother to believe it would. As Dad grabbed my burger to take a bite, my pleas for him to stop became louder and more urgent.

People in the restaurant were now staring at us, as Dad was trying to calm me. He told me that he was going to finish my burger no matter how I felt about it and I burst into tears.

"*No, Daddy, please stop!* Don't eat it or you will *die!*" I frantically tried to convince him.

Dad ignored me and picked it up to take a bite. I started screaming, repeating my warning not to eat it. I was hysterical and scared to death that he would die right there at the restaurant! I watched him finish my burger without a word. He paid the bill, took me by the hand and led me to the car.

"Why did you eat it, Daddy? My germs are going to *kill* you. I don't want you to die. Why Daddy? Why did you eat it? *Why?!*" I sobbed, uncontrollably.

He was kind to me as he put me in the car, reassuring me that everything would be all right.

As the hours passed, it became obvious that Dad wasn't going to die. I was very happy he was okay, but I was also very confused.

Now, for the first time, Dad realized that I had a germ phobia along with my other problems. He didn't have a germ phobia, but knew that my mother did. As time went on, he was starting to understand more about me. On top of issues that needed to be addressed, there were incorrect assessments made by neighbors and others. Some of these created new problems and challenges. For example: because I was very quiet and rarely engaged in conversations with adults, some neighbors and family friends believed I was actually retarded!

Fear followed me like a shadow. Sleeping was not an escape. I suffered from horrible night terrors from which I woke screaming. This happened almost nightly and, at times, multiple times during the same night. As a result, both Dad and I were sleep deprived.

The damage that had been done to me was much worse than Dad had previously thought. He became terribly concerned over my mental and emotional condition. He wanted a referral to a child psychiatrist and his doctor knew a good one. Some doctor friends also suggested the same psychiatrist, Elsa Gordon, M.D., and recommended her highly. Dad made an appointment for me. Dr. Gordon had a psychologist give me a battery of tests that included looking at inkblot cards and making up stories from pictures I was shown. The test results were not good.

At first, I was very afraid that Dr. Gordon might give me a shot, draw blood or otherwise hurt me. I didn't trust her when she said she wouldn't. She started me on Dexedrine to help me slow down and focus. In the beginning, I saw her twice a week. Months later, she reduced it to once a week.

During our first session, Dr. Gordon brought me into a big playroom full of toys. I never saw so many toys in one room. I was enchanted and a little overwhelmed. The first few visits, I played with the toys by myself and in silence. She tried to engage me in play, but I refused to interact with her much. As I remember, this went on for about a month.

Then, one day, Dr. Gordon offered me some candy. I looked at it wondering if it was safe to eat and whether I would somehow be in trouble for accepting it. I decided to try a piece anyway. She then gave me plenty of space and was on the other side of the room playing with some of the toys by herself. In a little while, she offered me some more candy. After I had a couple more pieces, she asked if I would like to play with her. Slowly and tentatively, I accepted her offer. From then on there was always candy available during therapy and I always left with a small bag to take home.

Dad was concerned about cavities and wanted the candy stopped. When I was an adult, he told me that he had talked to Dr. Gordon about this concern and was surprised when she told him that she planned to increase the candy. She explained that she had rarely used candy in treatment. However, after exhausting all other clinical avenues to try to get me to engage with her on any level, she concluded that using candy was the only approach she had left. He was unconvinced and complained that the candy would rot my teeth. She explained that I had been so badly hurt mentally and emotionally that if she was unable to work with me soon, she believed I might be mentally lost. She would then have no choice but to institutionalize me. She told him it would be better for me to lose my teeth than my mind, as teeth can be replaced if necessary.

She reminded him about the results of the psychological tests I had taken, which showed that I was suffering from severe and nearly incapacitating distress and that permanent damage to my mental health was a real possibility. The candy was no longer an issue.

The sessions consisted largely of play therapy and continued for four-and-a-half years, until I was almost eleven years old. My distrust of people extended to Dr. Gordon, as well. Sometimes working with Dr. Gordon and responding to some of the questions she asked was very painful. At other times, working with her was uncomfortable and obnoxious at best. Often we played with puppets, making up what they said as the playing progressed. This part of the therapy was the most painful as my puppet was put into situations and scenarios for me to demonstrate my deepest pain.

I kept almost all of my mother's abuse secrets. I was terrified to tell anyone, including Dr. Gordon. However, through play therapy she learned a lot about me and certainly got the general idea of some of the things I had suffered, even though I said very little. Today, I am grateful that she was there to help me.

Getting to Know My Dad

My dad was big and physically strong. At the drop of a hat, he could look and act as tough as nails. The timbers shook when he got angry and I would become petrified with fear, but he never lost control with me. By the time I ended up in his care, I was well trained to act as soon as an adult gave me a directive, to the point of blind obedience. I would never think for myself or question commands; doing so or hesitating in any way had brought me severe consequences in the past. My dad liked this obedient side of me; it was a good fit for his authoritarian style. Mostly driven by fear, I tried desperately to please adults. Dad enjoyed the fact that I would go out of my way to please him. However, I still didn't trust him, was afraid of him and never spoke unless he asked me a question. He became fed up with my plain "Yes," "No," or "I don't know," answers. He told me to add "Daddy" to them and I immediately did. The same rule applied to me saying "Please" and "Thank you." Single word sentences were the extent of most of my verbalization with adults. Why say more? It was my experience that the more words spoken, the more chances of being hurt.

As time went by, things started to look up. Although an authoritarian, my dad also had a playful side. He could magically create fun out of thin air! He had also been an only child, and knew the loneliness of it. He began to have my friends over, one at a time, for dinner. My dad made up a seating game for us. He hid treats for us to find and found happiness and joy in creating fun and games for us. He started to enjoy being with and interacting with my friends and me. He got pleasure out of seeing the joy on our faces when he would have us pick "which hand." He would do this to give us special treats or to determine who would go first.

This was a new world for Dad and he was king! He loved every moment of it. He often got down on the floor to play children's games with me, including board games like Candyland. He would always let me or my friends win and then he would cheer for us. We never knew that he had manipulated the game so we could always be the winners. It was exciting to win, but to be six years old and win a game against an adult was an absolute thrill! Every once in a while, on Sundays, he would treat one of my friends and me to Frontier Village, Happy Hollow, Big Basin State Park, Santa's Village or the Santa Cruz Beach Boardwalk.

These amusement parks, state parks and beaches were reasonably close to our home in San Jose.

Dad wanted me to feel like I belonged and that this was a permanent situation. Everything he owned became "ours." He never referred to anything as "his." It was always "our store, our house, our money, our home, our life together," etc. I was always included and this helped me feel more secure and, for the first time in a very long while, wanted.

My dad wanted to bond and make up for lost time. He shared his love of fishing with me. I loved the hills and streams as much as he did. He showed me how to read the water's flow to determine where the fish would most likely be hiding. He taught me which kind of bait or lure to use and how to rig and work it. When I had a fish on, he coached me on how to set the hook, play the fish and then land it.

"Never drop your rod tip or the fish will jump the hook and be gone in a flash," Dad advised.

When I landed a fish, Dad would praise me and join in my excitement. Until I was about eight, he always handled anything to do with a knife or a hook. He always baited the hook for me and transferred the fish from the hook to the stringer. I quickly realized that I loved to fish and became very good at it. I was completely hooked!

While we fished, I did not talk at all. To fill this space, Dad told stories about his childhood. They were wonderful. One of my favorite stories from his childhood was "Adventures with Coons." When Dad was nine years old, he was "farmed out" to a family in Walnut Creek. During this time, he had a pet raccoon he named "Coons," who loved ice cream cones and swimming with him and his friends in the local streams and creeks. Coons also enjoyed riding in a basket that was strapped to the handlebars of Dad's bike. He and Coons were inseparable. Coons loved to play with anything shiny, including the pocket watch of a stranger from San Francisco. This man thought Dad had taught Coons to steal pocket watches and marched them both down to the sheriff's office. Dad was afraid he might be in trouble. However, the sheriff came to his defense and explained to the man that all raccoons are attracted to shiny things and suggested that he return to The City, where he belonged!

Some years later, in an attempt to have a squirrel as a pet, Dad had lured one into a cage with some food. He rowed the caged squirrel out into the middle of a lake. Then he opened the cage door. The squirrel took one look at him and chattered, telling him off, before it jumped into the water and swam toward shore. Soon the squirrel tired and could no longer swim. Dad rowed over to the squirrel, put the oar under its body and lifted it out of the water so that it wouldn't drown. After the squirrel had recovered, it jumped back into the water again but tired much faster than before. Dad repeated the rescue with the oar and, when recuperated, the squirrel took off again! This went on for a couple of hours. After the umpteenth time of hoisting the squirrel out of the water, it looked at the water and looked at the open cage on the boat. It hopped up the oar handle and jumped into the safety that the cage provided. Dad had a low maintenance pet.

Dad told stories of the hardships of growing up during the Great Depression and that the only good part was that it brought neighbors and townspeople closer together. No one had any money to speak of, so they learned to enjoy and appreciate what they did have more than ever before, which included each other. Communities became tight knit. People often got together for picnics and dances. They told stories, made music, sang songs and played games. Without money for toys, the kids made their own kind of fun by making up games to play. Many young boys had to drop out of school to help support their families. Dad knew some boys who dropped out at sixth grade to go to work and never finished their schooling. His ex-business partner, John Cardoza, was one of these boys. After leaving the business, he became a photographer of some note. Dad learned how to drive at age six and had his first driver's license at the age of twelve. His mother, my Nan, never learned to drive. He told me that he learned to hunt and fish at a young age to provide meat for his mother's table.

Ever since he was a boy, Dad loved the mountains. At age seven, he made his first trip to the California Sierras with a friend and his family. I heard all about his great adventures on that trip. He told me the road to Yosemite had a super steep hill and none of the cars had the power to reach the top. A local man had a team of horses and for ten dollars, which was "a wad of dough in those days," he would pull your car up the hill. Dad told me about the park's grandeur, the waterfalls, camping out, hiking the trails, backpacking into the backcountry and how he caught his first fish. During his stay at Yosemite, Dad watched a man feeding a bear. When being fed, the bears seemed gentle and even tame. This man however, decided to get a picture of the bear behind the wheel of his brand new car. He lured the bear into his car with bacon and closed the doors to take the picture. All was going well, until the bacon ran out and the bear found that he was now trapped inside the car and went ballistic. It shredded the interior, then punched a hole through the window and made its escape. The man's car was ruined. Dad told me to remember that wild animals are just that: wild.

These were just a few in Dad's vast reservoir of stories. He talked, I listened and we caught plenty of fish in the process. Occasionally I would find the courage to ask a question regarding the story he was telling me and he would happily explain. He told me the greatest human needs were, "to want to be wanted, to be accepted and to be loved by others." Through fishing, stories and one-on-one time together, we got to know each other better and I felt less concerned about him leaving me in the middle of nowhere.

I began to realize that Dad and I had things in common. We were both "only children." Our parents separated when we were six years old and we were "farmed out" to multiple homes. We shared a love of nature, animals, fishing, and singing together. Both of us made and maintained lifelong friendships with others. We were flexible about the friends we made. We held our friends close and loved them dearly. They were important to us, as they were our extended family. Except for the love of music, my mother held none of these values, interests or childhood experiences in common with me.

With help from friends, neighbors and doctors, my dad created a stable home life for me. Life with Dad included consistent routines, rules that made sense most of the time and discipline that wasn't harsh or driven by anger. It also included stability, safety and fun. At some point, before I turned seven, I had started to forgive him for the mistakes he made with me in the past. There was no doubt in my mind: I wanted to continue living with Dad.

Meeting "Indian Joe"

Dad and I went to see a man he had known since he was young. On the way to the man's office, Dad told me a lot about him. I could tell by the way Dad spoke that he was nervous. He felt that this man, who was a lawyer, was the only person who could help us stay together. His name was Joseph Di Maria. Dad told me I was to call him Mr. Di Maria. The name went in one ear and out the other. When we arrived, Dad told me to sit quietly and not say a word. This would be easy, because I didn't speak to adults any more than absolutely necessary. When we arrived at his office, I sat in a chair and went into my fantasy world as Dad talked with this man. At first, they sounded friendly, but then their conversation took on an agitatedly serious tone, which quickly got my attention and snapped me back into the real world. The man told Dad he didn't handle divorce cases anymore, but for old times' sake, had read the material Dad sent to him. He had previously told Dad that he wasn't going to take the case and that nothing he had read had changed his mind. He said that divorces are always messy and my parents' divorce was going to be one of the messiest ever.

Dad started to beg the man and then began to praise him, saying he was the smartest attorney that had ever gone through Stanford Law School. Dad wanted to keep me safe and the only way he could do that was to get full custody of me. The man said that this would be next to impossible. Dad told him that if we had any chance at all it would be because he took the case and reminded the man that they had been friends for years.

"I need your help, Joe," Dad said, hopefully.

The man was getting irritated and started arguing with my dad suggesting other lawyers that could help him. He argued back. I was facing the man and studying his expressions intensely. I couldn't see Dad, as he had his back to me. However, I could tell that he was losing the argument. The tension was thick and their eyes were locked.

I got up quietly and slowly walked over to the man. Neither he nor Dad noticed me. Looking back, I think they forgot I was there! I looked at the man and remembered Dad telling me how important this man would be to help us stay together. I reached out, took the man's shirtsleeve and pulled on it. He whipped his head around and saw me. His face changed in an instant from irritation to surprise.

Before he could utter a word I said, "Please mister; please help us. We need you! Please mister?"

The man turned to Dad and in a booming voice said, "John, this isn't fair!"

Dad said nothing.

I was still tugging on the man's shirtsleeve. He looked at me again and I met his gaze.

"Please?" I pleaded.

He studied me for a moment then softly asked, "Do you want to live with your daddy?"

"Yes," I replied honestly.

"You are certain that you want to live with your daddy and *not* your mommy?"

"I don't want to live with my mommy, just my daddy," I said, still maintaining eye contact.

He looked down and muttered something under his breath. Then he turned to me and said, "Okay honey, I will take your daddy's case on a couple of conditions: first, that from now on you call me Indian Joe." Then he became very animated and said, "Why, I am the greatest Indian warrior there has ever been, of course your daddy must have told you all about me."

I shook my head.

"No?!" He shot Dad a look of utter disbelief and shock. "Well, I have known all the Great Indian Chiefs and smoked peace pipes with them. They made me an honorary member of their tribes and invited me along on many hunting trips. I have peacefully settled many disputes between the tribes as well," he continued. "Would you like to hear some of my stories?"

I nodded eagerly.

"And so you shall! Here Tracy, have one of these candies; they have made me what I am today: the greatest Indian warrior and buffalo hunter ever." By now, I was happily sitting on his lap.

Indian Joe looked at my dad who was still standing in front of his desk.

"As for you John," he said, "I will expect you to do *exactly* as I instruct you to do. I have known you a long time and you need to know this: If you deviate in any way from my instructions, I will drop this case in a hot second."

I looked at Dad, panicked that he might say something to anger Indian Joe. Dad agreed to his condition. Then no one said a word.

I broke the silence by asking what "deviate" meant.

"It means Indian Joe is the boss," my dad answered flatly.

Usually, I would be in big trouble for disobeying a direct command. I was told to sit and be quiet and I didn't do either. However, this time I wasn't in trouble. Dad looked like he was the one in trouble. They made an appointment and shook hands on our way out.

Mother and Dad

Me at 18 months

Mother and me in HI

My first day with Cinders.

Nan and me on my fifth birthday.

"But, I am smiling."

2

Justice: Blind or Biased?
A Little Girl's Fate Swings in the Balance

A New Beginning

I turned seven a month after starting second grade. Dad worked at the store during the week and I stayed at Mary Jane's after school until he came home. On Saturday, I stayed with Nan while Dad worked. Sunday was the only day of the week Dad and I had together. During the week, he laid out my outfit the night before and dressed me in the morning for school. He then made us breakfast and packed my lunch.

After school, I came home to Mary Jane's house, got my house key, then went two doors down to my house and changed into play clothes. Afterwards, I locked the front door and returned to Mary Jane's until my dad came home from work. Sometimes he would work late and I would eat dinner with Mary Jane's family. If he was going to be very late, I would sleep over with them. Mother was still in Agnews State Hospital. Although I was grateful that I had no contact with her, I was very fearful that she might show up at any time and take me away from Dad.

Dad had no idea how to dress a little girl. He was also significantly color blind with blue, green, red and orange. His ability to pick out matching colors for my outfits was limited. He also had no concept that polka dots, stripes and plaids didn't go together. However, the worst part was that he sent me to school in horrible, itchy, wool ski socks. The kids were teasing me terribly and I came home crying on several occasions. Mary Jane saw how upset I was and understood why. She decided to talk with my dad.

I was in Mary Jane's living room playing when Dad came over to pick me up.

Mary Jane said, "John, you don't know how to dress a little girl!"

Dad didn't defend his ability to pick out my outfits, but he did defend his decision to send me to school in the horrible wool socks!

"Tracy's feet are always freezing cold and she is often down with colds. The wool socks keep her feet warm. When her feet are warm she is healthier," Dad explained.

"That's the most ridiculous thing I've *ever* heard!" Mary Jane scolded. "My daughter, Janie, goes to school in girl's cotton socks and she doesn't have any more colds than the average kid."

They began to argue over the socks, and it got pretty hot! I listened intently and got very nervous about the raised voices. In my experience, when adults got into heated discussions it became a dangerous situation and often somebody ended up getting physically hurt. After a while, I decided to tune out what was happening in the other room and escaped into my fantasy world. At least there, I knew I would be safe!

Toward the end of the "discussion," I heard Mary Jane tell Dad, "I don't see why you spend all that money for Tracy to see a psychiatrist when you send her to school dressed like you do. All the kids tease her and she comes home crying. It doesn't make any sense that you're giving her more problems than she had in the first place."

Mary Jane was very outspoken, but was one of the rare women that Dad listened to and respected. Finally, he agreed not to force me to wear those terrible socks. After some discussion, Dad also agreed to send me over to Mary Jane's every day before school to be certain that I was dressed properly. I did this for at least a year. However, the best news was that the wool socks were history!

There were many times when Mary Jane argued with Dad about things she felt were in my best interest. Secretly I wished she was my mother or that she would adopt me into her family. I liked being there, eating dinner with them, and just being "one of the kids." I didn't want to leave my dad; I just wanted to be added to the Knudson family, as well.

When I ate dinner with the Knudson family, nothing was ever rushed. The meal was always started with a prayer thanking God for the food. This was the second prayer that I had learned:

"Bless us, O Lord, in these Thy gifts, which we are about to receive from Thy bounty, through Christ, our Lord. Amen." Mary Jane told me that she had learned the prayer from her parents who always said it before mealtime. Dinnertime at the Knudson's was a time to talk, laugh and share interesting things about our day. I ate at the same speed as the other kids. It was enjoyable and relaxing, just to share a meal with them. Mary Jane was an excellent cook, so everything was quite tasty. However, dinnertime was different at my dad's house.

There were no prayers, but often Dad would play his seating game with me to determine where we were going to sit at the table. Each dinner was served with a timer ticking away and a threat. He expected my meal to be finished within fifteen minutes. If not, for every minute over that, I had to sit at the table in silence after I finished. I learned to eat quickly. Dinners with Dad were stressful. It was not like the Knudson's house at all.

The lunches Dad packed for school presented another problem. Have you ever eaten a peanut butter and jelly sandwich with baloney, mayonnaise and lettuce? If you haven't, you're not missing anything! That was only one of his many "creations." The problem was, even though *he* enjoyed them, I couldn't stand the sandwiches. I felt sick every time I tried to eat them. None of the kids at school liked them either; so nobody would trade with me. The sandwiches he made for me ended up in the garbage and I ended up hungry. Usually, I could persuade some of my friends to share their lunches with me, which helped. However, there were days when no one shared. I remember being so hungry, I started to sift through the school garbage cans to find uneaten or partially eaten sandwiches. The kids didn't understand and started to make fun of me. One neighborhood girl saw me and told my dad. He was so angry with me that I got scared and denied it. I knew that if I told the truth I would be in terrible trouble and had no idea what would happen to me, so I lied. He told me if anyone ever told him again that I threw away my sandwiches or went dumpster diving, I would be made to feel very sorry. I could tell he didn't believe me. I stopped going through garbage cans and started begging for food from my friends again. Many times, I just went without. I was too afraid to complain to my dad about the sandwiches he made. I just kept telling him that I liked plain peanut butter and jelly sandwiches. Many months later, he started making them for me.

Despite these bumps in the road, overall my life was much improved and more predictable living with Dad than at any previous time. It made a big difference to be living with a sane parent. I no longer constantly feared for my life, nor did I have to sleep under my bed for protection. Nobody was attacking me in the middle of the night. No one was saying there were voices in the walls, killer germs everywhere or cars following us. No one was yelling at me to get in bed when I had been there all along. There were no more tortures, pills, burn sessions, ritual daily punishments or sexual contact. No longer did I live in minute-to-minute fear of when this would occur. No one held a knife to me or threatened to "slit my throat" if I didn't keep their disturbing and horrible secrets. There was no more violence in our home. Dad was consistent with his rules and, after a while, I knew what to expect. He was also fun! He liked to play games with me and take me places. Since I had started living with him, things in my life had improved greatly. However, living with my mother had taken a disastrous toll on my mental and emotional health. Dr. Gordon certainly had her work cut out for her. As a child, I had no idea how fortunate I was to be under her care.

When Opinions Collide

Mother had been an inpatient at Agnews State Hospital for eight-and-a-half months. During that time, she had sixteen shock treatments. The doctors' consensus was that she had improved in some areas. Her speech was coherent, but they seemed cautiously optimistic in regards to the degree of her overall improvement. They believed that she was much improved, but *not* successfully cured.

The doctors thought Mother could maybe hold some type

of job, which type was not clear. They still had many concerns. Because of this, she was not discharged, but released on an indefinite leave and was still considered a patient.

One month after Mother left Agnews she had a routine interview with Social Services. Mother wanted to know her rights. She denied responsibility and projected blame for the marriage problems and her illness onto my father. She also tried to convince the social worker that she was a little girl unable to take responsibility for the steps needed to resume a normal life. Mother had consulted a divorce lawyer, which I think she did previously. She also arranged to see a private psychiatrist. The social worker felt that while this gave the appearance of a focused effort, that Mother's goals seemed to be unclear. She did not mention any plans or have any desire to have me live with her again. Employment was not something Mother was actively seeking and she had no idea when she might start looking for a job.

It was the social worker's impression that my mother was still very disturbed and because of her high intelligence, she had the ability to hide or distract others from noticing some of her mental problems. The social worker also felt that she had a fixed delusional system involving mostly my father, but most likely everyone else in her life as well.

I don't know why Agnews released Mother. Maybe she acted in an acceptable manner and simply told them what she thought they wanted to hear. Perhaps the doctors felt that she had made as much progress as she could or that she was stable enough to manage adequately within society. I really don't know. I do know from the multitude of letters she had sent to Dad, which I read when I was an adult, that she wanted to get out of there in the worst way.

Just as my life started to settle down and become more

predictable, I was told that Mother had been released. The news shook my fragile little world to its core. All of the old fears came rushing back and I no longer felt safe. She came to the house to collect her things. I remember her driving away in my favorite car, the red and white Ford Fairlane, and my sadness to see it go. However, I was not sad to see *her* go! When the piano was moved to her new residence, I felt fairly certain that she wouldn't be living at the house anymore. However, my sense of security was shattered when, on several occasions, she broke into our house taking things she later claimed belonged to her. It was alarming and very frightening to know she was doing this. If she could steal our things, then maybe one night she would break in and steal me as well. My anxiety level sharply increased. I believed she had witch-like powers and might be able to pop in anytime she wanted. I was afraid that one night she would make good on her promises to kill Dad and me as we slept. I knew from experience that even when my dad was home, I still was not safe.

Unknown to me, in March of 1964, Mother filed for divorce. One of Mother's six demands stated that she wanted, "an order awarding Plaintiff [Mother] the care, custody and control of the minor child of the parties."

The *Cable v. Cable* custody war had begun. The first court action was to determine which parent was going to be granted temporary custody of me until the divorce and custody trial, which was set for January 1965. At this time, it was extremely rare for a father to get custody of minor children in the State of California, when the mother wanted custody. It was also very difficult to prove that a mother was "unfit." The courts also had the mindset, as they often do today, that women are more naturally capable of raising children than men.

The court ordered several investigations, including one

by the Santa Clara County Juvenile Probation Department. It was years before Child Protective Services was established. The results were submitted to California Superior Court Judge Rizzo on May 1, 1964. Tom Padmore, a Juvenile Probation Officer, made the investigation. Officer Padmore interviewed Mother, Dad, neighbors, family friends and doctors.

The consensus of neighbors and family friends was that I was in poor shape when I was living with Mother. They felt that while in her care I had been clingy and a crybaby, reacting to the slightest hurt. Some felt that I was a retarded child who would never be able to learn to ride a bike or engage in age-appropriate activities. After a year-and-a-half of living with Dad, they were all amazed at how much I had improved, how much happier I seemed to be and that I had learned to ride a bike. I also didn't seem to be retarded or a crybaby any longer. All of the neighbors and friends who were interviewed agreed that I had made remarkable improvement both in learning new things and in my own personal development.

Some of the people interviewed, included:

James Marshall, M.D., Mother's psychiatrist, suggested she go into Twin Pines Sanitarium for three weeks and, later, he also suggested she go to Agnews State Hospital. He said that Mother was paranoid schizophrenic and had been for many years. He stated that many doctors including the psychiatric staff at a hospital in Berkeley, California had treated her. He believed that my mother's condition was an ongoing chronic situation. If he had to choose the more adequate parent, he would *not* choose my mother.

Justin Perkins, M.D., my parents' physician, felt that living with Mother would be extremely damaging to me. He thought that my problems were the product of her mental illness. He said that Dad had his problems as well, but felt that he was a good parent. He said that Dad was not psychotic but Mother was; that she had been properly diagnosed and it would be a shame if the courts gave her custody.

Joseph Di Maria, (a.k.a. Indian Joe), said Dad had told him that he had seen me fondling my breasts. When he questioned me about this, I told him that Mother had taught me to do this by having me fondle her breasts.

Elsa Gordon, M.D., my psychiatrist, offered that Dad probably would have sought psychiatric help for me earlier, but was delayed. Dad had told her that he had left me to Mother because he did not want to tangle with her. Dr. Gordon had confidence in Dad's sincerity. She had interviewed Mother earlier in my therapy and was of the opinion that Mother was paranoid schizophrenic, as diagnosed by the State Hospital. Dr. Gordon stated that I had in fact acquired schizophrenic traits and characteristics from my mother. Dr. Gordon believed that I was suffering from severe emotional disturbance, and that this would progressively worsen if I were placed in my mother's custody. Dr. Gordon offered her professional opinion that she doubted my mother had normal mothering feelings toward me. Dr. Gordon also stated that I showed signs of extreme maternal deprivation. Dr. Gordon had full knowledge of my past neurological illness, Virus X, but that she doubted that there was a medical correlation between my psychiatric problems and Virus X. Dr. Gordon believed that my schizophrenia reactions were, in fact, largely acquired from Mother. Because of this, Dr. Gordon concluded that even limited visitation between Mother and me should only occur in the presence of a third party.

Daniel Hanson, M.D., my pediatrician, indicated that my illness, Virus X, was serious, but it was medically unrelated to my psychiatric problems. He stated that it would be a tragedy for me if Mother was to gain custody of me and that I had made remarkable improvement since Mother's departure from the home.

Alan Foster, M.D., a supervising psychiatrist at Agnews State Hospital, said that Mother received extensive treatment over a long period and that the hospital considered her a patient until she is *officially discharged.* She was only released on "indefinite leave." He mentioned that the social worker believed my mother was still suffering from her mental problems. Dr. Foster concluded that she was not a well person.

Officer Padmore was concerned about the genuine alarm my pediatrician and psychiatrist had expressed about my mother and if she were to gain custody of me. Both physicians had stressed that I was currently living in a period of mental recovery. Officer Padmore felt that the neighbors and friends of my parents supported this opinion and believed that I had improved since my mother had left.

Based on the interviews, Officer Padmore recommended to the court that temporary custody be given to my father.

Forced Visitation

When I was seven-and-a-half years old, the judge signed the order giving Dad temporary custody. Officer Padmore's investigation weighed heavily in the court's decision. Without this, Mother would certainly have been granted temporary custody of me. On Dad's behalf, Indian Joe sent a thank you note to Officer Padmore for his lengthy and thorough investigation. The letter reads in part:

It may be of some interest to you, and some gratifica-
tion to note the following makes this case quite different and apart from the general run of cases; that Dr.
Gordon, after a long and intensive study and treatment of this child, came to the firm conclusion that
the mother's psychotic condition caused very deep and
heavy damage to the child's mental health and equilibrium; that the mother was removed from the realm of
influence barely in the nick of time (and there is even
some question yet remaining on this point); that any
further continuation of direct influence by the mother
upon this child would have in very short order made
the child an "irretrievable case," and have caused her to
slip so far backwards as to make it impossible ever again
for her to retain any semblance of mental health.

Also, it may interest you to know that Dr. Marshall,
local psychiatrist, interviewed Mr. Cable on three separate occasions at the behest of Mrs. Cable's attorneys.
He could only report that Mr. Cable was a fit and proper custodian and that he recommended a continuance
of custody with the father. This is the first time I have
ever run up against a case in which an *opposing* psychiatrist took the view that coincided identically with those
of the opposition. His statements are in writing.

--Joseph F. Di Maria

Mother was granted temporary visitation rights. When
Dad broke the news to me that I would have to see her again, I
was horrified. My fear level shot off the scale. I also learned that
I had to see her four hours a week. Everything that was secure

and safe in my life started to crumble. I cried buckets of tears and pleaded with Dad not to make me go.

Why didn't the judge want to protect me from my mother? I wondered, *Wasn't that his job?*

I told Dad that the judge must hate children, but he assured me that the judge didn't feel this way. My tears turned to anger because the judge had made this terrible decision without even talking to me. I was frightened to think how powerful this faceless man was. I wondered if he had any idea how mean and hurtful his visitation order was to a little girl who had been hurt so much already. At least he had given temporary custody to Dad. However, it was just that: temporary. Dad told me that the judge believed all children needed contact with their mother. He felt a mother had a special kind of love for her child and that a child needed a "mother's touch," especially a young female child. I couldn't believe my ears! I had suffered for years from my mother's *"touch."*

Dad assured me that this was only a temporary visitation order. The final decision would be made at the next trial, in six months. Ironically, the judge decided that visitation with my mother would begin on July 4, 1964. The day we celebrate our country's freedom was the day the judge took away my freedom to choose whether I wanted to see my mother or not.

The judge forced me, against my will, to spend time with the person who had tortured, severely punished and terrorized me for years. I had nightmares every night. I was dreading that first visit and was very fearful about seeing Mother again. As the day grew nearer, the nightmares grew into night terrors. They would not go away, even when I opened my eyes. Dad was up all hours of the night with me. When he finally got me back to sleep the nightmares returned and I would wake up again, screaming.

It was well over a year since I had seen Mother. She had been in Agnews State Hospital and then needed time to resettle herself. She was now living in an apartment in Palo Alto. She took some secretarial classes when she was in Agnews, which helped her find a job as a file clerk at Stanford Hospital. Even though I had had no contact with Mother for over a year, I still was very afraid of her and what she might do to me -- especially if she got me alone. I told Dad that I was afraid and he told me that the court appointed Mary Jane to be the "third person." So I wouldn't have to be alone with my mother if I didn't want to be.

Throughout my young life and fearing for my life, I had kept Mother's secrets. Mary Jane had no idea what had transpired between my mother and me. Nevertheless, Mary Jane was very anxious about that first visitation. When I became an adult, she told me that she didn't know what to expect or how it would all go.

When Mother arrived for our first visitation, there were no happy tears or words that conveyed deep love or a longing to see me. She acted as if she hadn't missed me at all!

Mary Jane later told Indian Joe, "Tracy was very matter-of-fact. She just said, 'Hi Mom.' There were no tears on either side. There were no words or emotions that a mother would normally feel after being separated from her little child for so long, with no contact. When parting came, it was just a matter-of-fact goodbye." Mary Jane said that my mother had conducted herself and interacted with me, "as if she had just returned from a quick trip to the grocery store." Mary Jane said she was shocked by this and it left her speechless.

I was grateful that Mary Jane kept a watchful eye on us. However, I was angry that I was forced to see my mother and acted out as a seven-year-old child would under the circumstances. I did everything I could to annoy her and let her know, in my childish way, that I didn't want to be with her and wanted nothing to do with her. I *hated* her and everything she had done to me. Visitations were scheduled twice a week, on Thursday and Saturday. During this time, I tried to involve myself with the Knudson kids or other distractions, thus giving my mother as little time as possible. The more time I spent with the kids, the less time I had to spend with her. It was also nice to know that I was only two doors away from my home.

Even though Mary Jane was watching us, she was not always within earshot. Mother began a campaign to brainwash me, which she called her "little talks." She attempted to erase my memory of the past and turn me against my dad. She also ran him down to me. She started out slowly by trying to deny our history together. She insinuated that my dad had lied to me about the things I had actually witnessed. It angered me to hear her say these things. I was frightened to hear her threats of what she would do to me if I told anyone about *"our little talks."*

After I saw Mother a couple of times, Dad started saying some negative things about her. I felt that I was in the middle of a tug-of-war, between my parents. I was frightened that I would be torn apart by their efforts to alienate me from each other. To make matters worse, Dad was interrogating me after every visitation. "What did your mother say?" "What did *you* say?" "Does your mother talk about the past?" "Do you like seeing your mother?" And he asked many other questions. My anxiety hit a new high, as he would get angry with me when I wouldn't or couldn't answer him. He was also angry with me when he didn't like my answers, or felt I could have given better answers to my mother. He started coaching me about what to say, and how to say it, telling me how to reply to her questions and comments.

I was living in a state of continuous high anxiety, fear, sadness and insecurity. Some of this was caused or heightened by my parents' efforts to alienate me from each other. I was very upset and finally told Dr. Gordon about what was happening. She talked with my dad and he stopped the negative comments, but the grilling and coaching continued. Dr. Gordon called Indian Joe and told him about her concerns.

Indian Joe called Dad and told him to stop questioning and coaching me with anything that had to do with my mother. Indian Joe explained to him that this, along with his negative comments about my mother, had hurt me and could weaken Dad's position in court. He told Dad that if I offered information, he could only listen. Indian Joe warned him not to question or give me advice about anything that I offered to share with him. Dad immediately stopped. He told me about his talks with Dr. Gordon and Indian Joe. Dad apologized to me and asked me to forgive him, which I did. He never again engaged in any form of parental alienation.

Dr. Gordon and Indian Joe had no control over what my mother said to me. Her campaign to alienate me from Dad gradually increased in intensity and, as time went by, she started interrogating me about him.

By age seven, I knew what type of person Mother was, how dangerous she could be and that she was not to be trusted. I could tell that she had, what I thought at the time, was power over and ability to control adult minds. I also knew she could trick others by her words and hide the person she really was. Her lies could be very convincing!

Even though Mother tried to change our past, she was not convincing me! No one needed to tell me about my history with her. I knew all too well! Vividly, I remembered what had transpired and I was not afraid to tell her this fact. However, when she questioned me, I kept my answers short. It distressed her greatly that I could remember the horrible things she did to Dad and me. No matter what I said, Mother denied it vehemently. If she could blame Dad for the event, then she would try and I would correct her by telling her what actually had transpired. She only spoke of these things when she thought we were alone. It always came with a warning not to tell anyone else.

Often, when Mother thought we were alone, Mary Jane was peeking at us through a window. Unfortunately, she couldn't hear what my mother was saying to me. Mother would immediately change the subject any time Mary Jane or the kids came within earshot.

Mother's "little talks" became so overwhelming that I found it necessary to develop an "escape plan." During visitation, I always had my bike and my skates within easy reach.

Mary Jane testified to the California Superior Court on May 10, 1965. She stated that she had asked me why I always had my bike and skates at these visits. She told the court that I replied, "If my mother goes to say anything I don't want to listen to, I either ride off on my bike or I skate away."

At least I had the ability to physically escape from my mother and her poisonous words!

I became indifferent and nasty when speaking to my mother. I didn't pay attention to her directives. Every second of this forced contact with her was painful to me. I felt somewhat safe in showing and saying how I felt, but only to a small degree. I was certain she wouldn't abuse me in front of Mary Jane or her kids. Outwardly, I would ignore my mother as much as possible by distracting myself with toys, adults, kids or by escaping into my fantasy world. Inwardly, I was screaming from the depths of my soul.

Mother and I had visitation at Mary Jane's house twice a week from July 4, 1964, to January 1965. Mary Jane could no longer supervise our visits, due to surgery and health issues. She was our first "third person" and the best.

Parental Alienation and Fighting to Save My Sanity

The court proceedings for the divorce and permanent custody had just begun when my friends and I started to play a game on the walk home from school. We called it, "Step on a Crack, Break Your Mother's Back." While the other girls took great care to hop or jump over them, I stepped on every crack.

The next "third person," Mrs. Hayes, was chosen and we started to have visitation at her house in late January, or early February in 1965. The visitation times were changed from two hours twice a week to four hours once a week on Saturdays, as this better suited Mother's schedule.

At Mrs. Hayes's house, I no longer had the security and protection I had had with Mary Jane, who looked after me during the visitations, and had a personal interest in my safety. Mrs. Hayes was a stranger to me and lived several miles away. I couldn't bring my bike or skates. There was no opportunity for an "escape plan." Her children were older than I was except for two toddlers who were much younger. None of them were interested in playing with me, so I lost that distraction as well. Visitation was modified: instead of in the *presence* of a third person, it became at the *premises* of a third person. Because of this, I became even less protected and was more vulnerable. Mrs. Hayes was constantly busy with her own kids and stayed inside her house. This left me trapped in the backyard and isolated with Mother for long periods. Mrs. Hayes could not see or hear us from the house and no one in her family ever went into the backyard while we were there.

As time passed, Mother and I rarely saw Mrs. Hayes, except when we arrived at her house and when we left. At Mary Jane's house, Mother never got too far with her attempts to indoctrinate me into her ideal history and the lies she wanted me to believe about Dad. Mary Jane and her kids were always around and we were never left alone for long. Mother took advantage of our newfound privacy and went on a major brainwashing campaign with her "little talks." How I *hated* them!

Mother expanded on her endeavors by attempting to make me believe that Dad was at the bottom of all our troubles, as she continued her attempts to alienate me from him. She also tried to convince me that I would be better off without him. Sometimes she would use innuendos like, "You know who" had told me this or that, not mentioning Dad directly. Dad was always the person she would refer to as "that *other* somebody" or "that somebody you report to..." When she was frustrated with me, she would finally call him "your father." Often she used innuendos for other things as well. She also dropped hints, spoke in roundabout ways and was often obscure instead of direct in her approach.

From time to time, Mother reminded me that if I repeated anything she said, to anyone, the consequences would be "deadly" for both my dad and me. She told me that she could enter our house in the dead of night, so quietly that she would not be heard. Then she would "*slit our throats* as we slept." This increased my fear of her and her ability to pop in and out of places with "witch-like powers." Nighttime was *never* safe.

One day at visitation, Mother announced, "I want to do a little talking -- I never caused any problems at home. That 'other someone' caused *all* the problems. But you were too young to remember."

"I *can* remember. I remember *everything* you did to me!" I snapped back.

"You know who [your father] told you those things and they are *not* true. You can't *possibly* remember anything except what *he* told you to remember and they are lies, *all lies*!" she insisted, trying to control her anger.

"I do remember! Don't tell me what I remember and what I don't! *I know* what *you* did because *I was there!*" I said, resentfully.

"Now, calm down! There's no need to get upset. *We have to have our 'little talks'* and *you* need to listen to what I tell you because it *is* the truth."

"NO ONE HAS TO TELL ME WHAT HAPPENED, BE-CAUSE I REMEMBER! I *HATE* COMING ON SATURDAYS! YOU ALWAYS FORCE ME TO LISTEN TO YOUR LIES! *I HATE IT!* I'M GOING TO TELL MY DADDY!" I yelled.

Mother grabbed me by the shoulders and shook me hard. Then brought my face up to hers and hissed, "*Don't* you tell your father about *our* 'little talks!' They are between *you and me.* If you ever tell him, I will visit you in the night and you know what I will do to *you* and your *daddy!*"

The more Mother tried to brainwash me and deny responsibility for the other horrible things she did to me, the angrier I got with her. I became so worked up at times, I would yell the truth inches away from her face! Even though I was just eight years old, I could tell that she knew her words were lies. I could tell by the way she looked at me, her tonality and the way she rhythmically shook her head, which got much worse when she lied. Her eyes skittered away when she lied; otherwise, she was able to maintain eye contact. On the other hand, I could also tell when she *knew* I was telling the truth by the panic in her eyes revealed just before she looked away. Oh yes, she knew the difference between a lie and the truth! However, my response to her did not dissuade her. She only intensified her crusade, which infuriated me even more!

Ever since I was a young child, I fought to preserve my memories. Back when Mother had tortured and abused me, I forced myself to remember the details of each occurrence, repeatedly. I tried my best to retain my memories as *vividly* as possible. Even as a very young child, I knew that my reality was under fire. There was a lot of craziness back in those days! Between my mother's insanity and her hallucinations, she exposed me to a lot of unreal and incorrect information. The only place that these things were real was in *her* mind. My efforts to make myself remember those early years also stemmed from my search for reasonable explanations for the unusual events and all the torture and abuse I was suffering. There was no question about it -- I was under attack! Even though I was just eight years old, I knew I had to fight to continue to maintain my memories, as they were key to maintaining my sanity.

Mother soon realized she wasn't getting anywhere in her attempts to alienate me from Dad and to rewrite our history. She became more insistent that I believe her and resign myself to her way of thinking. I became extremely scared and agitated, yelling and crying as I denied her lies. It became an urgent, internal struggle to hold my fragile world together. Mother worked hard to destroy my memories, sanity and grip on reality with every poisoned falsehood that came out of her mouth! Her reality was *not* reality at all. Looking back, I believe she had evil intent and on some level, I knew this at the time. I felt I had right on my side, most of the time. She didn't see me as a living and breathing human being, but used me as an object, a pawn in her sick little game, which she was losing! Her response was to keep intensifying her efforts.

Then I began to realize something: the more I argued with Mother the harder she argued with me to sway me to her way of thinking. So, I tried something different. When Mother tried to change our history together and modify my memories, I would calmly tell her what actually happened. At first, this approach shocked and scared the heck out of her. She would beg me to say that I didn't remember. However, that did not stop me from explaining every little detail of exactly what she had done to me and set the record straight. She put all her effort into trying to convince me, but I calmly remained unconvinced. Sometimes I did this while crossing my arms and shaking my head with a big smile on my face. It wasn't easy, but it was working! When she realized her words had no effect she started hitting me or pinching me to make her points. I refused to let her win and I didn't waver. I thought I had found a way to dissuade her from her "little talks," but my plan didn't last for long.

When Mother realized she couldn't change my past memories she started to focus more on the present.

One Saturday she said, "Come over here, Tracy, I have something very important to tell you."

I walked over and sat down next to her. Nothing could have prepared me for what she was about to say.

"Your father doesn't really love you."

At first I was confused because I routinely asked him, multiple times a day and he always said he loved me. So, I replied, "My daddy says he loves me, every day."

"I know it's hard to believe, but he doesn't love you, he only *tells* you that so you will think he does," she insisted. She could tell that she had hit the mother lode of my insecurities.

I felt very vulnerable and weak. All of the strength had run out of my body. I tried to put on the bravest front I could as I stated, "*That's a lie!*"

However, my voice was quivering, which gave away how insecure I was about my relationship with Dad.

Then in the softest most understanding voice Mother could possibly muster she replied, "I know it's hard for you to accept. After all, you are only a child. I hate to be the one to break this news to you, but it's true. Honey, your father *only acts* as if he loves you, but he has *never* truly loved you."

My little world crumbled as I scanned Mother's face for any hint of a lie and detected nothing. She looked sad and deeply concerned for me. I started crying and she put her arms around me and held me close. I cried and cried. Nothing more was said until it was time to leave.

Mother expanded on this new campaign by telling me that I meant nothing to my father except to be a "robot" reporting to him about what she had said during visitations. Along with trying to convince me that he was to blame for all our problems, she also tried to convince me that *he* was the person who was trying to brainwash me. She transposed the things that she was doing with and to me, onto him. Then Mother tried to convince me that Dad had contorted my memories of the past, because I believed his lies! She gained a foothold by using my insecurities against me and attacking Dad in the present. Then she began to mix the present with the past and I was completely overwhelmed. I didn't have the inner resources to be able to cope with this new attack. It scared me terribly to think that some of the things she was saying about my dad in the here and now might have some truth to them. My night terrors increased dramatically. I was still somewhat uncertain about my relationship with my dad and had trust issues with him.

Mother's newest approach had rocked my insecure little world to its core. I didn't want her to know the fear she had created deep inside of me, so I denied the things she said and told her they were untrue. As time went on I became more convincing, which infuriated her. This was all going on with the third person in the house, out of earshot. Mother was doing everything she could to interject confusion, doubt, lies and chaos into my thought process. I fought her attempts at every visitation, which she had turned into mental torture sessions.

Although, I never verbally told Dr. Gordon what Mother had done to me when I had lived with her -- during play therapy I demonstrated some of those horrors. I also demonstrated what Mother was doing to me during visitations. Dr. Gordon testified in court that my actions in the playroom backed up my words one hundred percent, week after week, month after month and year after year. Because my actions and words were consistent with each other, she knew I was telling the truth. At some point, I became brave enough to tell her about the visitations in which Mother had told me that Dad didn't love me and I cried to Dr. Gordon about how horrible it was. Dr. Gordon became very concerned about the toll this had taken on me and she started to work with me in a different way. With her help, I found the strength to start pushing back again, by telling Mother that I knew Dad loved me and I *knew* that she had lied. I learned distraction techniques, which helped me in changing the subject.

Mother was impossible to detour for long and always came back to the subject, leaving me to think of another way

to distract her again. She had a million different ways of trying to convince me to see things her way. When I was feeling
vulnerable, I told her I could remember every terrible thing
she ever did to me; I knew it as well as I knew my name. I
told her that she didn't have the *power* to force me to think
differently and that nothing she did to me would ever force
me to bend. As the words came out of my mouth, I hoped
they were convincing. Often I felt very fragile and vulnerable, but I hoped that my words would hide these feelings
and convince her that I was strong. It was a continual fight
to maintain my sanity, as Mother continued her efforts to
destroy it on a weekly basis.

I stepped up my efforts to review and retain my memories.
I knew that if I exchanged my reality for my mother's that I
would be lost forever. I knew that what she was doing to me
was poisonous and maybe worse than *anything* she had done to
me before. I fought her attempts to brainwash me as if fighting for my life. I argued with *her* reality and told her she was
wrong to do this to me. I didn't care if she hit me. I didn't care
if she shook me until my teeth rattled, which she did out of
pure frustration. I knew that no matter what she did to me that
I had to fight for my reality and what I knew to be the truth!

I replayed my memories repeatedly, keeping them vivid
and alive in my mind. Sometimes I told my friends. Sometimes
I play acted my memories out in the privacy of my bedroom.
I hung onto them like a life preserver in a raging sea. I believe
that my memories and my courage to maintain them saved
me from irreversible mental damage. Mother didn't give up on
these crusades and pursued them into my teenage years.

With Mother's every attempt to brainwash me, change my
memories, challenge the reality of our past relationship, run
down Dad and tell me that he didn't love me, my relationship

with her deteriorated. I literally *hated* going to visitation and I *hated her* for what she was trying to do to me during the time we were together. It's interesting how Mother's efforts to alienate me from Dad had a boomerang effect, leaving me feeling negative toward her when she tried so hard to make me feel negative towards him. This was what visitation was all about. The result was that Mother was unable to develop any kind of positive, meaningful relationship with me. The only feelings she succeeded in instilling in me towards her were fear, distrust and hatred. My feelings toward Mother were directly reflected by her actions.

When There Is No Protection

One day at visitation, as Mother was trying to alienate me from my father and I was yelling at her that she was a liar -- something changed. As usual, we were alone in Mrs. Hayes's backyard. I was very upset and crying about things Mother was saying to me about Dad, when she opened her bag and pulled out some homemade cookies and candies.

"Would you like a special treat?" Mother asked slyly.

I was in no mood to eat and didn't want Mother's treat. I was very angry and hurt. I refused her offer several times.

"Eat one of these right now," she demanded.

"No! I don't want it."

Mother quickly grabbed the back of my head with one hand and pinched my nose tightly closed with the other. She held my head so tightly there was no escape.

When I opened my mouth to breathe, Mother jammed her "treat" into my mouth, filling it and making me choke. Then she wrapped her hand tightly around my nose and mouth making breathing impossible.

"Do you ever want to breathe again?"

I was barely able to nod in reply.

"Then chew that up and swallow it right now!"

Out of breath, choking and afraid I might die, I swallowed. Mother was angry and I was afraid she was going to kill me.

"Now that wasn't so bad was it? Eat another one, Tracy, or I will give you the same treatment."

I did what I was told.

Not too long after I swallowed Mother's treat, I began to slow down and felt very tired. My thinking was fuzzy and I felt like I had lost control over my own thoughts and actions. I was sluggish and clumsy. Somehow, Mother had gained control over me! She told me to repeat things she said and I did automatically, without thinking for myself. She had me draw pictures of us and write, "I love you Mommy," under them. I felt like I was losing myself as a person.

Mother made me do and say things that I would not normally say or do. She had me repeat over and over, "My father doesn't love me," "I love my mommy," and anything else she wanted me to say. On some level, I felt ashamed, but I couldn't control my words. I simply did what I was told to do like a mindless little robot! I thought that she had hypnotized me, but I wasn't certain. I had no free will and I was terribly afraid. I didn't understand what was happening to me.

The next Saturday Mother started by offering me some candy. Remembering what she had done to me last Saturday, I took a couple. I had the same strange feeling come over me. This time she had me write a note saying that I loved her and I missed living with her. I lost all sense of myself again and became a puppet for her to control at will. I became agreeable to her and felt compelled to do whatever she said, which wasn't like me.

After that visit, I felt very tired, my speech was slurred and I couldn't walk right. I knew something terrible was happening to me, but didn't know what it was. I thought Mother was using some kind of magical power to hypnotize me, because I only felt this way when I was with her. Fears of her being a witch came back to haunt me. I didn't know what to do, or what she might do if I told anyone about it, so I kept my thoughts and feelings to myself.

After visitation, Dad and one of his friends picked me up. They noticed something was wrong with me. At first, they thought I was sick. We drove home and Dad put me to bed. They checked in with me quite often and they came to the same conclusion. Dad called my pediatrician, Dr. Hanson and then Indian Joe, telling them that both he and his friend thought I had been drugged. However, I was not made aware of this concern.

Indian Joe hired an investigator who went to the Hayes's backyard and set up recording equipment, so Indian Joe could hear what was going on during visitation. The investigator also hid under the house and watched us through the ventilation screens. Neither Mother nor I were aware that any of this was taking place.

Dr. Gordon called Indian Joe asking if it would be legally safe for her to coach me about what to do or say when my mother told me untrue or hurtful things about my father. She told him that she felt these comments were destructive to me and counterproductive to my recovery. She wanted me to have a way of protecting myself. She went on to say that she was willing to go to court and give solid medical testimony to this effect. If she couldn't coach me about this, then she thought visitation should be stopped.

The following is an excerpt from Indian Joe's notes regarding their conversation:

I [Indian Joe] told her [Dr. Gordon] that I didn't think that we should terminate the visits, although she hinted very strongly that this is what she might desire at the present time. I said that we would look bad if we terminated them on our own, that we should have a court order before we do this, but I told her that I thought, first and foremost, that the child should be able to say something such as the doctor was suggesting, such as, "I don't think it's fair, Mother, that you talk to me this way, and I won't listen to you. If you keep talking this way, I'll go inside the house and stay near Mrs. Hayes." I told the doctor that once a child has to say this that it isn't so good because of the pressure [put upon the child by the mother], the up glances and the long [hostile] stares would be tough on her [the child]. However, we will wait to see what happens.

Then Indian Joe added his own personal thoughts:

Perhaps the best thing to do is to see whether or not after one admonition of this kind from the child, based upon advice and consultation with Dr. Gordon and the child, whether the mother would stop this sort of thing. If she persists or if the visits become intolerable because of her lack of cooperation or glares at the child, then, of course, I will go into court and the doctor will back me up. We will ask for termination of all the visitation rights.

In fact, I'll stop the visitations on my own. I didn't tell the doctor this, but I would at that point. I didn't want to appear to be too forceful, but first and foremost, I will protect the child. Nor did I tell her what plans we have and why I want her [Tracy] outside [in the Hayes's backyard] for the next visitation.

Starting with Mother's next visitation, Dr. Hanson either accompanied Dad to pick me up or was waiting at our house, every Saturday, immediately following visitation. Dr. Hanson wanted me to pee in a jar. This was very embarrassing. However, this became routine every Saturday following visitation. Despite Dr. Gordon's encouragement, I was not yet brave enough to tell my mother to stop saying terrible things about my dad, or to go stand by Mrs. Hayes. I was afraid my mother would view this action as a threat that I might tell the third person her *secrets*. Mrs. Hayes was a stranger to me. How was I supposed to feel safe under the circumstances?

The Tapes

Visitations were now audiotaped and sometimes the investigator was under the house watching us through the vents. The microphone was set up in the backyard where Mother and I spent most of our time. We had no knowledge of this, which was the whole idea. Indian Joe wanted to hear and have an eyewitness as to what was going on during visitation. The tapes that were pertinent to the case were transcribed at the time and submitted to the court as evidence. My urine test results were also submitted.

The following are conversations taken from these tape recordings. Note: At times, I added thoughts or clarification by putting my words in [square brackets] to distinguish my words from those of the speakers. Entered as Defendant's [Father's] exhibit "H" [minus the square bracket statements] on May 4, 1965 to California Superior Court:

Visitation on March 13, 1965

Mother: I want you to come over here because I want to do a little talking.

Tracy: Why?

Mother: Because don't you think that a mother and daughter ought to talk once in a while?

Mother: Are you worried about it?

Tracy: No.

Mother: Well don't be because I don't talk to you about things I shouldn't.

(Tracy sings a little bit)

Mother: You have a pretty new jacket. Did you get it at the store?

Tracy: At my daddy's store.

Mother: That's nice.

Tracy: It isn't new either, so don't say it is.

Mother: Well I don't know Tracy, you see I know very little about you because I haven't been able to see much of you, have I?

Tracy: Oh yes you have, every Saturday.

Mother: And you think that is -- that is a lot?

(They both talk at once.)

Mother: (garbled)

Tracy: Five hours. 2 million and 80 minutes, it is!

Mother: Four hours, not five. (Garbled) The thing is -- (they talk briefly about the bench). But the only thing, you know, this is very important for a mother to see her child. [It] should be important for the child too, shouldn't it?

Tracy: I don't know.

Mother: (Garbled)

Tracy: Anyway you have your own, don't you? (Referring to the candy.)

Mother: Yes I do darling, you don't have to share them with me. But would you if you had to?

Tracy: Yes.

Mother: Well that's good manners anyway. (Pause) Because if it were up to one person in the world, [your father] I wouldn't be allowed to see you. And it has been, and is, very very hard to understand that. Did you ever ask what happened to me when I left the house? Did you?

Tracy: (Garbled)

Mother: (Garbled) Poor honey. I'm talking about you sweetheart. You're a very good child, Tracy. And of course your father has told you what he wants you to believe.

Tracy: He says he is leaving you. (Garbled) I'm (garbled) leaving you because here we are. (Garbled)

Mother: Do you know why we're here?

Tracy: Because of, because of my (garbled) us a promise (garbled)

Mother: He [the judge] sent you to me in the first place because you're my (garbled) baby. And I had to find out if I could see you. I never committed any (garbled) problems (garbled). You see I had -- I had to go elsewhere. But the main thing is that I want you to know that I love you dearly. And that I made such an effort to come and see you. I'd like to see you very often.

Tracy: This tastes like peppermint.

Mother: And I don't ever want you to go away from me, Tracy. Do you think that you could manage that? You think you can manage to stay my little girl too? (Garbled) You see honey, I don't want to scare you or frighten you or anything like that. And I think you get worried about this whole business and I can see why you do. But, uh, now did you ask Dr. Gordon what happened between your mother and father? Or did you just ask your dad about it? Do you remember?

Tracy: I remember what happened.

Mother: What happened honey?

Tracy: Not going to tell you.

Mother: Why? Does it hurt you?

Tracy: Not only that, it makes me sad.

Mother: Honey why do you insist that you remember? Please don't say that.

Mother and I got into a discussion about my deceased cats, Cinders and her kittens. She insisted I could not remember and tried to alter my memories about it. She told me that she had *never* hurt my cats and had not had them killed. She said that I could not possibly remember what had happened to Cinders and her kittens. She had underestimated me. Not only could I remember what she had done to my cats, I remembered it *vividly*. She further tried to convince me that my "so-called memories" must have come from my dad and that his version was a lie. I was inconsolable and very angry about the falsehoods that she was forcing upon me. She was not just lying to me, but attempting to brainwash me and to make me believe that I couldn't perceive reality correctly, which in itself is *crazy making*. I was crying and denying her untrue statements. I told her that I knew exactly what she did to my cats. The argument escalated, as I refused to replace my memories with her fiction. The kittens were dropped and the discussion focused on Cinders.

…**Mother:** It makes no difference; I'll buy it [a replacement kitten for Cinders] sooner. However, I am going to tell you something else, you were told this [by your father that I had Cinders killed] to make you unhappy, but I don't want you to believe it. Now, I had a lot of problems myself, but I would never hurt your cat, I never would and I'm so very glad you told me that. This is a most important thing for me to know how you are getting along. And I did not…

(Tracy interrupts her mother with crying and the following)

Tracy: I'm getting along *fine* with my daddy. Don't tell me, don't tell me. I *want* to *live* with him too.

Mother: All right. Will you be quiet honey? You don't have to cry over it. You don't have to cry over it. WILL YOU STOP CRYING so I can get a peppermint ["treat"] in your mouth? Hmmm?

(Tracy sobs very loudly.)

Mother: If you're going to cry like that then everyone is going to come running out and maybe that's what you want. I don't know.

Tracy: (Crying) I want to go home.

Mother: Your father has done -- please don't say that. You and I are going to have to talk together once in a while, honey. Please stop crying, please stop crying. Tracy! You know something; you don't have to go home. I'll go home. Will that make you happy? I'll go home and you go ahead and yell as much as you want to.

Tracy: I'll stop crying if you go home.

Mother: Yes, but I have *never* made you cry. You have made yourself cry (garbled) because

(Tracy interrupts)

Tracy: I HAVE NOT! I HAVE NOT! I HAVE NOT!

Mother: Okay, okay. Honey, honey, honey, honey.

Tracy: YOU! In a minute I'm going to burst. I'm going to go and tell Mrs. Hayes. (Tracy cries)

Mother: Wouldn't that be dreadful because you know what they would do then?

Tracy: What?

Mother: Honey you know that it is the court who orders -- just a minute, just a minute. I'm not hurting your feelings. I want to tell you it was the court who ordered… Tracy, I'm going to have to go because I can't stand it if you weep and accuse me unjustly. Do you know what unjustly means? I'm a woman who has loved her child and because you were told that I gave the cat away frightfully…

Tracy: I was not, I was not, I was not! [Told this.]

Mother: All right, all right, I believe you. I love you, honey. Put your arms around me and tell me: Mother I love you because you had a hard time. Don't you say anything to me about …

Mrs. Hayes: [Finally comes out to the backyard to see what's wrong] Tracy, what's the matter? (Garbled)

Tracy: She killed my cat! She did it, she did it! I can remember; *she* did it!

Mother: (Garbled) Today I don't know.

Tracy: I want to go home to my daddy and stay with him. (Tracy cries)

Their talking fades as they go into the house.

During most visitations Mother engaged me in poisonous conversation -- sometimes by dropping innuendos and sometimes painfully spelling out her intentions to turn me against Dad. She denied our history together, while creating her own version to replace it. She often attacked or denied my memories and what had transpired between us. The above is an example that was caught on tape. Never once, over the years, was Dad contacted when I cried, asked or pleaded with the third person to call him to come and take me home. No matter what Mother did or said to make the situation unbearable, I was never allowed to go home early. I was forced to suffer through anything she chose to dish out.

Later the same day...

Tracy: I didn't say I wanted to live with you last week, did I?

Mother: If you wanted to live with me?

Tracy: Uh huh.

Mother: Well I should think you would want to live with me, part of the time anyway -- you could you know.

Tracy: Did I say that I wanted to live with you?

Mother: Part of the time?

Tracy: No! Last time when I saw you did I say I wanted to live with you?

Mother: Why do you ask that?

Tracy: Oh never mind, forget it!

Mother: I can't forget it though, because you see if everyone says to forget it and they don't give me any reason, it's like a child when they just tell you to do this, do that, and that's not right, is it?

Tracy: Let's play horsey!

Mother: I don't know what's wrong with you living with me. I told you once you could see all your old friends; you could see your father.

(Tracy changes the subject)

Tracy: Mother you don't really want me to, do you?

Mother: Mother I am, gee, mother I am going to be sad if you don't do as I tell you to do mother. [She was trying to be funny.]

(Tracy giggles.)

Mother: Will you tell Dr. Gordon that? I'm going to tell my mother I'm going to be sad unless I stay with my mother. Will you tell Dr. Gordon that? Oh boy, I want to stay with my mother! That's going to fall back and break the glades. [Meaning it would destroy my father's custody case, if I were to ask to live with my mother.] (Garbled) almost had me weeping today, tell her [Dr. Gordon] that. Tell her I felt so badly I almost killed myself and my mom. Boy I felt blue enough to do that. Don't be afraid to say you want to come home to me. This is to be expected. You are only a child. You love both your parents, I think. You just go ahead and say that. Because you can bring it about if you want it bad enough.

Tracy: What should I say? What should I say?

Mother: I don't dare say, because you might say, Oh I feel sad! My poor mother will go kill herself. I feel sad. I want my mama. Take me to my mother's, I feel sad. (Laugh) Wouldn't that be dreadful [for your father] honey?

(Subject changes)

<u>Visitation on March 20, 1965</u>

This visitation started with Mother feeding me drugs, which she had concealed in her "treats." When the drugs took effect, she intensely interrogated me about Dad's activities. She had questions about whether I was sleeping at someone's house, if Dad had gone away somewhere, where Dad was every night, what time he generally arrived home, whether he was home the day before, how many days a week he worked late, who watched me when he was late, whether he was there in the mornings when I woke up and lots of other questions about his comings and goings. I answered the best I could. Although I didn't like to be interrogated about his activities, I liked it a lot better than Mother's attempts to change my reality.

...Mother: Tell me something, how do you feel about last week? (Garbled) last week? Hmmm?

Tracy: Why do you ask me that?

Mother: Why do I ask you that?

Tracy: Yes.

Mother: Because (garbled)

Tracy: Ah blau!

Mother: (Garbled) (Walking noise) Did somebody (complain or explain) to you honey about being depressed?

Tracy: Yeah.

Mother: They did?

Tracy: Yeah, Daddy. DA! [Duh.]

Mother: Did the doctor check you?

Tracy: Stop! Stop! Stop!

Mother: But Tracy...

Tracy: Stop, stop.

Mother: Or don't you want to talk about it?

Tracy: No stop!

Mother: (garbled)

Tracy: No!

Mother: Okay.

Tracy: DO YOU GET THE MESSAGE?! (Shouting)

(Subject changes)

Mother: You're not going to get too hot running around? Do you want to take off your underwear or anything?

Tracy: I don't want to. I (garbled) it's cold. (Pause) Don't pull that down!

Mother: Just a little down so your neck can get some fresh breeze on it.

Tracy: No!

Mother: Now don't be so cross.

Tracy: Oh it's cold (garbled) it's cold. I'm freezing in this thing. Are you nuts?

Mother: You know you don't call mothers nuts. What's your father say, your mother is [a] nut, huh? If you have something to say about it [you should say] you love her and how!

Tracy: 'cause he [my father] isn't a nut.

Mother: Oh, he just thinks I'm a nut, huh?

Tracy: No.

Mother: (Laughing) you (garbled) gave yourself away.

Tracy: Come on, come on!

Mother: And do you think I am too?

Tracy: We-e-e-l-l-l.

Mother: He thinks that because he doesn't know any better. He doesn't bother to come [to visitation] and see, does he?

Tracy: Come on!

Mother: Think about that. People who don't bother to come and see someone [for themselves] and [then] call [that person a] something something...yeah. [Sic.]

Tracy: Come on!

Mother: Gives you something to think about doesn't it? He never did bother to come [to visitation]. Think about that. If you think I'm a nut I want to tell you something. You want to come and talk to my doctor about it? A doctor would know wouldn't he!

Tracy: I guess so.

Mother: Yeah he sure would.

(Tracy changes the subject.)

Mother: May I do a little talking?

Tracy: Yeah.

Mother: (garbled)

Tracy: You love me, right, huh. (In a laughing, not buying it, kind of tone.)

Mother: Do you want to say you love me right! Sure you do.

Tracy: No I don't. Not right now.

Mother: Well.

Tracy: Why Mommy (garbled) cannot scream, not now.

Mother: I think you're just trying to avoid the question. (She laughs) You know something Tracy it is a good idea to love your parents. Even your mother. Especially your mother, who bore you, who (garbled).

(Tracy changes the subject to snails.)

Mother: Do you love me?

Tracy: (Makes some high-pitched whining sounds, very loudly.)

Mother: Are you crazy about me?

Tracy: (Again the loud whiny sound.)

Mother: I'm not coming to this (garbled).

Tracy: NO! (In a whiny voice)

Mother: Are you mad about me?

Tracy: NO! (In the loud whiny voice)

Mother: Huh -- yeah?

Tracy: No.

Mother: You aren't? Well that's your tough luck.

(Chuckle) That's your problem. That is your problem.

(Tracy changes the subject.)

Visitation on March 27, 1965

Tracy: No announcements this afternoon?

Mother: No what?

Tracy: No announcements this afternoon?

Mother: No, no announcements. Have you any announcements from your side of the family that you would like to tell me about -- to make known?

Tracy: (garbled)

Mother: You aren't supposed to talk about any of the things we talk about. Did you know that?

Tracy: Where?

Mother: When you and I talked together, (Pause) except to Dr. Gordon. Least that's a good idea, huh?

Tracy: I can talk to my daddy about things.

Mother: *Don't* you talk about what *we* talk about. Just like you don't talk to me about what you and he talked about. What do you think of that?

Tracy: (Garbled)

Mother: Don't you see it wouldn't be right, would it? Otherwise -- (something clanks) Now what did you find? A sliver, aren't you lucky. It's big as a sword.

(Giggle) Like a needle. Well not really honey, but I'm trying to show you what is fair and what is right.

(Both talk at once)

Mother: That's all I...

Tracy: My daddy loves me.

Mother: Who says so?

Tracy: (In a very excited tone) *I did*, because *I know*, because *I live* with him.

(Noises and mumbling then Tracy gets very excited and yells a lot.)

(Subject changes)

Later... (Playing a game [Cowboys and Indians].)

Tracy: You can shoot me. You can shoot me.

Mother: (Garbled) I don't want to shoot you.

Tracy: Don't you want to win the game?

Mother: I'd like to win the game but I don't want to shoot you. (Garbled) I want you to turn around and give me a kiss on the cheek. You wanted to shoot me ever since you've been having your heart-to-heart talks with somebody [my father]. Now who could that somebody be? Yeah... That somebody that you report to all the time.

[Again, "that somebody" or "that someone" always meant my dad.]

Tracy: NO!

Mother: Tracy...

(Tracy interrupts)

Tracy: You can shoot me first.

Mother: Why, don't get angry with your mother honey. It's a good idea to remember that your mother (garbled) is a part of your growing up, and a big part of it. Turn around and I'd like to see you act nice. Okay? That ought to make sense doesn't it? (More is said that cannot be understood.)

Tracy: No!

Mother: You feel you're going to do something (garbled) that your father doesn't like.

(Tracy changes the subject.)

The end of the tapes.

My Doctors Take the Stand

My urine test came back positive for a couple of different types of tranquilizers, but mainly one called Meprobamate. Even with these lab results, the tapes and the eyewitness accounts of the investigator, the court was still not convinced that my mother was drugging me. Mother was blaming Dad, but of course, she had no evidence to back up her claims. Every time Mother wronged me or did something horrid to me, she always turned the tables and accused my dad for her actions or words, as if they were his. She tried to convince anyone who would listen. She was well practiced and was very convincing.

The court was convinced that one of my parents had given me Meprobamate and was interested in pursuing the responsible party.

In court, Indian Joe questioned Dr. Hanson and then Dr. Gordon regarding their involvement, and the effects Meprobamate had on me. The following is a portion of their testimonies, starting with Dr. Hanson. Taken in part from the California Superior Court transcript dated May 4, 1965:

...**Q:** Now, you were requested by Mr. Cable to participate in an effort to get some urine of Tracy Cable's here sometime back?

A: Yes.

Q: Then what did you do?

A: I stayed with her until we obtained a urine specimen, which would be about 30 to 45 minutes, after we picked her up [from visitation].

Q: Was there anyone else in the bathroom with her?

A: No.

Q: Then mailed it [the urine sample] where?

A: To the -- I forget the exact name of the laboratory, but it is a laboratory in San Jose, to analyze the contents.

Q: Would it be The Laboratory of Criminology of Santa Clara County?

A: Yes.

Q: Now, did you request any specific chemical analysis?

A: I requested it be analyzed for tranquilizers, barbiturates, and any other sedatives that they could analyze it for.

Q: What were the results?

A: That it [Tracy's urine sample] contained Meprobamate, which is a tranquilizer, sold as Equanil or Miltown.

Q: Considering the possible use of Meprobamate by a layman, is there a large or small margin of error with respect to the use of such a drug from the standpoint of its possible serious or *fatal* consequences?

A: A fairly small margin of error.

Then Indian Joe questioned Dr. Gordon. Taken in part from the California Superior Court transcript on May 4, 1965:

...**Q:** Now, Doctor, with reference to this point about this sense of unreality that Tracy carries with her, is there any danger in administering any type of barbiturate or sedative type of tranquilizer to a child in that condition?

A: I feel so. When a child is given something without the child's knowledge that disturbs her state of equilibrium, Tracy could only feel that something was happening inside of her that she had no knowledge or understanding about, and she became extremely distressed.

Q: And with a state in which she were, let's say, submerged by the ingestion of some type of drug such as I mentioned, would such a state increase her state of unreality?

A: It actually did, she stated she couldn't understand what was happening to her. She was actually losing her sense of control over her own self, her own feelings or what she was saying. She felt she could no longer control this.

Q: And you noticed what specifically in her, then, at this time with respect to this business of her sense of reality being tied in with reality?

A: She was -- she was much more anxious within the playroom, she would jump about, she couldn't settle down to any particular activity, she complained about the visits and said she didn't know what was happening to her. She just felt different and she couldn't understand why or what. She was afraid that she was saying things that she didn't mean to say. She didn't know why she was saying them.

Q: To her mother, you mean?

A: To her mother.

The transcript of Dr. Gordon's cross-examination reads in part:

...**Q:** Anything else that she [Tracy] reported to you as having happened about this trial coming up?

A: Simply that she was afraid that she wouldn't be able to say what she felt like saying, that her mother would hypnotize her into saying things that she didn't mean.

Q: Where do you suppose an idea like that might have come from in a child?

A: Well, she said that she hadn't been able to say what she wanted to say when she was with her mother, that it seemed like she couldn't say the things she wanted to say, that she was made to say things just the opposite from what she wanted to say.

Q: When she was with her mother?

A: Yes.

Between direct and cross-examination, Dr. Gordon's entire testimony was fifty-eight pages long.

Truth, Lies and Deceit

After Mother drugged me, forced me to write notes stating that I loved her and wanted to live only with her, it all felt like a dream. However, it wasn't a dream at all. Mother's attorney submitted these writings and drawings to the court as evidence. The expert stated that someone was trying to copy my handwriting style. His opinion was that I did write some of the notes submitted to evidence, but not all. I would have never written or made these notes and drawings if I had not been in a drug-induced state. Never at any time did I want to live with my mother. The only time I told her I loved her was when she forced me to, after she gave me her tainted "special treats."

With my doctor's testimony, the judge became very interested as to which parent was drugging me. My mother immediately stated she believed my father was responsible. The judge made it clear that the responsible party would be held accountable. I believe the court felt certain that it was inconceivable for a mother to drug her child.

Dad and I went to Arcata to visit our friends the Gibsons over Easter vacation.

Indian Joe sent the following telegram to my mother's attorneys:

Cable and daughter left today on vacation in the country and will return Friday, April 16.

--Joseph F. Di Maria

On the trip home, I broke down and begged Dad not to make me see my mother the next day. I recited some of the horrors of seeing her. Dad told me he was sorry, but that I had to see her. I begged, pleaded, and finally cried myself to sleep. Dad contacted Indian Joe, told him what was going on and wanted to know what could be done.

Indian Joe sent this Western Union telegram to one of my mother's attorneys, stating:

Please inform Mrs. Cable visitation is not possible this weekend. The child registers too many unhappy affects about visiting with her mother.

--Joseph F. Di Maria

Their response was prompt. Mother's attorney went into court and convinced the judge to sign a restraining order against Dad to stop him from interfering with visitation.

Shortly after the Meprobamate issue was brought to the court's attention, and these telegrams were sent, Indian Joe pressured the court to stop the visitations. However, he could only convince the judge to stop visitation temporarily. It was done and I was overjoyed. Not long after the judge made this decision, my mother convinced him that I should see her one more time. The judge agreed with her and ordered one more visitation. I was devastated at this turn of events and cried and cried. The visitation took place at Mary Jane's house. We never again had visitation at Mrs. Hayes's house.

My parents agreed to take separate lie detector tests to help determine which parent was responsible for drugging me. Dad took his test first. The Associates Security Agency gave my dad the polygraph examination. They asked many questions including: whether he had ever given or had ever instructed anyone else to administer tranquilizers to me, whether he had ever given me Meprobamate, whether he ever had Meprobamate in his possession, and whether he ever put tranquilizers in my food or drink. He answered, "No" to all of the questions.

Dad passed the test. The report to the court stated:

There were no significant emotional disturbances indicative of deception in the Polygraph Records of Jonathan Cable. Therefore, it is the opinion of this examiner, based upon the subject's Polygraph Records, that he is telling the truth in this matter.

A few days later, Mother was asked the same questions. After she had completed her polygraph test, she questioned the person who administered the test and learned that my dad had passed. She immediately questioned whether her polygraph would be considered valid because of her history of mental illness. The polygraph examiner submitted a declaration to the court stating that he was not informed that Mother had been released from a mental hospital and because of this, her answers would not be considered valid. She got her attorney to motion the court not to have her results disclosed. The judge agreed and the entire Meprobamate matter was immediately dropped. If she had passed her polygraph test, why would she not want the results to be known?

Then Mother's attorney wrote the following letter to the judge:

Dear Judge Riley:

I should like to request that before the court make any order with respect to custody and visitation, an opportunity be afforded to each the plaintiff and defendant to meet with you privately in chambers for a discussion. I understand that Mr. Cable's polygraph examination showed a favorable result for him; I am happy that this occurred because it cleared the atmosphere and will perhaps allow these people to join in their interest for the welfare of Tracy.

From the point of view of our client, it is, of course, so important that she be able to reestablish herself fully in the world of her daughter without the hampering effects and restrictions of the visitation agreement previously made. I think it is clear to all of us that these have only served to create problems for this child and for our client, and perhaps both parents.

We do not wish to impose upon the court but want to do everything, which will assist it in making a decision in the matter.

Thanking you, I am.
Very truly yours,
Peter J. Molino

Mother's attorney now wanted the entire Meprobamate issue swept under the rug. Considering the overwhelming evidence that she had drugged me, her attorney now wanted to put me in a worse situation by increasing visitation and eliminating the minimal protection of the third person. Her attorney's view was simple; he couldn't pin the drugs on my dad, so the whole matter should be dropped without any consideration for my safety.

The judge completely dropped the Meprobamate issue as if it never existed. He said there would be consequences for the parent responsible. The whole matter was tossed out when that parent turned out *not* to be Dad. Shortly after this, the court ordered me to have visitation with Mother again on a regular basis.

The Court Appointed Psychiatrist

Judge Riley appointed Helen Rothenberg, M.D. as the Court Psychiatrist to interview my parents and me. She would then report to the court about her opinions and recommendations, relative to custody and visitation.

Dr. Gordon sent a letter to Dr. Rothenberg before she began her interviews with my family. It read in part:

Enclosed are reports of the first and second psychological testing examinations of Tracy, plus two communications from Mr. Cable which give some flavor of the general nature of some of the problems which existed. The cat [Cinders] incident was corroborated repeatedly by Tracy in play sessions. The exact nature of the sexual play was never repeated by Tracy to me, but many times Tracy's play and physical movements indicated the presence of bizarre sexual fantasies and great anxiety.

[During] initial examinations at age six-and-a-half, Tracy was extremely timorous, hesitant in her actions. There was an overall sense of helplessness, confusion, and enormous anxiety. Her voice had a peculiar baby-ish lilt. Some of her responses were inappropriate. Tracy impressed me as an extremely disturbed child with flightiness of movement, severe personality disorganization. She relates in a tense, gritty manner, extremely fearful, was almost mechanical in her responses. I was not a person, only a fearful unknown object.

Dx: pre-psychotic disorder.

Course of therapy:

All of Tracy's play sessions have been characterized by intense random, essentially disorganized non-directed activity which has shifted gradually to more realistic ego-controlled working through conflicts, which at first were essentially on an extremely primitive level. Notes on each session were recorded. Tracy's fantasies and conflicts involve primarily the following:

1. The struggle for an identity, at first Tracy was a Mr. Nobody with extremely disoriented body imagery; her body was filled with bad parts, confused sexually. She then became the frightened animal, lost and unprotected; she verbalized the fantasy that her mother wished for a boy. Tracy acted out fears of being eaten by her mother. Tracy spoke of seeing her mother hit her father with pots and pans, she was fearful for his safety, and stated her mother would murder her father if she returned. Repeatedly, she saw herself as needing to be strong, a giant, to protect her father from her mother.

2. Tracy verbalized her mother's disposing of her cat, and was sure her mother had magical powers against which no one was safe.

3. Tracy worried about her brains and was afraid she would be like her mother *if* she grew up. She characterized her mother as being a liar, who abandoned her.

4. Birth fantasy: "being born is like dropping out of the nest; a new baby will be murdered or not taken care of."

5. Tracy verbalized her mother screaming at her at home, telling her to get into bed when she was in bed.

6. Tracy acted out her fears around her hospitalization, when Tracy was in Stanford Hospital, but associates the frightening darkness with her mother.

Concomitantly, during these first several months, her father and Mrs. Knudson were allaying Tracy's fears when possible, and giving much needed realistic direction to her everyday living. From time to time there were anxiety attacks at night with Tracy screaming hysterically and crying out in fear of her mother.

Tracy would make statements such as "My mother doesn't love me, but she keeps repeating it… Her face looks different from what she says… If I go to live with her she'll take me twice around the world and then leave me… She lies. She's never told the truth. She tells me my daddy lies, but that isn't so." By this point Tracy was quite aware of the realistic struggle for her between her parents, and finally realized they would never get back together. After the first visit [with her mother at the Hayes's house, and] during the next two days, Tracy was acutely anxious, [and] crying; [she was] on the phone and cried to me stating "I don't know why I feel so bad….. My mother blames me for everything." She finger-painted five hills; her mother was on two hills, Tracy on the other two, and the therapist in the middle. During the next few sessions Tracy displayed strong guilt feelings, repeatedly washed a puppet that she named "Goodie," whom she hid from the therapist because it was scared the therapist would take him away. Escape fantasies from bad mothers followed in the next few sessions. Whenever questioned about the father's role, it was usually non-influential. (I must add that in the beginning there were negative, frightening feelings towards her father. These were worked through and disappeared from the sessions after the first few months.)

During the month of March, Tracy became increasingly hysterical, begging not to have to see her mother. She stated that her mother kept telling her bad things about her father, and sometimes hit her for no reason. During the last two weeks I've known that Tracy has been given some sort of drug by her mother, presumably Miltown on two occasions, something else on the third. Tracy was not told [about this], but during these sessions was extremely anxious and said she felt "funny" when she was with her mother, that her mother could make her say "I love you" and she could not stop herself. The visits were stopped. Tracy was immediately relieved, but then, visitation was reordered for this week. This was shattering to Tracy, [as it] became further evidence to her of anyone's ability to protect her from her mother. This week Tracy became hysterical about seeing the judge. She viewed him as mean, saying he would believe her mother and make her [Tracy] live with her. She was very afraid of having to talk to the judge. Tracy said, "My mother will hypnotize me into saying things I don't want to say."

In conclusion, Tracy, in my opinion has been subjected to extensive psychological damage by a chronically psychotic mother, during the first six years of her life. She [Tracy] was barely holding herself from a complete psychotic break at the start of therapy and separation from her mother, over this almost two-year period, Tracy made extensive gains but is far from being recovered. The ongoing unsettled custody battle has had devastating effects. The visits with her mother were at first helpful in removing distortions but during the last three months in particular have created almost unbearable anxiety for this eight-year-old child. The use of drugs in the deceptive manner they were administered is appalling and only further loosened this child's controls and sense of reality, pulling her closer to psychosis. I cannot state strongly enough that Tracy's mental health will be destroyed if she lives with her mother, and her best interest in all respects can best be taken care of by her father.

I believe this covers in sufficient detail the essence of what Tracy has been struggling with these past two years. Any part of this is documented in dated notes. My impression, and again it is only impression, is that Tracy who now may represent to Mrs. Cable an extension of her husband, may be subjected to actual physical harm if ordered into Mrs. Cable's custody. The risk of either total psychological destruction or physical assault is too great.

--Elsa Leiter Gordon, M.D.

I think it was amazing that Dr. Gordon could figure out so many things about the horrors I had been through without my actually having told her. This shows the benefits of "play therapy." I never told her about the tortures and punishments my mother inflicted on me. However, some of this was revealed through my actions and the way I played in the playroom.

Often children can't talk about the horrible things that happen to them; however, they can demonstrate the events by playing. That's why child psychologists and psychiatrists go through extensive training in play therapy. Through this form of therapy they can learn how children are doing, what they are feeling and what has happened to them. Sometimes this type of therapy can very specifically pinpoint information that a child could not, for whatever reasons, verbalize. Dr. Gordon was able to obtain a great deal of information from me, without me saying a word. As a child, I never knew how important Dr. Gordon was to me. As an adult, I am amazed by her skills and efforts on my behalf. I am extraordinarily grateful that she was in my life at such a critical time. I believe Dr. Gordon was an example of excellence in the psychiatric field.

Mother had more than a deep-seated anger towards Dad. She wanted to *destroy* him. If she could not achieve this on her own, then she was determined to destroy him through *me.* She gave no thought nor had any concern for my well-being while using me in this capacity. My facial features resembled my dad. This enraged her because when she looked at me, she saw him.

I was afraid to see Dr. Rothenberg. I knew she was going to interview Mother and Dad, too. I was certain Mother had power over people to get them to do or think whatever she wanted. Because of this, I didn't think anything I said would make any difference. Still, I did my best to show Dr. Rothenberg how I felt.

Dr. Rothenberg's report to the California Superior Court reads in part:

> Dr. Ruth Brown's report [of] testing done in 1963 (June), indicates that Tracy has high natural intelligence. There are some suggestions of organic brain damage, but clearer indications of the presence of schizophrenia. Some of her T. A. T. stories showed bizarreness of content. All of the people she saw on the Rorschach test cards were somehow distorted, grotesque, or inhuman. Dr. Brown saw Tracy as severely ill

and in need of psychotherapy. On her second testing with Dr. Brown in July 1964, Tracy presented much the same basic character structure. She was still seen as a frightened, depressed child pursued by devils and afraid of being torn apart in the struggle between her parents. There seemed to be improvement. A mean looking witch seen on card one of the Rorschach was now a devil sticking out its tongue (still threatening but more playful), and the mad giant on card four was now a dog sitting down. The bad ant, a real mean one, seen on card six was now only a cat. T.A.T. stories contained less killing and fear of death, and generally had optimistic endings. Testing, done in April 1965, showed more generous and free responses, indicating that the child has blossomed.

In my interview with Mr. Cable, he appeared to be a large man who was initially covertly hostile and anxious, but who became almost too friendly and trusting as the interview progressed. He talked of verbal and physical abuse he suffered at the hands of his wife, and his inability to cope with it prior to getting help from Dr. Cooley, of whom he spoke in a warm friendly manner. He spoke with what seemed to be genuine pride of the way Tracy was progressing and how they were managing since his wife went to the hospital. He described his wife as being ill prior to hospitalization to the extent of hearing voices in the wall and blaming him for everything that happened to her, when she apparently couldn't find her way.

In my interview with Mrs. Cable, she talked of feeling

JUSTICE: BLIND OR BIASED?

the need for psychiatric treatment for herself long before she went to either Twin Pines or Agnews, but claimed that her husband blocked her chance to get such treatment by refusing to pay for it and at the same time telling her she was crazy. She offered explanations for many of her husband's accusations of her. For example, she gave Dr. Marshall a fictitious name when she consulted him because she felt her husband would stop her from going if he heard of it. Mrs. Cable was meticulously dressed and carefully organized in her conversation with some rigidity and lack of spontaneity. She seemed to feel a need to justify and explain everything.

In my interview with Tracy, she was anxious and needed to touch my hand in a ritualistic manner before entering the office, probably to alleviate her anxiety. She had a free, friendly manner which made her rather appealing. She talked of coming to see me as having something to do with the court and whether she would live with her father or her mother, and whether or not she would have to see her mother again. She readily, spontaneously and repeatedly stated that she did not ever wish to see her mother again. She said her mother lied and that she was afraid of her mother. She was quite busy during the hour, and if I would pause a minute, she would take over leadership immediately. She laughed and played happily, but she always maintained some distance and avoided some questions.

I conclude that Tracy is an emotionally disturbed girl who was even more disturbed two years ago. Tracy's illness is serious. Slowly she has begun to develop trust and confidence in her father, which has been helpful to her. Any covert or overt criticism of him frightens her. If she cannot trust him, she may well fear becoming sicker again. Because Tracy's illness is serious and because she is making progress, I recommend that she continue in the custody of her father. The expressed fears of such a sick girl must be taken seriously in considering placement for her. Since she is so frightened, I recommend that visitations with her mother be quite limited and supervised to limit Tracy's anxiety. I also strongly recommend that Tracy's psychotherapy be continued.

--Helen Rothenberg, M.D.

The High Cost of Silence and Family Secrets

The trial now turned to the issue of permanent custody and visitation. Uncle Les, whose family I lived with when Mother went to Agnews, had planned to testify on Dad's behalf. He was Mother's youngest brother. His testimony would surely have convinced the court to grant custody to Dad.

Uncle Les's parents and siblings became aware that he was planning to testify for my dad, against his sister. His family joined my mother in putting terrible pressure on Uncle Les to get him to change his mind about testifying. His mother (my grandmother) phoned him and told him, in her gruff Hungarian way that she would disown him if he testified against his sister. He also received negative letters and phone calls from infuriated family members. They all lived back east and believed everything my mother had told them. Sadly, they had no idea what was really going on.

Meanwhile, unknown to anyone outside of their immediate family, Mother was introducing Aunt Nita and Uncle Les to her own special brand of terror. My aunt and uncle told me all about it when I was an adult. On several occasions, my mother broke into their house and snuck up behind my aunt, who had no knowledge that she was there. Sometimes, when my aunt was working in the kitchen, she would turn around to find my mother standing in front of her with a butcher knife in her hand! She told my aunt that my uncle had better not testify against her. She said things like: "I watch your children come home from school," while holding a butcher knife in her hand. My mother made other threats against my aunt, uncle and cousins' lives and their family as a whole. She slammed the knife down on the counter and left the house when she was finished. She conducted this form of terrorism quite a few times. Even though my cousins were old enough to walk to school, which was just down the street, my aunt would accompany them every day as a precaution.

Mother broke into Aunt Nita and Uncle Les's house several times during the day and a couple of times at night. One night my uncle discovered my mother hiding just outside the master bedroom with a butcher knife. She hissed her intentions to slit his and his wife's throats as they slept. He overpowered her and physically removed her from the house. She made it known to them that she had several plans for the demise of their family. One plan was to kill them both; another plan was to kill only their children. This was followed by her later plan to kill only my aunt so that my mother could then live the rest of her life with her brother. She told him about this plan and how she wanted to "marry" him.

Mother had the ability to pop in and out of my aunt's and uncle's house undetected. This, along with all of her threats, terrified them. They took it all very seriously. They taught their children never to let "Aunt Kathryn" into the house. They showed their children where all of the important documents and insurance papers were kept, in case their parents were killed. It was during this time of great stress that my uncle developed type-one diabetes. My aunt and uncle felt that they could not risk their children's lives or my uncle's health any further. Without an explanation or telling anyone what was going on, my uncle declined to testify for my father.

Uncle Les and Aunt Nita also decided that any further contact with me could possibly bring my mother's reign of terror back into their lives. Not wanting any contact with my mother, they decided to sever all contact with me. My four cousins and I were like sisters. I hadn't seen them for about a year. When this decision came down, I thought I would never see them again and was devastated.

I was almost eight years old when I wrote my first letter to Aunt Nita and Uncle Les, begging them for some kind of contact with my cousins. Year after year, I continued to write. My letters went unanswered. Dad didn't understand why the problems among the adults had to be taken out on the children. He felt terrible about it, but there was nothing he could do. Dad didn't know what had transpired between my mother, Uncle Les and his family. I felt that they didn't want me or love me anymore, although Dad said he was certain that was not the case. I had no idea why I was banished and felt guilty that I had, again, done something terribly wrong to deserve this treatment.

My oldest cousin Linda, four years my senior, shares her memories from this time:

My parents, Tracy's Aunt Nita and Uncle Les, were secretive as well as quite authoritarian. Discipline in our
household was swift and often severe. My sisters and
I never received any answers to our questions about
why we could no longer have contact with Tracy. I
especially felt bad because Tracy and I were very close
and I missed her terribly. It was as if someone had
taken my little sister away, with no explanation why. I
remembered asking my father, throughout my growing up years, why I couldn't see Tracy. My dad would
simply answer, "End of discussion." And that would
be the end of it. Repeated questions would result in
a swift spank or the dreaded hard knuckle rap on the
top of the head, so I didn't push it. However, Dad was
a pushover compared to my mother's punishments,
as they were severe. Because of my parents' actions,
my sisters and I learned quickly not to ask questions
about Tracy or her mother.

I had known that Tracy's mother, my Aunt Kathryn,
often broke into our house and threatened my parents
with a butcher knife. Sadly, however, this did not hor-
rify me as much as it might have. Due to a childhood
attack, my own mother had a disconcerting habit of
screaming hysterically and throwing up her hands if
anyone accidentally walked up behind her. All of us
had had the experience, at one time or another, of
having walked up behind her when she was slicing
something with a butcher knife and seeing the knife
fly up in front of us and hearing her ghastly shriek,
"Eeeeeehhhhhhh!!!!!!!!" This experience had somewhat
dulled me to the horror of butcher knives. It was far

more devastating to lose a cousin, who was more like a beloved little sister, with no reasonable explanation.

--Linda Malnassy

The court never knew about Mother's threats to my uncle's family. I think the outcome would have been different for everyone in our family if my uncle had informed the court. However, Uncle Les and Aunt Nita had been terrified into silence, as I had been. I believed that if I just kept quiet no one would get hurt. I am certain, after many discussions with them that they shared this opinion. Mother was a dangerous and unpredictable person who thought nothing of terrorizing others to fulfill her own needs. It gave her great power over others while causing them pain and suffering. If my eight-year-old self had the wisdom of my present years, I would have sung like a jaybird! I would have told *all* of the adults in my life every horrid detail! Terror was my mother's way of sealing mouths shut, both young and old. This is what she used on me to "keep Mother's secrets."

Without any explanation or the court having any knowledge of Uncle Les's reasons, he was simply dropped from the list of witnesses and that was the end of it. The trial raged on without him.

Evaluating My Mother and Her Ability to Parent

John C. Archer, M.D. was a psychiatrist who evaluated Mother during her five visits to his office, three in April 1964 and two in March 1965. Below is a condensed version of his testimony of his findings and observations from the Superior Court of California transcript dated May 5, 1965:

Dr. Archer testified that this particular evaluation of my mother was based on, "Her emotional reactions, intellectual reactions, her emotional behavior, her feelings, her thought processes, her ability to cope with reality, to seeing reality and to use judgment." Dr. Archer added:

Intellectually, she [Kathryn Cable] was oriented to time and place, she knew why she was there, she knew where she was and she had considerable difficulty in either recalling or relating to the circumstances of her life and her current difficulties. The difficulties manifest itself in a considerable amount of evasiveness and inability to answer questions directly. She spoke in a very circular fashion, through a very long, involved and sometimes irrelevant course in order to pursue the point that I was seeking. She was frequently unable, even after a rather prolonged questioning on a certain point, to answer the question.

Dr. Archer described Mother's thinking as "tangential," which he explained as:

Starting at a certain point, which is the question or the issue about which we are discussing, and then leaping off into some other area in attempts to answer the question.

Dr. Archer testified to other observations of my mother:

She was superficially friendly, she smiled, she was cooperative and she was somewhat ingratiating in that she attempted most of the time to maintain a friendly and pleasant facade. Emotionally -- the best way I think to describe her emotional reaction was that she was flat, except when she discussed her husband; only then did she show emotion and that was anger, but even that was flattened.

Dr. Archer defined schizophrenia to the court, saying:

It is a very complex illness and it takes on many forms, and it takes on many changing forms within the same individual. However, there are certain indicators, such as impairment of one's intellectual functioning, one's ability to think clearly to organize one's thoughts, to [be able to] test and perceive reality and also to have and express appropriate emotions. There are other symptoms which are characteristic of the illness which stem from these more basic intellectual and emotional impairments, such as: delusional or paranoid thinking, bizarre thought patterns, which, again, are related to the ability or inability to perceive reality, hallucinations and impairments in judgment. I would say that the clinical findings were consistent with a diagnosis of paranoid schizophrenia. What I brought out or discovered in interviews were symptoms and signs characteristic of schizophrenia and these she did manifest.

Dr. Archer went on to state that it was his opinion my mother had the chronic type of schizophrenia and that, "It is considered to have a very guarded or poor prognosis in the terms of recovery to a healthy well-integrated state."

Dr. Archer was asked if he tried to elicit any response from Mother as to whether or not she was able to perceive the nature and extent of her previous emotional problems and/or mental illness, centering around the time she went to Agnews State Hospital. He replied, "She denied having any emotional problems at that time." The doctor added that she was suffering from a very disturbed mental state and that her *inability* to perceive or have any insight into her illness would prevent her from recovery or responding to treatment. The doctor stated, "A successful treatment requires that the patient be able to recognize that there is a problem in the first place in order to deal with it."

To my knowledge, Dr. Stern and Dr. Lynwood were the only two psychiatrists who testified on Mother's behalf. They were her sole medical/psychological witnesses. Dr. Lynwood only saw her twice and Dr. Stern saw her three to four times. Their first appointments with her were after her release from Agnews State Hospital. They didn't know her before then. Neither doctor ever saw my dad, me or the three of us together.

Dr. Stern's declaration reads in part:

I am a physician and surgeon in the State of California. I specialize in neurology and psychiatry. I have specialized in the field of psychiatry, neurology and psychology continuously since 1934. I have reviewed the records of Mrs. Cable at Twin Pines Sanitarium and at Agnews State Hospital and have consulted with and examined Mrs. Cable, psychiatrically.

It is my opinion that the diagnosis of paranoia and schizophrenia imposed upon Mrs. Cable at the time of and prior to her stay at Agnews was not correct and that in fact her condition was only one of great emotional upset arising from family discord; that she was rationally and in good faith seeking relief from an intolerable emotional stress which was in my opinion being manufactured and created by her husband.

Mrs. Cable is a rational and sound person with all of the natural maternal instincts.

In the beginning of the trial, both Dr. Lynwood and Dr. Stern felt that my mother should be granted custody. As time went by and they heard other doctors testify, they seemed to become less certain.

This is part of Dr. Stern's and Dr. Lynwood's testimony. It was copied from the California Superior Court transcripts, and entered as Exhibit "A" by Indian Joe on August 11, 1965:

...Mr. Di Maria: I object. The question is too general. What does he mean cope with?

Mr. Molino: To have the custody.

Mr. Di Maria: It is [a] question of which parent can demonstrate the best ability, not who can cope with it.

The Court: What is the question as it now stands?

Mr. Molino: The question is whether in his [Dr. Stern's] opinion, she [Mrs. Cable] was mentally and emotionally capable of coping with the situation of having the custody of her own child, Tracy.

The Witness [Dr. Stern]: May I -- I have never seen the child. I would say I would like to answer it and say that I think that Mrs. Cable is competent and capable of coping with or managing the care of an average six-, seven- or eight-year-old child. I have heard some disquieting reports which have -- which is the reason I do not become involved in this specifically.

...Q: (by Mr. Di Maria): And you would say, Doctor, that schizoid parents tend to transmit their schizophrenic condition to their children?

A: I would say so.

Q: One more question, Doctor. Is it your opinion chronic schizophrenia has a poor prognosis for recovery, long-standing, seven, eight, ten years?

A: Relatively, yes.

Q: You don't think that Mrs. Cable is an ideal parent, do you Doctor?

A: That I don't know.

Indian Joe entered Dr. Don Lynwood's testimony as Exhibit "B,"

...Q: [Mr. Di Maria]: Before I get to that, Doctor, just deviating for a moment here, would you have to see Mrs. Cable with her daughter under a variety of conditions and particularly with her husband and daughter present at the same time to form a worthwhile opinion whether she could be a good mother to that daughter?

A: [Dr. Lynwood]: If you will let me use the word "adequate" instead of "good," since I don't know that anyone has defined what a "good" mother is, I would agree, yes.

Q: In other words, you cannot now form a worthwhile opinion as to whether she would be an adequate mother, because you have not seen her in the presence of her daughter and in the presence of her husband and daughter together?

A: Right.

...Q: So that you really didn't look to see or to go as far in your determination as to try to establish whether Mrs. Cable was, specifically speaking, creating a very dangerous or sick environment for her child, is that correct?

A: That's correct.

The declaration submitted to California Superior Court on August 8, 1965 of Justin Perkins, M.D. reads in part:

I am a medical doctor licensed to practice in the state of California and have been a medical doctor since 1940.

That beginning with the year 1951, I was treating, as medical doctor, Kathryn Cable, the plaintiff in this action, and that I saw her a significant number of times to form an opinion stated herein.

That based on my general knowledge of the subject, I considered her from the time I first treated her and never had any grounds to change this opinion, as a person seriously and chronically mentally ill; that I also advised her husband, Jonathan H. Cable, of this at that time. I have, at all times, been of the opinion that she could be dangerous to the physical safety of others.

Dr. Archer, who had psychologically evaluated my mother on five separate occasions, also questioned her about her relationship with me during those interviews. Dr. Archer gave the following testimony to Indian Joe's questions in California Superior Court on May 5, 1965; the transcript reads in part:

...**Q:** Did you attempt to obtain any manifestations of her [Kathryn's] feelings towards her daughter, Tracy, on the topic of whether or not her feelings were that of a typical mother towards her daughter?

A: She was very reluctant to talk about her daughter. In response to the direct question, "What are your feelings about her?" She said, "I have a mother's love for her." I tried to get her to elaborate on this to get to a more significant and meaningful level, but I was unable to do so. She was quite evasive about this.

Q: Were your observations that her concept of her role to her daughter was not that of a typical mother?

A: Yes, I would say so.

Q: In what respect?

A: Well, she seemed -- she lacked conviction in what she was saying about her feelings about her daughter. When

I first saw her in April of 1964, she had been discharged from Agnews, I believe about, oh, five months or so, and hadn't seen her daughter, and I couldn't elicit any explanation for this. She was quite vague and unable to really say why. She was unable to describe any personal interaction between the two of them. When I asked her about her [daughter's] future -- about the future possibilities of a life with Tracy how she envisioned that in her planning, her response was that she would be able to watch for Tracy when she came home from school as she crossed the railroad tracks in order to protect her from being hit by a train. And I asked her further about it and she said, "Well, I would like her to have ballet lessons." I think -- I would consider these responses quite liberal and concrete in nature, and rather limited in their scope.

Q: Did she manifest to you any other programs she had in mind for her daughter than those two?

A: No, she did not.

Dr. Gordon's declaration submitted to California Superior Court on December 21, 1965, reads in part:

In my studies made on her [Tracy Cable's] case I established to my satisfaction that essential contributing causes to emotional mental condition were the irrational conduct of her mother when she was living with her mother and father and also the coldness of the mother towards her and the inability of her mother to feel and act as a mother.

I found that for a considerable period of time before the trial of the Divorce Action between her parents and consistently up to and through the point of termination of that trial, Tracy suffered from the following fears: fear of harm from her mother; fear her mother would hurt or harm her father; fear that her mother was some kind of a colossus or evil genius that could not be contained or controlled; and finally, great fear that her mother might get custody of her. These fears were great contributing factors towards her emotional disturbance. Regardless of the reason or basis for her fears, her fears are real.

One of the present sources of anxiety in Tracy that works detrimentally against more rapid improvement is that her mother keeps telling her that her father does not love her, according to Tracy, and her account is certainly credible. Her mother has been doing this during all visitations in recent weeks. Tracy feels essentially she has only her father to depend upon and this assault by her mother on the topic of the lack of love of her father for Tracy is very disquieting and very disturbing to her.

Up to this point and time Tracy has not developed anything that resembles a relationship of the typical daughter to a typical mother. In my earlier medical examination of Mrs. Cable I concluded that she was unable to consider Tracy as her daughter, but considered her only as an object. I know that Tracy wants a true mother relationship to develop with someone, if not with her own mother. I can only assume from the failure of Tracy to develop this feeling of a daughter towards her mother that the cause is Mrs. Cable's inability to feel and act toward Tracy as a mother would towards a daughter. If it is argued by Mrs. Cable that the reason no such development has taken place is that she has not been given an opportunity to act as a mother towards her daughter, then this suggests that a new medical examination should be made of Mrs. Cable. However, the fact that she is trying to destroy the relationship of Tracy with her father, which is a firm and sound father-daughter relationship, strongly suggests that there has been no essential improvement in the mental condition of Mrs. Cable as I found it when I examined her.

I feel strongly that it is harmful psychologically to this child to force her into any position toward her mother that she does not naturally wish to assume, and certainly she does not wish to have visitation take place.

During the trial, Dr. Gordon was also questioned about her interview with my mother. The following is her testimony to Indian Joe's questions on May 4, 1965; the transcript reads in part:

...**Q:** Now, you had an opportunity to interview the mother, Kathryn Cable, did you not?

A: On one occasion. [The interview lasted one hour.]

Q: Within any kind of limits were you able to form an opinion as to whether or not this mother bore a meaningful relationship to that child?

A: It was my feeling that Mrs. Cable essentially

demonstrated no real feelings for Tracy. Instead she seemed to be bound up with trying to exhibit her anger towards her husband.

Mother demanded that her psychiatrist, Dr. Marshall, interview Dad. Her hope was that Dr. Marshall would find some kind of mental illness or issues in my father and declare him an unfit parent. This was also presented in court. Below is the body of the letter from Dr. Marshall to one of Mother's two attorneys.

Pursuant to your request, Mr. Jonathan Cable has been examined psychiatrically by me to determine his suitability to continue as a parent and guardian. Examination consisted of a total of three hours of interview.

I find no evidence of any psychiatric illness or mental condition that would impair Mr. Cable's parenting abilities. He has assumed the responsibility for his daughter's care for the past year without any unusual difficulties and has been able to seek competent medical guidance when indicated.

--James Marshall, M.D.

A Lunch Date with the Judge

There were several times when I was brought to the courthouse and had to wait outside the courtroom for hours, most of the time with an adult. I was told I could be called in at any time to testify. It was scary to think of being put on the stand and grilled in front of Mother, Dad and everyone else.

I still had no knowledge that Mother had drugged me during visitation. I believed she could "hypnotize" me at will to gain control over my mind and force me to say whatever she wanted as she had done during visitations. This was so frightening. There are no words to describe it. I shook in my shoes as I waited for hours, holding my breath every time a door opened, terrified that they might be calling me in to testify. Usually by the end of the day, I felt sick to my stomach. Mother wanted me to testify in open court, so her attorneys could have the opportunity to cross-examine me. Each time this came up somehow, Indian Joe was able to stop it from happening. Instead, he made an agreement with the judge to have lunch with me in his chambers.

When told that lunch with the judge was coming up I was terrified. I didn't know if Mother could hypnotize me from a distance or maybe even hypnotize the judge. Due to his visitation orders, I already felt that the judge was on Mother's side. Why would he listen to me? After all, I was just an eight-year-old kid. My experience told me that most adults tended to stick together. The day finally arrived. Dad packed a brown bag lunch for me and took me to the courtroom. I was left alone, sitting on a hard wooden bench outside the judge's chambers awaiting his arrival.

A young man walked by me and went into the judge's chambers. He didn't acknowledge me and I thought that he was too young to be a judge. A moment later the man came back and frowned at me.

"Are you coming?" he asked impatiently.

"I'm waiting for Judge Riley," I replied, clutching my lunch bag in my tight, sweaty grip.

The man looked even more irritated as he glared down at me and said, "I am Judge Riley; *come on.*"

The judge walked back into his chambers.

I followed him.

The room contained a big desk and a big chair behind it where he sat. He seemed irritated as he told me to sit in front of him on the opposite side of his huge desk. I was very nervous and my legs were shaking as I walked to the chair.

After we were settled, he stared at me for an uncomfortable moment.

"So, I don't look like a judge to you?"

I thought to myself, *Boy this is getting off on the wrong foot.*

The only judges I had ever seen were on TV and the only ones I ever paid attention to were on *Daniel Boone*. They were all old men who had long white hair. Judge Riley did not look like any of those I had seen on television.

"Are you going to wear your white wig?" I asked meekly.

The judge seemed very confused by the question.

"My white wig?"

"Yes. All the judges on *Daniel Boone* wear white wigs, are you going to wear yours?"

Judge Riley's confusion turned to laughter. He explained to me that judges don't wear those wigs anymore and that not all judges were old men. His laughter broke the ice between us.

I relaxed a bit, but that didn't last for long.

I was still quite worried and wondered, *Would I be able to say what I wanted to say to the judge? Would Mother somehow be able to control my words as she had done during visitations?*

The judge asked me about the shows I watched on TV, who my closest friends were and what I enjoyed about school. I worried what would happen when the easy questions ended and he started talking about my parents. The judge had brought a lunch as well and started to eat. Nervously I opened my bag and began to eat too. I was so anxious I could hardly swallow. When I did, it felt like the food was stuck in the lower part of my throat.

Judge Riley abruptly changed the subject.

"Tracy, do you know the difference between a lie and the truth?" he asked in a serious tone.

"Yes," I croaked, wondering if I was in trouble.

"Can you give me an example?"

I was starting to shake as my mind raced reviewing what I had just said. I was certain he thought I had lied to him. I swallowed hard and replied, "The truth is what honestly happened and a lie is a fake. Lies are the opposite of what honestly happened."

The judge looked at me and sighed.

"Is it good to lie or is it good to tell the truth?" he asked.

"Telling the truth is the right thing to do. It is wrong to lie."

Judge Riley seemed satisfied and told me he wanted me to tell him the truth, which I promised I would.

"Do you want to live with your mother or your father?"

I looked into his eyes and told him that I wanted to live with my dad. I searched his eyes for some kind of clue as to whether or not he believed me and was agreeable or open to my thoughts and feelings, but his eyes remained unchanged and distant.

"Why don't you want to live with your mother?"

"Because I don't like her, I am afraid of her, and I don't feel good when I am around her."

The judge looked at me as if he didn't believe me. My anxiety level was through the roof.

"Do you want to continue seeing your mother?"

"No," I replied, feeling the distance growing between us.

"Please don't make me see my mother anymore. Please don't make me live with her," I pleaded. I held my breath, as I waited for his response.

He frowned at me and then threw me a curve ball.

"Did your dad tell you to say this?" he asked suspiciously.

"No," I replied. I was completely confused by his question.

The judge continued with his line of thought, "Did your dad practice these answers with you or teach you what to tell me?"

"No," I insisted, wondering how I could convince this man that my answers came from me and not my dad.

"Are you telling me the *truth*?" he asked in disbelief.

"Yes." Even though I was telling the truth, I could tell that the judge didn't believe a word I said. I felt completely lost and very sad. Not only was the judge questioning my honesty, but I had somehow gotten my *dad* in trouble as well. I panicked as my anxiety level shot toward the stars. I met his gaze and wondered what he was going to do with me. This man had the power to decide whatever he wanted. He could make my life, or break it. I was frightened, extremely uncomfortable and did not know what to say to make the situation better. I decided that if I tried to explain myself, it would just make matters worse. I was almost frustrated to tears not knowing what to do. Then I suddenly realized, on some level that it didn't make any difference what I said; this man wasn't going to believe me anyway!

The judge finally went back to small talk as we finished our sandwiches.

Leaving his chambers, I felt completely defeated and guilty that I had somehow let down both Dad and myself. It was obvious to me that the judge was on Mother's side and didn't like or trust my dad. I thought that maybe she had hypnotized him when they were in court. By the time I got into the car,

I was sick to my stomach from the meeting. I knew it had not gone well and that somehow I would end up suffering the consequences. Dad could tell by the look on my face that I was upset. He had been well counseled by Indian Joe and Dr. Gordon not to ask me any questions about anything to do with my mother. We drove home in silence.

Some nights, after Dad had put me to bed, I would sneak back down the hall toward the living room where he sat in his easy chair. There was a place at the end of the hall where the wall jutted out about a foot and a half. There I would hide and listen to his many phone calls. I think most kids eavesdrop on adult conversations, when there are so many questions in their lives and they don't know what might happen to them next. When there are so many pieces of the puzzle that are missing, kids naturally try to gain more information by listening in on adult conversations, when the adults are unaware that this is happening. Dad would be in his easy chair, secure in the knowledge that I was in my room asleep with the door closed. Sometimes he would talk about my mother, what was going on in court, issues with the store or how I was doing. I would listen and try to make sense out of the adult conversation. Most of it was extremely boring and a lot of it I didn't understand. I would eventually fall asleep and my dad would find me on his way to bed. I guess he must've understood, because in the morning, I always woke up in my own bed and nothing was ever mentioned.

When the Gavel Fell

Things were not going well for Dad in court. Toward the end of the trial, Mother's attorney filed a document that had to do with their "position" through the Proposed Finding of

Facts, Conclusions of Law and Proposed Judgment Submitted by Plaintiff [Mother]. Here is a portion of Indian Joe's filed response and rebuttal to their document:

There is no evidence of any substantial nature that Plaintiff became ill, either mentally or physically, as a result of any acts committed by the defendant [father] or that she underwent any suffering of any kind because of acts ever committed by the defendant.

There is no substantial evidence that the plaintiff [mother] is a *fit* person to have the custody of a child, and specifically of the minor daughter of the parties.

That the uncontroverted evidence establishes beyond any doubt that there is a long history of mental damage to said child, resulting right down to the date of trial, on account of the association of the plaintiff [mother] and said minor child, and that this uncontroverted evidence, both medical and lay, and entirely uncontroverted, establishes that any further association [between Mother and Child] could be fraught with frightful consequences to the integrity and mind of said child, and that records, being both notes of psychiatric treatment and examination over a two year period; as well as tape recordings as well as other objective and undeniable evidence presently existing, establish this serious danger.

That the court was sufficiently interested in the question of who had administered and from whence came the Meprobamate found in the urine of the minor child of the parties so as to require the defendant [father] to undergo a Lie Detector Test; that while said Lie Detector Test incontestably cleared the defendant of any connection with said drug, nevertheless, certain questions arose with reference to the validity of the Lie Detector Test taken by the plaintiff [mother] on her own Initiative, without forewarning either the court or the defendant as to her taking the same; that since the court was sufficiently interested in the question of guilt in connection with said Meprobamate to make said request of Defendant, it is urged by Defendant that the evidence in the trial is not complete on the question of visitation and that the court should reopen the case for further evidence touching on the question of the conduct of the plaintiff [mother] and statements the plaintiff made in connection with her Lie Detector Test and touching on the general validity of such a test given to such a person as the plaintiff; that this objection is presented on the grounds of the terrible implications of the use of such Meprobamate under all the circumstances brought to the attention of the court during the trial, and that the future safety of said child and her mental integrity demands that all of the evidence pertinent thereto should be before the court, before the court makes a decision on visitation.

Some of Indian Joe's questions to the court included:

What is the general tenor of the substantial evidence upon which to base a Finding that the plaintiff [mother] is a fit person to have custody of a minor child, namely the minor daughter of the parties?

Was it proven to the satisfaction of the court and by a preponderance of the evidence that the plaintiff [mother] administered within a period of several months of the date of the trial a drug known as Meprobamate, also known as Equinol, to the minor child of the parties?

If the answer to the above question is in the affirmative, did this fact have any effect with reference to the degree of rights of visitation according to the plaintiff?

If it was so proved to the satisfaction of the court that the plaintiff [mother] did so administer Meprobamate to said child, was it further proved to the satisfaction of the court that the intention of the plaintiff was to brainwash or deprive the said minor child of her independent mind with reference to the issue of custody?

If the court accepts as proved, in the case of administration of such a drug by the plaintiff to said child, was it proved to the satisfaction of the court that under the circumstances the administration of said drug to said child constituted a real threat to said child's sense of reality and sanity?

Was it proven to the satisfaction of the court that the testimony of Dr. Elsa Gordon was true with reference to the conduct of the plaintiff [mother] in relationship to the minor child of the parties being the essential cause of the mental and personality problems suffered by said child?

If it be the determination of the court that the mental and personality problems of the minor child of the parties was occasioned by the contact of the plaintiff with relationship to the minor child of the parties, then is it the determination of the court that the association of said minor child with the plaintiff no longer presents a hazard of mental or personality damage to the said child? If this determination be as stated, namely that there is no reasonable probability of further damage to the personality or mental condition of said child by association with the plaintiff, then upon what evidence does the court base its determination?

Defendant objects to the language of the proposed Interlocutory Judgment requiring him to "take the attitude that it is a normal and customary thing for a mother to visit with her child." On the following grounds: that while such a statement as to normalcy and as to custom is undeniably true in the vast majority of instances and while the defendant heartily endorses such a view, nevertheless, under the special circumstances pertaining to this particular mother and this particular child, it would be most damaging to the process of psychiatric therapy and to the process of obtaining a realistic appraisal that would aid in the mental recovery of said child to require the defendant positively to adopt such an attitude. This is because said child, for sound medical reasons evinced in the evidence by medical doctors, is expected to and does spontaneously react against any abnormal relations with one in the position of her mother, and that it is impossible, if such relations be abnormal, to accomplish anything with such a positive attitude other than to cause said child a feeling of desertion and a feeling of dangerous unreality: that these statements by the defendant in no way imply that he ever has or that he ever intends to depreciate the natural mother of this child.

-- Joseph F. Di Maria

The court did not respond to any of Indian Joe's ninety plus questions or objections. Despite the overwhelming evidence he had produced during the trial, the court's decision was to side with my mother.

Indian Joe attempted to reopen the case with new evidence that reinforced and validated Dr. Gordon's testimony plus more declarations from other doctors as well as other new evidence. The judge denied it.

Superior Court of California, Findings of Fact and Conclusions of Law [the court order] signed by Judge Riley on August 20, 1965, in part:

The above-entitled cause came on regularly for trial before the court sitting without a jury, Peter J. Molino appearing as counsel for the plaintiff and cross-defendant, and Joseph Di Maria appearing as counsel for the defendant and cross-complainant, and the court having heard the testimony and having examined the proofs offered by the respective parties, and the cause having been submitted to the court for a decision. The court being fully advised in the premises now makes its Findings of Fact as follows [in part]:

Findings of Fact

It is **TRUE:**

A. That there is one child of the marriage, to wit, Tracy L. Cable of the age of approximately 6 years old at the time of the filing of the complaint.

B. Since the marriage the defendant [father] has wrongfully and without provocation treated the plaintiff [mother] in an extremely cruel manner which has caused the plaintiff much humiliation and great physical and mental suffering, making her sick in mind and body and rendering the marriage relation no longer endurable.

C. That the plaintiff is entitled to an interlocutory degree of divorce from the defendant on the grounds of extreme cruelty of Defendant.

D. That *both* parties are *fit persons* to have custody of the minor child, Tracy. It is, however, at the present time in the best interest of the minor child that custody be granted to the defendant. Plaintiff is entitled to reasonable rights of visitation and until further order of the court or agreement by both parties; such rights are defined as the right of Plaintiff to visit with Tracy for two hours once each week at the premises of the third person agreeable to both Plaintiff and Defendant.

E. Both parties must use their best efforts to facilitate and make fruitful the relationships with the minor child.

*It is **NOT TRUE:***

1. That Plaintiff and Cross-defendant [Mother] has been guilty of extreme cruelty towards Defendant and Cross-complainant [Father].
2. That Plaintiff and Cross-defendant is unfit to have care, custody and control of the person and education of the minor child of the parties hereto, nor is it true that the association of Plaintiff and Cross-defendant with said minor child would be extremely detrimental to said minor child.
3. That each and all of the allegations and denials that the defendant's answers to the plaintiff's complaint herein are inconsistent with the Findings of Fact hereinabove are untrue.

Conclusions of Law

1. Plaintiff is awarded a decree of divorce against the defendant on the grounds of extreme cruelty.
2. The custody of the minor child Tracy be awarded to the defendant, subject to reasonable visitation with the plaintiff.
3. Reasonable visitation rights of Plaintiff with the minor child of the parties hereto are presently defined as being once each week for two hours at the premises of a third party agreeable to both Plaintiff and Defendant.

The gavel fell and it was done.

My Opinions about the Order

I was eight years old when custody was awarded to Dad and visitation to Mother. I was later told that this was the first case in California in which the father was granted full custody of a young daughter while the mother, who also wanted the child, was declared a "fit person" to parent by the court.

I was very grateful that my dad was granted custody and my home life would remain unchanged and stable. I no longer feared that I would be forced to live with my mother and have to face the terror of daily life with her. I was, however, very unhappy that the judge was still forcing me to have visitation with her. I couldn't understand why the judge refused to protect me from the emotional and physical abuse she was inflicting on me weekly. As an adult I still don't understand it, let alone how she could be considered "fit." I do believe that the judge held the misconception that it was inconceivable for a mother to harm her child, but I don't know this for certain.

Both my dad and I were victims, first from my mother's abuse and then from a court blinded to the truth. The judge discounted the evidence and accusations of physical, mental and emotional abuse by my mother towards both my father and me. The judge claimed that it was not true -- but he didn't have to suffer through it or even witness it. He discounted a lot of the solid evidence brought to him by Indian Joe. The judge disregarded my words and discounted my doctor's testimony and the testimony of others who knew me well.

The judge was also incorrect in believing that my dad was the one who was alienating me against my mother, it was the other way around. It was my mother who was working hard, during every visitation, to alienate me against my father. The visitation order allowed this to continue.

I came back from visitations every Saturday enraged over Mother's "little talks." I was angry with her most of the time and, at this time in my life, had no trouble verbalizing exactly how I felt. After the trial had ended, I was surprised and dismayed that Dad began to stand up for Mother! As an adult, I have read documents stating he was directed by the court to say only good things about her to me. It was very disheartening and painful to listen to him tell me about her good points. At times, this infuriated me. I thought to myself, *Here I am being continually hurt by my mother, fighting her every attempt to bad-mouth my dad and brainwash me against him, while trying not to go crazy. Now Dad is standing up for her! He doesn't seem to care about my feelings at all!*

"Remember, your mother has a lot of good points," Dad said. He would go on to say that she is very smart, a great cook, excellent pianist and could read at the speed of light. He told me that because of her reading gift, she was employed at fifteen, in preference to adults, for proofreading and part-time secretarial positions during the Great Depression. He told me that, as a teenager, my mother would stand in line for ten to twelve hours, in the cold Chicago winters and the hot and humid summers, with hundreds and sometimes thousands of other applicants, just to get an interview for a single job opening. These proofreading jobs helped to keep her, her brothers and parents sheltered, clothed and fed.

Of course, I knew Mother had good points. However, when I was eight years old and under fire every Saturday, I certainly didn't want to hear about them!

The judge was *unconvinced* that my mother was a threat to me. His order forced me to see her once a week for two hours, *not* in the *presence* of a third person, but at the *premises* of a third person. This left me again with very little protection.

When a child is forced to stay two hours with a person he or she is terrified of, it feels like an eternity!

Judge Riley's visitation order made me feel that I had been sentenced to endure ongoing pain, nightmares, mental and physical abuse, continual brainwashing and psychological torture. He ordered visitation with my mother to continue until I was legally an adult, which at that time was age twenty-one, thirteen *long* years away. His order gave Mother countless opportunities to continue abusing me. He turned a blind ear to the tapes that were presented in evidence and he didn't give credence to my feelings when I talked with him over lunch. He never asked *why* I was afraid of my mother. He obviously didn't believe me or the evidence that Indian Joe brought forth as to why visitations were so detrimental to me. In his own words the judge stated in his Finding of Fact document: "nor is it true that the association of cross-defendant [Mother] with said minor child would be extremely detrimental to said minor child." How much *more* evidence did the man need? I believe that the thirteen-year sentence he forced on me was an injustice as it put an innocent child, me, in harm's way.

New Challenges

The teachers and staff at Meyerholz Elementary School undoubtedly knew about my family situation. They did an excellent job of not leaking any information about it or about my mother's mental issues. However, the kids *knew* I was different.

I was one of the only kids from a divorced family and I was the only girl in school who lived with her father. Shortly after I started the fourth grade, three boys in my class started following me home. About halfway they jumped me and beat me up.

This was during a short period of time when Dad came home from work before school let out.

When I arrived home my dress was torn and I was scuffed up and crying. Dad soothed me while tending to my scrapes and tears.

I told him about the three boys and their threat to beat me up every day after school.

"Why?" Dad asked.

"They said they would because I don't have a mother," I cried.

At eight years old I had learned a painful lesson, being different made me a target for bullies.

Dad phoned the school and wanted them to intervene. He was told that because this happened off the school grounds, the school would not get involved. Dad asked for the last names and phone numbers of the boys involved, so he could speak with their parents. The school would not release any information. The following two days the boys kept their promise and continued to beat me up. Dad decided that it was time to teach me how to defend myself. He told me that if any kids hurt me or intended to hurt me that I was to kick them in the shins as hard as I could. He gave me a stern warning never to start a fight. However, if someone started one with me, I was to defend myself in this manner.

The next day the boys followed me off the school grounds as I walked home. I was scared as they closed in on me. Then one grabbed me by my arm and swung me around. He tried to punch me, but I quickly kicked him in the shins and he doubled over in pain. As the other boys were grabbing me, I kicked them in the shins as well. All the boys were crying and hobbling away. It worked! I jumped for joy, ran home and told Dad. Those boys never bothered me again.

Saturday was coming up and I dreaded the thought of

visitation with Mother. The nightmares came back almost every night. *What kind of judge does this to a kid?* I wondered. My horrors were far from over. Mother wanted me to have visitation at the house of an acquaintance of hers. The "third person" was supposed to be a neutral person unknown to either of my parents. We ended up having visitation at the Children's Health Council in Menlo Park. The new third person was a hired babysitter from a babysitting service. This woman came to Dad's sports store to pick me up at 9:45 AM, every Saturday. She usually sat on a bench and read a book during visitation. At noon visitation ended, and she drove me back to the store.

There was a playground by the creek at the Children's Health Council. Mother started taking me down into the dry creek bed. At first, the babysitter came with us, but then Mother stated that she wanted to be alone with me in the creek. After that, the babysitter sat on a bench in the playground area and read her book. Mother often took me down to the creek bed, out of sight and out of earshot of the babysitter.

One Saturday, when we were down in the creek, Mother and I had wandered out of sight of the third person who had lagged far behind us. I found a large nut, which looked like a chestnut. I had never before seen one this big, so I showed it to Mother. She said it was a "buckeye" and told me to eat it. I was hungry, but I had never seen one before. I stood there studying it, listening to her insisting that it was delicious and that I should eat it right away. Her insistence and urgency struck me as odd and I became suspicious. I thought of Dad's new instructions to bring home anything Mother wanted me to eat and show it to him first. I told her I wasn't hungry and I would eat it later. I put it in my pocket and quickly found something else to distract her.

Later that day, I told Dad that I was going to eat the big

chestnut I found in the creek. He asked to see it, so I showed it to him. As I handed it to him, I told him that my mother called it a buckeye and was pushing me to eat it. I told him that she said it was delicious.

Dad's face darkened with concern as he asked me if I had eaten any of these or anything else she gave me.

"No," I replied.

He searched my face for a second and phoned the local hospital. He told them that his eight-year-old daughter might have eaten a buckeye a couple of hours ago and asked what he should do. A doctor came on the line and asked Dad some questions.

"Tracy, are you certain you didn't eat any buckeyes?" Dad asked again.

"I didn't eat any, Daddy, *honest!*"

The doctor informed my dad that buckeyes are deadly poison to children and had I eaten one, hours ago, I would probably be dead by now. He said that the poison acts quickly and by the time we could have arrived at the hospital it would have been too late.

Dad hung up the phone. Then he told me that when my mother had come out from Chicago and they were dating, he had shown her some of the plants she should avoid here like poison oak. He told me that he had showed her a buckeye he found while they were out walking. He told her that they were poisonous and never to eat one. My mother said that she already knew about buckeyes, because her father had taught her never to eat them when she was a child.

During visitations, Mother continued telling me that Dad had never loved me and that he just wanted to take me away from her. She kept telling me that my dad was only using me as a tool to make her miserable. If Mother felt she wasn't getting through to me she would sometimes hit, slap, punch, pinch or otherwise hurt me. She kept hinting to me that my father having custody was not a permanent situation. I returned to the store upset and told Dad what she had said to me. He contacted Indian Joe to pass along this information and told him about the buckeye incident. Indian Joe contacted the babysitting service and requested that the babysitter write reports on the visitations. Indian Joe stressed that neither Mother nor I were to know about the reports.

The Sabers Rattle Again

My mental stability decreased as Mother's campaign to turn me against my dad increased. Dr. Gordon became quite concerned about this and discussed it with Indian Joe. Then Indian Joe, unknown to my mother or me, requested that the third person submit written reports to him about our interactions at visitation. In the report, the third person was also referred to as the "operative" or "babysitter." The following are excerpts from these reports:

<u>October 9, 1965</u>

Mrs. Cable asked the operative [third person] if Mr. Cable had told her to follow herself and Tracy closely. The operative [third person] replied, and then asked what Mrs. Cable wanted her to do. Mrs. Cable said that the operative was just a "dear heart" for being so cooperative. She further said that she "just wondered" because when she and Tracy were alone in the creek bed Tracy kept asking, "Where is the babysitter [third person]? Why isn't the babysitter with us?" Mrs. Cable then asserted that the only reason she was concerned about these things was that she wanted these two hours to be perfectly happy for Tracy and that Mr. Cable's motivations were exactly the opposite.

October 16, 1965

Tracy was climbing on the monkey bars. When she was hanging from one bar, with her back balanced on another, she began to cry. During the first five seconds, the sound of activity was like that of any ordinary playground accident. However, the activity and sounds of Tracy's cries continued for perhaps as much as 45 seconds. During this time, Mrs. Cable was directly behind Tracy and seemed to be trying to help her. The out-of-the-ordinary aspect of this incident was the result of two things: the rather long duration of the incident, and the contradiction in what mother and child said about it. Mrs. Cable said that Tracy slipped and was in a position where she was stuck with pressure on her spine. Tracy said that her mother caught her and pushed her down on the bar.

October 30, 1965

10:40 AM Mrs. Cable called from the gate to the playground that she and Tracy were going down to the creek bed for a little while. She had her hand on Tracy's shoulder and seemed to be firmly guiding her out through the gate. She seemed to be in a hurry. This was the first time that she and Tracy had gone to the creek bed alone. Up to this point, the operative had gone with them and waited on the side of the creek bed.

November 6, 1965

The operative sat on the bench and watched. Mrs. Cable seemed to be speaking in an insistent manner [to Tracy]. The operative came up to them from behind. Mrs. Cable was saying, "Let's go down to the creek bed, dear." Tracy had been shaking her head "no." Mrs. Cable seemed to be startled that the operative was there. She turned away.

In the car on the way back, Tracy began what has become a pattern of verbal behavior following the meeting with her mother. After singing and telling jokes she said, "Can I tell you a secret?" Initially, the secrets were minor, such as her birthday.

This time she told the operative about "how different" her mother was today. When questioned, Tracy revealed that her mother says things "differently" when the operative is not around. Ordinarily, the minute Tracy and Mrs. Cable are alone, Mrs. Cable begins asking Tracy such questions as, "Why don't you want to live with me?" and "Don't you know that your father doesn't really love you?" Tracy's reaction to this could be seen in her spontaneous comment to Molly [a playmate] on the playground. "We [my mother and I] don't live together because we don't get along very well together."

December 11, 1965

10 AM As soon as Tracy and the operative arrived, Mrs. Cable suggested they go to the playground for just an

hour. The operative sat on a bench while Mrs. Cable followed Tracy around and talked to her.

12 Noon On the way back, Tracy said again that her mother "spoke differently" when the operative was not near. Tracy said her mother told her that her father never told her [Tracy] the truth, and that she should believe only her mother. Tracy also said her mother wanted, again, to take her away in the car.

January 22, 1966

10:15 AM Tracy ran after the operative and began crying -- saying "take me home." Mrs. Cable came up behind closely observing Tracy and the operative. Tracy became progressively more upset. Her mother asked what was wrong and Tracy said, "You know what's wrong. You did it yourself." At this point, the conversation broke down into Tracy's accusations and Mrs. Cable's denials.

Tracy indicated that her mother was a liar; her mother said terrible things about her father and made her feel very sad; she hated to come on Saturdays; she was always very sad on Saturdays because she had to come; she loved her father; she knew her father loved her; and that her mother really didn't love her but was just trying to take her away from her father.

Mrs. Cable began to actively solicit the operative's support when Tracy said that she didn't like the operative either. The operative led Mrs. Cable to believe that Tracy's statements were discounted.

10:30 AM Mrs. Cable went to get a Kleenex. The operative winked at Tracy, which calmed her down, and went to the other side of the playground and engaged Mrs. Cable in conversation.

Mrs. Cable indicated that she thought Mr. Cable might be drugging Tracy "like the last time" since Tracy was so unhappy to see her; that Tracy's not seeing her enough in December was causing alienation of affection; that a substitute for her own "mother's love," in the form of a different woman was being attempted; that the only reason she did not have custody of Tracy was because she did not have the money for a high-powered, high paid lawyer, and that something definitely was going to have to be done to change the whole situation.

Just when I thought that everything had been settled between my parents, Mother made contact with the court, again. On December 8, 1965, she filed the following declaration with the California Superior Court:

I the undersigned, declare:

I was unable to visit with Tracy on Saturday, November 27, 1965, because Mr. Cable took her to Eureka for the Thanksgiving holidays. Mr. Cable now says that I will be unable to visit Tracy on Christmas Day, which is a Saturday. He has advised my attorneys through his attorney that he has made plans with others involving Tracy for Christmas Day.

I want very much to see Tracy and be with her whenever

and wherever I possibly can. If a normal mother-daughter relationship is ever to be reestablished between us, we must see each other at times and places that do not present such awkward and embarrassing circumstances as now exists.

Signed, Kathryn Cable

"Awkward and embarrassing circumstances" meant in the presence of the third person and at the Children's Health Council.

On December 18, 1965, Dr. Gordon wrote the following letter to Indian Joe:

Dear Mr. Di Maria,

Following my discussion with you and preparation of the Affidavit you now possess, I would like to add several psychiatric comments which pertain to Tracy and the question of an extension of visitation with the mother, Mrs. Cable. Since I will not be in town for the hearing December 21st and I will not return until December 27th, I submit the following with the hope that you will present it in court in my absence.

First, let me say that at this time, I am unalterably opposed to any extension of the visitation rights either by lengthening of the individual visit, increasing frequency, or by the exclusion of the third party who is now present.

Tracy, who was diagnosed as a borderline psychotic child when I first began to see her two-and-a half years ago is still extensively disturbed and does not have the inner resources with which to deal with another person's [her mother's] threatening and anxiety-producing behavior. According to Tracy, since the establishment of custody with her father she no longer fears her mother will gain her in custody. However, Tracy reports that her mother persistently and at every visit [still] tells Tracy that her father doesn't love her, that she, the mother, is the only one who does. Whether Mrs. Cable does this from conscious intent or cannot help herself, I cannot judge, but the effect upon Tracy is hardly bearable. On several occasions she has subsequently broken down and has cried to her father asking him whether he loves her or not and why her mother says these things. Mr. Cable does not feel free to make any comment about Mrs. Cable's statements. Therefore, Tracy remains confused and anxious. Under these current circumstances Tracy's only aid is the presence of a third party [third person, operative, babysitter, etc.]. I have instructed Tracy, without Mr. Cable's knowledge, to inform her sitter if the pressure becomes intolerable that she wishes the visit terminated. My last concern is this child's mental health. She is entitled to an uncomplicated and as helpful a progression as possible.

Let me further state that Mrs. Cable's visits with Tracy have two positive values. One is by realistic contact Tracy can form a realistic concept of her mother and is not limited to her own fantasies. Secondly, there is always a possibility that Mrs. Cable's mental status might improve and she would be able to provide Tracy with a meaningful mother relationship. However, these positive values become less of a possibility as Mrs. Cable continues to attempt to disrupt Tracy's relationship and sense of security with her father. When I feel the negative aspects of the benefits outweigh the positive, I will not hesitate to request a discontinuance [of visitation].

Sincerely yours, Elsa Gordon

Not long after this letter, Dr. Gordon let it be known that she felt the negative aspects of visitation outweighed the positive. She requested the California Superior Court to grant a two-year discontinuation of visitation. She was deeply concerned because of the extreme anxiety my mother was causing me during visitation. On December 21, 1965, Dad filed his declaration with the California Superior Court, which in part reads:

...At the same time that the child was exhibiting characteristics of being drugged, she also exhibited a fear that her mother was trying to dominate her mind, and have the child reiterate whatever the mother wish it to [sic]; that I took a lie detector test on the question of whether I had administered such drugs to my child and was absolutely cleared; that my wife could not be cleared by the party who gave her a lie detector test of such a charge, because of her history of mental illness.

That the Interlocutory Decree of Divorce provides: "Neither party shall criticize the other, directly or indirectly." The premises of a third party were specified by the trial judge. I have repeatedly objected to the place of visitation now being employed, which is the Children's Health Council in Menlo Park; that this means open grounds and ground privileges which are taken by Mrs. Cable to mean that she can take my child, as she habitually and regularly does, down to a creek bed away from the babysitter I have hired for the purpose of being close during visitation periods; that she does this in order to further her campaign of hatred towards me and damage to said child by telling said child incessantly during the last few months that I do not love the child.

That on account of the visitations and as they have been conducted by said wife, Kathryn Cable, the emotional condition of my said daughter has deteriorated the last few months, and that she seems very insecure as a result of this campaign of telling the child that I do not love her; that it is for the best interest of said minor child that, in accordance with Dr. Elsa Gordon's recommendations, she [Tracy] not see my wife for approximately two years, when she can as a more mature and stable person determine whether or not they will develop a significant mother-daughter relationship; that the only medical doctor who has treated my child and knows her thoroughly for her mental and emotional conditions is Dr. Elsa L. Gordon; that in the summer vacation months when for some five or six weeks she fails to see her mother, she is a much improved child -- far more stable, far more happy, and far more secure.

Executed the 17th day of December 1965.

Signed, Jonathan H. Cable

My Leg Hurts!

One fall day, after I had just turned nine years old, Dad watched me run as I played with the Knudson kids. As my left foot struck the ground, I collapsed screaming in pain. Dad ran to my side. He saw that it was the same leg that I had been complaining about, on and off, for months. He picked me up and carried me to the car. Then he drove us straight to Dr. Hanson's office. Dad had always believed in the pain I had reported and had never called me a "liar" or a "faker," as other people did. This wasn't the first time he had taken me to the doctor for my intermittent leg pain.

Dr. Hanson told Dad that he had examined me before and found nothing wrong. However, by the time he had seen me the pain was temporally gone, only to return later. I could tell Dad was getting more irritated by the second. He didn't want to listen to any more reasons not to X-ray my leg because of high radiation exposure.

"Order the X-ray *now!*" Dad demanded.

Dr. Hanson immediately did.

The X-ray lab was a few doors down from his office. Dad carried me over and then carried me back, while I held the X-ray films.

When the nurse put the film onto the light box, Dad and I saw that my thighbone contained a four to five inch elongated circular mass, located up toward the hip joint. There was a tiny space between the edge of the mass and the bone's exterior.

"What the *hell* is that?" Dad asked, under his breath.

Not noticing his concern, I was delighted and completely relieved that the X-ray had proven I was not a "faker" or a "liar."

"See Daddy? See it?" I asked happily, "I told you my leg

hurt. I was telling the *truth,* Daddy. I bet that thing in my bone is why it hurts so badly."

Just then, Dad went pale and started tearing up.

"Oh dear God," he cried.

Dr. Hanson flew into the room.

"It's a single cell growth, it's a *single cell.* It is not cancer. *IT'S NOT CANCER, JOHN!"*

I was alarmed and puzzled as to why my doctor was so excited and my dad was crying.

The bone-eating cyst had eaten out the entire inside of my thighbone, which had made the bone as thin as a piece of construction paper. The only treatment available was amputation. I was immediately put on crutches and taken out of school. Dr. Hanson warned me not to put weight on it and that any slip or fall, even a minor one, could shatter the thighbone. Dad, again, consulted every doctor he knew as to the best orthopedic surgeon available for this type of situation. One name kept coming up and that was Dr. Grannis. Dad and I went to talk with him.

Dr. Grannis was a very kind and gentle man. He told my dad about an experiment that they had recently done at Stanford with a chimpanzee. They removed a portion of the chimpanzee's thighbone and replaced it with layers of calves' bone and alternating layers of the chimpanzee's shinbone. The experiment had been successful and the chimpanzee had made a full recovery. Now, they were looking for an adult to use as a "guinea pig" to see if the operation would be as successful in humans. Because I was only nine years old and facing total leg amputation, Dr. Grannis got the okay to try this experimental operation on me. I would be the first person to have this surgery. However, there were several concerns about this operation being performed on a child. The thighbone area involved was an area of growth for the bone. The researchers and doctors were uncertain whether the operation would permanently stunt my leg's growth. They were also uncertain whether the surgery would be successful on a human. There was concern that my immune system might reject the cow's bone altogether. Dad discussed it with me. He gave me the opportunity to choose -- the experimental operation or amputation of my leg at the hip. A few days later, I saw an old man in a wheelchair, missing one leg. I thought, *If I have my leg amputated, I will never be able to run with my friends again.* Even though the doctor told me that amputation would be the less painful of the two, I chose the experimental surgery.

Before I went into surgery, I was half Hungarian and half English. When I came out, I was part Hungarian, part English and part Heifer!

The surgery took eight and a half hours. After I had recovered sufficiently to be put in a regular ward, Indian Joe sent a telegram to my mother's attorneys and told them that I was in the hospital recovering from leg surgery. In another telegram to her attorneys, Indian Joe waived the two-hour visitation limit. He made it clear that my mother could have unlimited visits with me while I was in the hospital.

Much to my dismay, Mother took time off work and visited with me almost every day. I was constantly in severe pain and was very afraid that I was dying. On top of that, I had to contend with her popping in whenever she felt like it. At first, she read children's stories to me, which was something she had never done. These visits were quiet and more enjoyable than any other visitation. Soon, though, Mother was back to her old campaigns. She would only do this when no one was around. When people were nearby, she was *overly* sweet. She also started a new campaign to rally the nurses for their sympathy, which she planned to use later for her own advantage. The nurses began to side with my mother and told me that she had a right to visit me in the hospital. They scolded me for not wanting to see her and not being better behaved towards her. At times, hospital volunteers took turns acting as the third person. However, there were other times when my mother and I were alone for hours. The volunteers and nurses felt sorry for my mother and there was no understanding or protection for me.

One day, when no one else was around, Mother again started saying terrible things to me about Dad. She told me that he didn't want me anymore and he had decided to turn custody of me over to her. I was angry and crying, denying her allegations and yelling at her to leave me alone. All of a sudden a nurse flew in the room. She immediately took my mother's side and started yelling at me because I was "misbehaving" and "not being fair to my *poor* mother." I started thrashing around in my bed crying and yelling that I wanted Mother to leave. Just then, I heard a BIG booming voice enter the room.

"WHAT IS GOING ON HERE?! *WHO* IS THIS WOMAN?!"

I looked up to see Dr. Grannis. His face was flushed, bright red, in anger.

The nurse started to explain that I was throwing a tantrum, misbehaving and sassing my mother.

"*Nobody* upsets *my* patients. This girl has had *major* surgery and if she does not want to see her mother then her mother needs to *leave*," Dr. Grannis ordered.

"We can't throw her out; she's the girl's mother," the nurse replied defensively.

"I don't give a damn *who* she is, she needs to leave *now!*"

"You can't order me out of this hospital!" Mother interrupted defiantly.

"Madam, you have one of two choices: either leave on your own power or I will have you *thrown out!*"

Mother chose to leave under her own power. After she left, Dr. Grannis was so kind to me. He stayed with me for some time speaking to me softly, while he held my hand and gently stroked my forehead and hair until I was completely calmed down. No one had ever stopped Mother from upsetting me before and no one had ever successfully forced her to leave me alone. That day, Dr. Grannis was my hero!

After the incident with Dr. Grannis, Mother's visits were shorter and less often. She did not spend much time with me, but instead kept soliciting the nurses, nurses' aides, volunteers and even the teenage candy stripers for sympathy. What she was really after were affidavits from these people in support of her position. I was in the hospital for two-and-a-half weeks. I was relieved when I could finally go home.

Surprise!

Mother had a nasty surprise up her sleeve. She had gotten her psychiatrist, Dr. Stern, and one of the nurses at El Camino Hospital to submit declarations and affidavits to the court. Her attorneys felt that they had enough to reopen the custody case and had scheduled a hearing for this purpose. Mother was demanding full custody of me, seven months after the custody case was settled. Her attorneys filed the following motion with the California Superior Court on March 17, 1966. It states in part:

> Plaintiff and Cross-defendant [Mother] will motion the court for an order modifying terms and conditions of the Interlocutory Judgment of Divorce made herein

on or about August 20, 1965, to the effect that Defendant [Father] is not a fit person to have custody of the minor child of the parties; that legal and physical custody of the minor child should be awarded to the plaintiff; and that the defendant be precluded from all visitation with the minor child.

Said motion will be made on the grounds (1) that Defendant is in fact an unfit person to have custody of said minor child, (2) that it will be for the best interest of said minor child that she not see Defendant or visit with Defendant at all, (3) that a substantial change in circumstances has occurred since a judgment was made.

The declaration submitted to the court by one of her attorneys reads in part:

Plaintiff [Mother] has pending before this court on motion to declare Defendant [Father] to be an unfit person to have custody of Tracy Cable, and ordering that Plaintiff be awarded custody of said minor child. Tracy Cable has been a patient of Elsa Gordon, M.D. for over two years for the care and treatment of certain emotional problems suffered by Tracy. Plaintiff contends that these emotional problems were caused by Defendant and perhaps were even intentionally inflicted upon Tracy by Defendant.

In Mother's declaration to the California Superior Court dated February 21, 1966, she stated:

Tracy and I have been seeing each other on a once

JUSTICE: BLIND OR BIASED?

a week basis since about July of 1964. These weekly
meetings have been in the presence of a third person
and always in an artificial and strange environment in
that they have been in homes of outsiders, at the Children's Health Council, and, for a while, at El Camino
Hospital. Despite these handicaps and conditions, Tracy and I have managed to get along with each other
very well and we have begun to reestablish the healthy,
normal mother-daughter relationship we once enjoyed.
Tracy was apprehensive during the early visits, but as
time went on, we got to know each other again. We
were able to laugh, to play games, to read and to tell
stories. We have progressed in our relationship to the
point where I feel strongly that Tracy should come live
with me. I would, of course, stop working in order to
be with her and to provide the proper home life and
environment. I would continue to provide any and all
psychiatric counseling necessary for her good health
and well-being.

The only place that this relationship between my mother
and me was a reality was in her mind!

Only two months later, on April 25, 1966, Mother submitted another declaration to the California Superior Court,
stating the exact opposite:

That the general tenor of the relationship between my
daughter and me in our visits has deteriorated in the period commencing *immediately prior* to the divorce trial
and continuing to date, as compared with the prior period. That she more frequently adverts to matters which
occurred in our family life but in which she has been

given a wrong version and one adverse to me, that is, she says that I "deserted" her by going to Agnews Hospital, that I never took care of her, that I had told her the world would come to an end "tomorrow" indicating to me a purposeful attempt by her father to alienate us. Since the Interlocutory Decree her attitude towards me, her upset, her tirades, her hostility have become more intense at our "formal" visiting times. Tracy and I have no problems in our personal relationship except such that have arisen from the continuing antagonism of Mr. Cable towards me; the vague fears he has planted in the child; the suspicion, and the uneasiness he has thrown into our relationship. The problems in my visits with Tracy are arising with greater frequency and a greater degree, but they do not occur in our meetings; they are present when she arrives. She is upset at the beginning of our visit. Mr. Cable is making the prospect of visits with me so unpleasant and is so hostile toward me in every respect that my daughter is being torn apart and destroyed. I believe in fact Mr. Cable is even destroying the foundations of any lasting relationship of his with our daughter. I must have the custody of my daughter for a full and free relationship with her and to remove her from the harm which is being done.

Both of Mother's declarations were written and signed under penalty of perjury. They were submitted only two months apart. The second stated: "Since the Interlocutory Divorce Decree [back in August] her [Tracy's] attitude towards me, her upset, her tirades, her hostility, have become more intense at our 'formal' visiting times." During the same timeline, Mother also stated that our relationship significantly improved: "Tracy and I have managed to get along with each other very well and we have begun to reestablish the healthy, normal mother-daughter relationship we once enjoyed." She also stated: "We have progressed in our relationship to the point where I strongly feel that Tracy should come live with me." Her declarations stated events and issues that were diametrically opposed to one another, while occurring simultaneously. That is impossible and in court should be considered perjury. On multiple occasions, Indian Joe brought this to Judge Riley's attention. The judge chose to overlook it. Judge Riley didn't even give my mother a warning or correct her in anyway, nor was there any consequence for her perjury. Maybe the court doesn't hold mentally ill patients responsible in this regard, I don't know. Yet, this same judge had deemed my mother to be a "fit person." How could she be deemed a fit person and a mentally ill person at the same time?

Mother stated that Dad's attempts to alienate me from her were tearing me apart and destroying me. She was correct about the effects of parental alienation on a child. However, *she* was the one engaging in parental alienation. At every visitation, year after year, Mother attempted to tear apart my relationship with my father. The things that Mother blamed on Dad, she alone was guilty of doing to me. Perhaps this was part of her mental disease and she truly thought *he* was doing this to me, instead of her; I don't know. Maybe it was just part of her delusion, since it had nothing to do with the reality of the situation. The only thing I truly know is what I experienced, which was horrible.

Parental alienation was not just a problem between Mother and me. Unfortunately, it is alive and well in many divorced families, today. I have witnessed parental alienation used on children of divorce, whom I have known personally. I have seen the familiar negative effects on these children and have stood up for them! The parent who practices parental alienation (running the other parent down to the child) is determined to harm or even destroy the relationship between their child and the other parent. However, these effects can boomerang, harming or destroying the alienating parent's relationship with their child, as it did with my mother and me. Sadly, the real casualty of parental alienation is the child, who ends up being hurt mentally and emotionally.

Mother was responsible for destroying any chance of a relationship with me by consistently telling me her negative beliefs, thoughts and feelings about my dad. Every Saturday at visitation, she attempted to alienate me from him by tearing him down to me and by telling me that he didn't love me. She didn't care that she was tearing *me* apart in the process.

As a child I would say, "I am half Hungarian and half English," because I perceived myself to be half of my mother and half of my father. It is understandable that kids think this way. This perception goes way beyond nationalities, as children are compared to both parents, from birth: "she has her dad's eyes," or "he has his mom's nose," etc. When children are older they hear: "you're just like your mom," or "you're a chip off the old block," and so on. Therefore, when my mother was badmouthing my dad, she was tearing down a part of me as well.

Parental alienation hurts the child by putting the child in a double bind, creating sadness, fear, pain, insecurity, confusion and great anxiety. Children do *not* have the inner resources to be able to cope with these negative feelings. The alienating parent is attacking a parent the child loves and, in so doing, is attacking a part of the child! I have learned, through many painful years of experience that parental alienation can cause devastating effects on children, because it is painful, manipulative and abusive.

If both parents are engaging in parental alienation, the child feels caught in the middle of a tug-of-war, torn apart by

JUSTICE: BLIND OR BIASED?

the two people who are suppose to love, cherish and protect
the child. I think if more parents and adult family members
were aware of these facts, the occurrences of parental alienation
would drop dramatically. If you are divorced with children,
please help to keep your relationship with them positive and
healthy by refusing to practice parental alienation. Please protect your children and all children!

When I was a child, I wanted a caring mother so badly. I'd
see other girls out with their moms, laughing, shopping and
enjoying each other's company. I saw a bond between them
that I craved down to my core. Unfortunately, Mother never allowed this type of relationship to grow between us. Her efforts
to turn me against my dad were the most important things
to her, not building any kind of loving mother-daughter relationship with me. I prayed to God that one day I would go to
visitation and my mother would be magically transformed into
a loving and kind mother, but that never happened.

Before the hearing, I was at the neighborhood market with
some of the Knudson kids. As we were leaving, Mr. Rush, the
neighbor that lived in between the Knudson's and me, took me
by the shoulder and firmly guided me away from the other kids.

Mr. Rush started asking me many questions about my
mother like: "How do you feel about your mother? Would you
like to live with her or see her more often? Has your father
been saying anything against your mother? Does your father
make you unhappy about seeing your mother? Do you love
your mother? Do you love your father? This whole situation
must be very hard on you, isn't it?"

I became very anxious and shrugged my shoulders as he
quickly asked his questions. I knew that Mr. Rush was a private
investigator. He was never interested in any of this before.

I wondered, why now? My suspicion grew with every question.

Mr. Rush smelled of alcohol and I thought he might be drunk. I wondered if he was working for my mother. My mind raced as I tried to figure out what he was up to and what I should do about it. I finally told him I would talk with him later, but right now, I had to go. I caught up with the Knudson kids who had already started on their way home.

That night I told my dad what had happened at the market with Mr. Rush. I told Dad that I didn't know what to say, so I didn't answer his questions and told him I had to go. Dad listened and told me that I handled the situation very well. Then he went over to Mr. Rush's house and had a long talk with him. Afterwards, Dad came home and explained that Mr. Rush had been hired by my mother's attorneys to obtain information from me to use against him in court. Mr. Rush promised my dad that he would not take the case or ask me any more questions. Just to be on the safe side, Dad told me if Mr. Rush asked me anything along these lines that I was not to answer him.

Back to Court Again

A hearing was set to decide whether to reopen the custody case or not. Indian Joe was not given copies of the affidavits or declarations, from my mother's attorneys, until the afternoon before. So, he had no time to get counter affidavits or declarations ready for this hearing.

In the early morning hours on the day of the hearing, Indian Joe phoned my dad. He told him to pack a lunch and an overnight bag for me and bring me to the courthouse. I waited in the lobby clutching my overnight bag fearful about what was going to happen to me next.

The hearing took many hours. I remember how hard it was to wait. I was anxious and worried about what was going on in court. I was sitting on a long, hard, wooden bench. I remember nervously pacing, sitting and singing softly to calm myself. I was alone and practiced reciting the Lord's Prayer, which I just learned. Later, I ate my lunch as I waited. I wondered if the real reason that Dad had packed an overnight bag for me was because I was going to have to stay with Mother. I was very afraid that this might happen. I knew she was at the courthouse. Whatever reason I had an overnight bag with me certainly couldn't be good. The hours seemed like days. Meanwhile in the courtroom, my parents' attorneys argued their positions, as my parents sat silently across the aisle from each other.

The following was quoted, in part, and verbatim from the California Superior Court reporter's transcript dated April 26, 1966:

[As I have done, throughout the story, I have continued adding [square brackets] with my words to aid with comprehension and ease of reading. [Sic] is placed at the end of an ill constructed verbatim sentence to flag that it is not a typo.]

Mr. Molino [Mother's attorney]: If your Honor please, I feel that the effect of these declarations, in a broad sense indicate that the premise upon which your Honor made his order at the time of the interlocutory decree with reference to custody and visitation does not exist.

…The child is being upset. The child is being subjected to an atmosphere of antagonism [by the father]. I think the declaration of [the nurse's aid from El Camino Hospital] is highly significant that a declaration with respect to events which took place at a time when both of the parents should be having the greatest consideration for a child, [when I was in the hospital] demonstrate quite clearly that there is an inability on the part of the father to divorce himself from the antagonism which he apparently continues to feel towards the mother.

The fact is that this is having a very bad influence on this child. So that, first of all, the premise upon which your Honor's order for custody does not exist, that an attempt would be made to have an environment for the best interest of this child.

Secondly, the next thing that these declarations show is that there is, aside from the attempt to do so, lack of an attempt to make a good atmosphere for this child, that there is apparently a purposeful and willful attempt to alienate the child from the mother, to further make the actual visits with the mother unproductive. That the child is being harmed [sic]. That in the declaration of Dr. Stern setting forth that Mrs. Cable is a normal individual, with a normal motherly desire to do for this child, and she is being prevented from so doing [sic].

...It shows that there is a continuing attempt by Mr. Cable in the supposed carrying out of the order of this court for visitation to harass Mrs. Cable by reporting and indicating that she is a mentally deficient individual [to the third person].

This, again, is harming the relationship of the mother

and child. It is so serious that your Honor knows, we had agreed that this was the date to determine whether or not your Honor would open the matter up. I certainly feel that the declarations show and form a basis for opening the matter up and it is so serious that I feel there should be a complete and full investigation of the matter for the welfare of this young girl. And it is a girl child, of whom we are speaking, and I do represent the mother, and it is the mother who is concerned at this time.

With reference to your Honor's second – second matter that you broached [sic], I had at the time of the previous hearing indicated that I felt that this was an instance where, not to put over the responsibilities nor the prerogatives of the court to some other group, but where it might be productive, in effect, to have a panel psychiatric review to advise the court in the matter [sic]. This panel psychiatric review to comprehend both of the parties and the child [sic].

Mr. Molino goes into detail, explaining how to construct such a panel: what records should be turned over to them, which professionals should be on the panel and who they should interview.

...turn over these Agnews records to them, [the panel] hear -- or have the records of the psychiatrist Mr. Cable saw previously, see this child, and themselves interview the child, Mr. Di Maria and I both have the opportunity of sitting down with them and expressing ourselves and our opinions [sic]. This should be more of an investigational board.

Although I certainly haven't had all the custody matters that exist, I have handled quite a few. I have seen many domestic relationship matters, and this is the most serious one from the point of view of the welfare of the child that I have ever had the opportunity of dissipating. And that is why I make a suggestion for a little different type of investigation.

...I must say that when a doctor [Dr. Stern] will make a declaration in which he says that he thinks that Mrs. Cable and this child are being psychologically strangled, although we may differ with this conclusion in degree, they certainly would indicate that he places a great deal of emphasis and a great deal of seriousness on the circumstances [sic]. I recognize that this is not the daughter's psychiatrist; he has not examined this girl. But he has examined the information which has come to him from Mrs. Cable.

So, we will submit, if your Honor please, that the matter should be completely and fully investigated, and a failure of ours to have this done at this time would be a tremendous detriment to this child. It may be too late that it be done at this time [sic], but we can't wait any longer.

Mr. Di Maria [Indian Joe]: If your Honor please, I don't believe that after a full and fair consideration of these affidavits there is anything at all in them. I want to say it with the utmost of fairness in the sense of reasonableness, but, really, number one, they don't bring out anything new.

Number two, on the very major one or two points in each of them, they are directly contradictory to other things in the record on this hearing on this motion. They are argumentative almost completely. They are full of tirades, full of conjecture, and this goes as well for Dr. Stern's so-called affidavit.

An affidavit, as I understand it, must be sufficiently particular in specifics so that a charge of perjury can be made.

Indian Joe tore apart the nurse's aide's affidavit, sentence by sentence, point by point and then did the same with Dr. Stern's affidavit.

... **Mr. Di Maria:** Since when does custody hinge on whether or not a woman is satisfied with the court order? There is still the best welfare rule in this state, and the best welfare rule is satisfied only by what is best for the child and what is best for the child depends almost entirely on who is the better custodian.

I do have a proposal. After all, everything that is in these papers, I don't dignify them by calling them affidavits, everything that is in them touches on the question of whether or not this is a child that is being steamrollered, terrified, coerced, [and] bullied by her father. Now this happens to be an intelligent girl, considerably above normal intelligence. She is articulate and vocal. I must say that if you had seen her at the time of the separation of these parties you would've deemed her to be clearly a case of a retarded child. But she is intelligent. I propose that your Honor talk to her, not just for an hour, you can have her [for] as long as you like as far as we're concerned; you can keep her for the weekend; you can keep her for four hours; you can take her out for dinner; you can have ice cream with her. She will talk. She will tell you how she feels. And, after all, it isn't too hard to tell what's in the mind and heart of a little girl that is nine-and-a-half years old. They aren't quite that astute at evading and outwitting adults. I don't know any that are. They haven't been exposed as much. This would clear up anything; if there were any residual doubts after what these papers purport to say.

I submit there is nothing here to go to trial on. There is nothing in Stern's affidavit. He bases it on telegrams and a junk affidavit of [the nurse's aide from El Camino Hospital]; he bases it on how Mrs. Cable apparently feels about the matter.

As far as Mrs. Cable's affidavit is concerned in the same motion, the same matter, it is diametrically opposite on the key points.

Now, if your Honor feels there may be some doubt here, we even have the girl here today; she is downstairs. You can talk to her now or you can have her over the weekend, for two hours, four hours, any number of times. I would be happy to have the matter settled that way.

As far as the proposal made by Mr. Molino, this panel business, it is, of course, unconstitutional. I cited the authority for it last time, and I don't want it, your Honor. In the first place, it is the job of this court to make that decision, and I know it [the panel] is going to be usurped by one aggressive member of the board; the other members are going to lie around and do nothing. That is the history of committees, of course.

And, secondly, I want the right to cross-examine. That is what we have in court, we have a panel, in effect; we cross-examine and find out what they think and what they base it on. I wouldn't want to give up my right of cross-examination where the very life of a little child is involved. I maintain that nobody can say that this girl has not been going up [improving]. She has been getting stronger and better. There is nobody who has examined her who says that she is deteriorating. There is not one word in these affidavits that this child is getting worse. Just her relations with her mother are getting worse. On that point, your Honor, maybe that is true, I don't know. We don't know exactly, because we are not allowed to ask questions [to the child]. She [Tracy] complains [about visitation], as she said before, consistently. She has no protection. She is a human being, she is an individual. This is what Dr. Gordon tried to tell the court, she [Tracy] has had no protection. It is very hard for a little girl to spend two hours each week, that's a much longer time than two hours to us [adults], with someone whom she fears, with someone, who is to her, irrational.

I haven't mentioned anything that I can't put in on this. Believe me, I have a case ready. I am not without a case. There have been things that have been happening. This girl is under fire. Those two hours with this person who is her mother have not developed into anything as her mother says, and I believe this to be true. I don't think

the [mother's] first affidavit is true that they are getting along just beautifully and she is ready to take her
[Tracy] back, she [the mother] will stop working and
everything is fine, that was two months ago. Now she
[the mother] says that there's nothing but difficulties
with her [Tracy]. I more likely believe that. And why?
Dr. Gordon said that there is nothing in the way of a
mother-daughter relationship [that] can take place at
this time.

So, what are you going to have when you put a little
child in a context like this? Her mother can't be just a
neutral nothing to her. Either there is a relationship,
[of] a positive nature, or a negative relationship. And
what we are seeing here probably is exactly that, a negative relationship. There are things her mother does I
haven't put in an affidavit form, but they are not going
to make her look like a real solid person who can really
develop this relationship.

And your Honor knows that, after all this time, if this
woman can't develop this relationship, the hard question is why, why can't she? I haven't said she has to be at
any one place for two hours [during visitation], nor has
Mr. Cable. I said repeatedly, as telegrams to Mr. Molino
state, pick anyone you want [for the third person], just
so it is a neutral person. Don't ask us in on the confer-
ence even.

I must admit my knees knock a bit when I say that, but
I want to be safe. Anyone you want. We will go for it.
Get a babysitting agency. Just so she is not known to
you or to us. And we are satisfied. But she [the mother]

wants somebody known to her. That's what these tele-grams are about. She is just bucking, and they are try-ing to get that third alternative, someone known to her [the mother]. Why, why, why, why?

And these little drawings [which I drew, a year ago at visitation -- while I was drugged, which Mother had included in one of her current affidavits], your Honor, they go back to the days of Meprobamate.

The Court: All right. Is there any final thing you want-ed to say?

Mr. Molino: Yes, your Honor, just to clarify in one re-spect. It is our position that the contrasts shown here, the so-called ordinary visits, this girl is getting to dislike them and hate them, because they are times that represent to her when she is being conditioned for them by her father, conditioned so that she will dislike her mother.

Mr. Di Maria: I'm going to object, your Honor, he doesn't know that, there is nobody who testified.

Mr. Molino: A climate is being created by Mr. Cable, as Mr. Di Maria referred to, an affidavit -- or a telegram that Mrs. Cable could have unlimited visitation [in El Camino Hospital]. I refer to the one that followed shortly thereafter, because of the misunderstanding of the nurse in charge. Mrs. Cable was told that visitation would be limited to an aggregate of two hours. Who told her this? Why? How did that misunderstanding occur? Why are the babysitters told by Mr. Cable that Mrs. Cable is schizophrenic, that she doesn't know what she's doing?

Mr. Di Maria: Now, quit testifying, Mr. Molino that is what you have done with all of these things.

Mr. Molino: In whose presence [of the third person] we have visited [during visitation]. [The third person has been] advised by Mr. Cable, in various ways that I am mentally ill [sic]. [I am certain Mr. Molino meant to say that my mother was mentally ill, not himself.] They cannot lead to a reasonable relationship with the child, if your Honor please, and if this is the tactic, then it is being done purposefully, then it is a vicious thing. If it is being done in a misguided fashion, then it is at the least a very bad thing and we ask that the matter be fully explored, and we be given an opportunity actually to bring in as witnesses many other people, and who would substantiate these declarations that we have here.

The Court: Well, I don't feel that the declarations indicate enough new changed circumstances to justify having an entire new hearing or a panel procedure of the type that you suggested. Some of the things that are talked about in the declarations go back to the whole previous history, which we did go into at the trial with psychiatrists testifying and being cross examined, and I talked to Tracy myself in chambers, and have been over all that once in a full, prolonged trial.

Others relate to, I think, the mechanics of the visitation, and in that connection, I think there may have been a misunderstanding about the interlocutory degree. It was not my intention that this third person had to be physically in the presence of Mrs. Cable and Tracy during this visitation. [The judge intended that the third person's role was just to provide a meeting place for visitation.] It appears that may have been a cause of confusion.

Mr. Di Maria: Now, your Honor, as I understand the reason why limitations were placed on visitation is for protective reasons, [the third person's role] and if we're going to have protection [for Tracy] we are going to have protection. If we are not, [then] we are not. And, frankly, I fear that if this child does not have somebody there who is at least neutral and who at least is within earshot, I fear the consequences. Dr. Gordon fears the consequences. I think I understand the psychiatry of the situation well enough to say I fear the consequences. I will go one step further and say that there are matters that we haven't had a chance to bring out; I hope we don't have to, that represent what Dr. Gordon has indicated in her testimony and in her affidavits, represent some substantiation of physical danger, again, to this child.

Your Honor must bear in mind, this is an unusual case. It was established that Mrs. Cable has an overpowering hatred of this man [Mr. Cable]. This I think is the key to the whole thing. Otherwise, by now no daughter who wants a mother as badly as Tracy does, and she [does] want a mother. No daughter would get this way towards her own mother. It is impossible.

The Court: Well, of course, it is obvious from the decree that I was concerned at that time about Mr. Cable having the right attitude about these visitations, and it does seem to me that there is a degree of obstructionism being indicated by this difficulty over just the place where the visitation is going to be, the fact that Mrs.

Cable suggested that a person whose premises should be used, therefore you are against it. I mean --

Mr. Di Maria: Yes.

The Court: That's what bothers me.

Mr. Di Maria: With all the rest of the world to choose from that is acceptable to us, we don't want this, because, your Honor, I have been in this case for four years, and I don't think I'm a person of undue fears. I know Dr. Gordon, I couldn't even talk with her for the first six months, she is definite, she knows this child, [and] she thinks the dangers are very real. She thinks the harm and trouble that could come to Tracy through her mother is a very real thing.

The Court: Well, I obviously didn't accept all of her opinions of the child.

Mr. Di Maria: I think that is true. But I think it is a real risk, your Honor, and I don't see why charming, agreeable people, who exist by the hundreds, should be objectionable to Mrs. Cable; and this one person [the one known to her] should be the one person to please her.

The judge and Indian Joe went over a list of prospective neutral babysitters and third persons. My dad added two more to the list and Indian Joe pointed out that these people had been involved in our visitations, on a substitute basis, and that they were all liked by me. We had visitation with the woman my mother wanted, once, and I didn't like her. Indian Joe told the judge to pick somebody, anybody, as long as they are not known to my mother or my father.

...**Mr. Molino:** All right. Now, if your Honor please, may I interrupt at this point? This is a very important part of the whole picture. Mrs. Cable is being worked on by these means. This child is being used as a tool unconscionably, and unmercifully, to torture Mrs. Cable, and the torture is being done to the child, too. They insist upon a stranger. We see these things, we come into court, and we accept the restraining orders and things of this sort. It becomes necessary that these things be done on occasion. But here we come into an extreme circumstance affecting the welfare of two people. Three, because I honestly believe that Mr. Cable does not, perhaps, realize how great the injury is that is that is being done here.

Mother blamed my dad for the things she was doing to me at visitation. The parental alienation was her doing, not his. Mother's attorney went on and on about how restraining the third person was to our relationship. Then Mr. Molino came up with an idea. He wanted Mother and I to visit alone in her apartment.

...**Mr. Di Maria:** Now, your Honor, I would like to say this about the apartment, I would dread it. I would dread it. I would rather there be a hearing, your Honor, and open up the whole thing rather than to have that. Because, as I said, we have evidence; it doesn't fail to accumulate, and I think that this girl might cross that line. She is afraid of her mother. She is secure in the order, she knows there is an order, she knows she lives with her father, she knows that she goes through two hours of this [forced visitation], she hollers and screams, he [her dad] says, but he has been instructed by me, and I would knock his ears off if he did, I told him in unequivocal English that he must never hurt his position or he would have a new lawyer in four seconds [sic]. Haven't I?

Mr. Cable: Yes.

The Court: All right, you are against the apartment?

Mr. Di Maria: I am afraid of it, is all.

The judge and Indian Joe spoke a little longer about the third person and the place where the visitations would be held. It seemed that all parties, including myself, liked "the operative/babysitter" (the third person who was with us) back at the Children's Health Council. The judge was looking upon this third person favorably.

Believing that my mother and I should see each other without a third person, but realizing that wasn't going to happen, Mother's attorney came up with another idea. He thought Mother should be able to take me on outings to the park, stores, museums, etc. He wanted some more flexibility with the visitation, so it was not confined to one place. Indian Joe had no objections to what he was proposing.

...Mr. Di Maria: The third person would, however, go on these --

The Court: If they [Mrs. Cable and Tracy] go to the park or something she [the third person] will go along with them.

Mr. Di Maria: And the third person would be in the house?

The Court: It [the third person] doesn't have to be right in the same room.

...The motion for change of custody will be denied on the basis that I have described.

After hours of pacing back and forth, silently praying and worrying that Mother might gain custody of me, Dad came downstairs and took me by the hand. He said that the hearing was over and I was going home with him. I was elated, exhausted and extremely relieved.

8 years old at Disneyland

10 years old

The Knudson Kids – 1967

Jeff

Janie

Rich

Brian

Barry

Mary Jane & Darrell (1954)

Brian, 12½ years old.

Tracy, Janie and Barry.

Tracy, Janie and Santa.

Uncle Les, Aunt Nita and Cousins

Gwen, Uncle Les, Leslie & Linda (1958)

Aunt Nita and Uncle Les (Late 1980's)

3

When There Is No Safe Place

Endings and New Beginnings

Mother and I now started to meet at the third person's house. Dad told me that during visitation the third person, my mother and I could now go places together in Mother's car. I was very leery of this idea, as I didn't want to go anywhere with her, let alone in her own vehicle. He tried to soothe my fears by telling me the third person would always be with us. At first, I flat out refused to get into Mother's car. With Dad's persistent support and confidence that everything would be okay, as well as the encouragement from the third person, I finally went along with the new court order.

Mother took us to the duck pond, the Junior Museum, parks and shopping centers. Soon I realized that this was much better than just sitting around or being in a confined place. The third person was with us all of the time and my mother had less time for her "little talks."

A couple of times Mother drove us to her apartment and tried to convince me to go in with her. Each time I refused to leave the car. The third person said that she would go up with me, but I still refused. Mother suggested that I venture up the outside stairway to look through the window while she and the third person stayed in the car. I refused to do this as well. I never saw her apartment. Just the thought, frightened me terribly. I never let on how scared I was, but, no matter what anyone did or said, I wasn't getting out of the car!

All of this new freedom did not change my opinion about visitation. I still hated to go. Yet with all the new distractions of things to see and do, it was easier to keep Mother focused on that and not her campaigns. However she soon started a campaign with the third person to win her sympathy. Mother worked diligently to get the third person on her side. Little by little, as time went by, she succeeded.

There was only one time I saw Mother outside of visitation. When I was ten, my dad and I were at the symphony. During intermission, everyone milled around. I saw her and pointed her out to Dad. He suggested I wave at her. She was looking right at me, so I waved. She turned her back on me and never acknowledged me. Dad made excuses for her, saying that maybe she didn't see me or was with friends who didn't know about me and she didn't want to explain. I felt a little sad and a bit angry that she ignored me.

Despite the problems with Mother, for the first time ever my life was predictable, routine and stable. Things seemed to finally be falling into place with consistency and continuity. A few months before my eleventh birthday, Dr. Gordon felt that I had made a good recovery. I was retested and scored in the normal range. After almost five years of therapy, all signs of childhood schizophrenia, psychosis and their effects were gone. I was happy (except for visitations) and was enjoying my life. Dr. Gordon felt that her work was done and it was a good time for us to end therapy. It was a very easy transition for me.

About six months later, after a bimonthly orthodontist appointment, I returned on my bike to the Knudson's house. The kids were outside playing as I walked in the front door to tell Mary Jane that I was home from the appointment. She was in the kitchen. As I approached, I could tell she was very angry. She started yelling at me saying that I never tell her where I am going and that I was too much of a problem to take care of anymore. I was shocked, as this came unexpectedly. I was also confused because other than these appointments, I was always at her house after school. I reminded her of my appointment and then showed her the calendar where it was written down. Instead of this having a calming effect, she became angrier. She stated that I never told her where I was going and would just come and go as I pleased. I told her that she always knew where I was and then asked her to give me an example of what she was talking about. She didn't. Instead, she announced that she was done taking care of me. She told me that I was old enough to take care of myself, which I didn't believe was true. She told me to collect my things, take my house key and go home. Without a word, I did what I was told.

I was too stunned and shocked to cry. The Knudsons were my second family. Mary Jane was my substitute mother. I knew all of that had ended. I had no idea why, but I knew it wasn't from the explanation she gave me. I remember going home, sitting on the couch and just staring into space. I was extremely sad, and felt the old feelings of abandonment again. Looking back, I think I was in a state of shock. I don't know how long I sat there before I thought about how I was going to explain all this to Dad. I wasn't worried about it, because I knew that in the end it was all going to be my fault, anyway. I didn't even care. Any punishment Dad could give me would be so minor compared to what just happened. Whether or not it was my fault really didn't make any difference; what was done was done and there was no going back. Somehow, I knew there would be no fixing it. I felt like a flower yanked up by its roots and thrown onto the hot pavement to wither.

When Dad came home, I explained what had happened.

"After dinner I will go over and talk with Mary Jane and find out what *you* did to upset her and what really happened," Dad grumbled.

In an interesting turn of events, my dad didn't go to Mary Jane's after dinner.

About an hour later, there was a knock at the door and there stood Darrell, Mary Jane's husband. He asked to talk with my dad in private and I was sent to the backyard. Every once in a while I would look in and see Dad's feet sticking out from his easy chair and Darrell sitting on the couch. Darrell must have talked with Dad for at least thirty minutes before he got up and left. Dad called me into the house and told me what he and Darrell had discussed.

Darrell told my dad that when he came home from work he got an earful from Mary Jane about how this was all brought on by my not telling her about the orthodontist appointment. After listening to her, he felt compelled to come over and talk with my dad. Darrell told Dad that he didn't feel it was right for a kid to take the blame when it wasn't my fault to begin with. Darrell said there were certain family issues that were causing difficult times at home and he told my dad about some of them. He wanted my dad to know that what had happened that afternoon had nothing to do with me. He also said that Mary Jane was going to have to start working again to help with family finances. Even though we only lived two doors down,

Darrell had walked all the way around the back of the block, so Mary Jane wouldn't see him pass in front of her kitchen window. He didn't want her to know that he was talking with my dad. Darrell said that Mary Jane thought he was in the garage working and he had to get back before she called him to dinner. He left and took the long way back home.

After dinner, Dad talked some more with me in the hope that I would be able to better understand what happened that afternoon. As I listened, I wondered how kicking me out of their nest was going to solve anything. I was too young to understand the connection that Dad insisted existed. I felt it could have been handled in a better manner and that it would have been more reasonable for Mary Jane to simply tell me that she had to go back to work. It would have been a lot less painful too. The way she left it made me feel that I could never go back, even to visit. Again, there was that feeling of not being wanted and being discarded. Dad told me how important it was to keep my mouth shut and never tell the kids that Darrell had come over, stood up for me and shared some of their family concerns with us. Dad said if I talked with the kids about it that there would be a fight between their parents and this would be my fault. *Great!* I thought, *More secrets to keep and more things to feel guilty about!* Dad never apologized for not believing me.

Starting the very next day, when I returned from school, I was on my own. I wondered whether Mother might come to the house, while Dad was at work and I was home alone. For my own safety, I decided to never let her know that I was home alone. In this way, perhaps she would never find out. I thought she might find out anyway and that worried me. I felt that under the circumstances, I was too young to be left alone, but there I was.

Word that I was home alone got around the neighborhood. A week or two later, one of the neighbor men, whom I had known for many years knocked on the door. To my utter shock, as I opened the door, he grabbed me and kissed me hard on the mouth! Then, without a word, he left. I was speechless and didn't understand why he did this. I had no idea what to do. I felt very strange and a little sick. I decided not to tell Dad. I didn't understand what had happened and didn't want it to end up somehow being my fault. Unfortunately, the next day the man was back at the front door. Again, I opened it and he grabbed me and kissed me hard and long on the mouth. I tried to resist and push him away, but I didn't have the physical strength. He finally finished.

"Why did you do that?!" I asked disgustedly.

"Because I like it," the neighbor replied as he walked away.

I felt ill, all over, and went to the bathroom to wash my mouth. When Dad came home, I decided to tell him about it. I asked Dad to talk to the man and tell him not come over anymore. Dad refused. He told me not to open the door if the man came back and to tell him that my dad said for him to go home. I was afraid and didn't want to do this because I thought the man might get angry and hurt me. The upper half of our front door consisted of multiple glass panes. When we were locked out of the house, it was easy to remove a glass pane to get in. I felt I could be in danger. Regardless of my feelings in the matter, my father insisted that I deal with this man by myself.

The next day I made sure the door was locked after I returned from school. My heart felt like it was going to jump out of my chest as I waited alone. The only sound I heard was my breathing as I wondered whether this man would show up or not. Then there was a knock at the door. I fearfully held my breath as he told me to open the door. I refused and through the bolted door, I told the man what my father had told me to say. As he turned to leave, the man looked irritated and angry. I was afraid and didn't know what to do. I wondered if he would come back and try to get in the house. Hiding under the bed was no longer an option as I had outgrown the space. So I hid in my closet until I heard Dad's key unlock the front door.

My dad asked about the man and I told him what happened. Dad looked at me and said, "Keep this quiet."

I nodded and wondered if the secrets would ever end.

"After all, Tracy, this man has a family and if you tell anyone about what had happened then you will be responsible for creating a broken home. So, if you like his kids, then keep your mouth shut!" Dad warned.

I stared at him in disbelief.

Dad didn't have to worry about me keeping quiet. At this point in my young life, I was an expert secret keeper.

For several days after school, I hid in my closet until Dad came home. When I felt reasonably sure that the man was not coming back, I stopped hiding. From this moment on, I never again was alone in the front yard when my dad wasn't home. I stayed inside, watched TV and kept the doors and windows locked.

Shortly after this, there came a small knock at the front door. I thought that maybe the man had come back. When I looked out the window I was surprised and relieved to see Barry, the youngest Knudson. I opened the door.

"Is it okay if I stay with you until my mom comes home?" he asked.

"Sure," I replied as he came inside.

Even though Barry was six years younger than I was, it was good to have his company and I was thankful he had come over. He told me his mom, Mary Jane, had found a job and came home a little after 5 PM on school days. My dad didn't come home until about 6:30. After that first day, Barry came over every day after school and stayed with me until his mom came home from work. We watched *Daniel Boone* and *Gilligan's Island,* then played a board game, made forts, made taffy or played in the backyard for the remaining time.

After a while Brian, who was the second youngest, came over with Barry. Occasionally their brother Rich, who was eighteen months younger than me, would join us. I was elated to have part of my second family back again! Every day I looked forward to their visit. I also felt safer being with the kids. I was certain that man wouldn't come over, because I was no longer alone. Even though the Knudson kids came over to my house, I didn't feel I could ever go over to their house again. That last interaction with Mary Jane left me feeling unwanted and unwelcome.

New School Bullies

I was looking forward to starting seventh grade at Miller Junior High. The school was a mile away, so I took the bus. I liked junior high right away because we went to different classes for different subjects; there was a cafeteria where kids could get a hot lunch and riding the bus was fun! There were other activities like clubs and dances. Miller brought together kids from several elementary schools, including some kids from my neighborhood who had not attended Meyerholz. Many of these kids were my friends. A few knew about my family's history. The secret of my mother's illness, which was guarded so well in elementary school, had now started to leak out. Before long it seemed that everyone knew about Mother's mental problems. Some of the kids I didn't know would boldly come up to me and ask if my mother was crazy. Some asked if I was crazy too. No matter what I said or didn't say to the kids, I was fast becoming a target at school for bullying.

During seventh grade, many of my neighborhood and elementary school friends started smoking and taking on the attitude of rebellion, which didn't interest me. I knew these choices were the first steps towards bigger things that would lead to nowhere good. I kept my mouth shut about it, not wanting to "rat out" my friends. These friends took a road that I didn't want to travel. As a result, I pulled away and didn't hang out with them anymore. I didn't have the inclination to invite trouble or to cause it and, despite all I had been through, I was not rebellious. I also had a gut feeling that if I smoked, did drugs or got into other trouble, Dad would not be able to deal with it. He would then have no other choice but to hand me over to my mother. I had to be as good as I possibly could for my own sake. When I was an adult, Dad confirmed these feelings.

There had been many challenges, losses, traumas and too much chaos in my short life! Because of this, I looked at the world differently than most twelve-year-olds. I still endured weekly brainwashing and parental alienation sessions at visitation, plus the stress of settling into a new school where many of the kids knew about my mother's mental illness.

Soon, I realized I needed to make a completely new set of school friends. It was very difficult and painful to let go of my old friends and look for a new group to hang out with. And, all the while, I wondered who knew about Mother and how that would affect any possible friendships. I was miserable. I soon discovered vending machines at school that sold candy and cookies. I bought this comfort food every day to help fill the aching void in my life. I was always in the normal weight range, but during the end of my eighth year, I hit a growth spurt and became very slender. When I started to learn about comfort food in junior high, I began to put on extra weight as I soothed my pain with high calorie snacks.

In the beginning of seventh grade, Bobby Sherman became my idol. Looking back, I am amazed that a total stranger could help me as much as he did. Once a month he would write to his fans in the teen magazine, *Tiger Beat*. I still had great difficulty reading and avoided it whenever I could. However, when it came to Bobby Sherman, I would read and hang onto every word he wrote or that was written about him. He shared his thoughts and feelings, and gave advice on how to handle things in life that were age-appropriate to his fans. Besides idolizing him, I also felt that I had a very special big brother. Bobby Sherman was the only adult "advising" me on how to deal with life. My room was plastered with his pictures and posters. I played his records constantly. I knew all his songs by heart -- and still do! Dad wanted to know more about Bobby Sherman and was concerned about my interest in him. After Dad listened to his songs and read some of the articles, he approved and encouraged my enthusiasm.

Things worsened at school as the bullying increased. Some kids were now spreading rumors that I was mentally ill, too. This was creating major social problems for me. Some kids made cruel fun of my situation and when I started to make friends, they would learn about my mother's issues and bail or turn on me. I felt empty and isolated. I also felt betrayed by my old friends to whom I had been loyal. This hurt the most. I talked to a couple of these friends and asked them why they talked to the kids about my mother's situation. They told me they thought *everyone* knew. Well, now they did! I was angry with the friends involved, but I was too young and too hurt to understand their explanation. Looking back now, I understand where they were coming from. It was information that was an accepted fact while my friends and I were growing up. They honestly felt it was common knowledge and did not tell others to hurt me. As the bullying at school increased, I felt I was at the end of my rope.

I talked with Dad and he said to ignore the teasing and bullying. It did not calm the situation when I started ignoring their cruel words. When their words were no longer effective, some kids started to punch or hit me as I passed them on my way to and from classes. I didn't even know who most of them were. I told my dad and he contacted the school. The school was reluctant to get involved.

The bullying escalated and the need arose for me to defend myself. Kicking shins was no longer effective and only served to anger my attackers. In response, they hit me harder and increased the amount of punches they delivered.

One Friday I came home roughed up and fed up! I threw my books down on the floor as I entered the house.

"Dad, I am quitting school!" I announced seriously. "I don't have any friends. All the kids know I have a crazy mother and accuse me of being crazy too! Every day I am being bullied. The kids are constantly punching and hurting me. Besides, I am so far behind that only a miracle can bring me up to grade level! Nothing you can say or do to me will change my mind or make me go back. My mind is made up. I am *done!*"

Dad looked at me thoughtfully for a moment.

"If you quit school, then the bullies will win and you will lose, both now and in the long run. You can't run away from your problems, Tracy, or they will follow you like shadows for the rest of your life."

Dad spoke to me softly, which helped calm me down. His kindness amazed me and he seemed to really understand my situation. He wasn't angry with me at all! He had a plan to get the bullies off my back once and for all.

"Stand up to a bully and they will respect you and leave you alone," Dad advised.

Dad held a black belt in jujitsu. He never believed in looking for trouble or starting fights. As a former state narcotics officer he learned how to protect himself and put an end to any physical fight that came his way.

Dad wanted me to stay in school. He believed that learning self-defense would end my problems with the bullies. He devoted the entire weekend to teaching me how to defend myself. We put all of the cushions on the living room floor. I paid keen attention and learned well. With my newfound skills and confidence, I could handle most anything dished out to me. I agreed to return to school on a trial basis.

The next day, three of the meanest bullies, all boys, cornered me in front of the temporary class units.

"We're gonna teach you a lesson about being crazy and do you a favor by pounding it out of you," the biggest one said.

"Go away and leave me alone," I replied.

Their response was immediate; like a pack of snarling wolves, they attacked!

I was surprisingly calm and fearless as I systematically defended myself.

They continued to fight with me as other kids ran up and made a big circle around us to watch. When the fight was over, I was the only one left standing. The kids clapped.

Word spread quickly that I stood my ground and "taught the bullies a lesson." Some kids even congratulated me and respected me because I had successfully defended myself against these boys.

Dad was right; no one tried to hurt me again! Almost over-night my social situation at school improved. Shortly after this incident, a group of nice girls, whom I hadn't known previ-ously, invited me to eat lunch at their table. They loved Bobby Sherman as much as I did and we spent hours talking about him and exchanging the newest information about him. I con-tinued to have lunch and hang out with this group. We became good friends and remained so throughout high school. By the end of seventh grade, I was overweight for the first time in my life, but the kids at school finally accepted me. I made many new friends and had my Bobby Sherman facts down pat!

When Innocence Is Shattered
(Sexual Content)

My body was starting to develop when I was in sixth grade. Men started to treat me differently. This was not just limited to the man from the neighborhood, but others too, even my own dad. He became less fun and more distant, stern and mechani-cal with me. He began to say more negative things about wom-en, too. I was still a child, so at this point I didn't understand, take offense or feel bad about his comments. As time went on, I began to wonder more and more about Dad's views and how they might later relate to me.

By the time I was twelve, I had learned to be blindly and often fearfully obedient to Dad. He was an authoritarian and I followed every command without question. I had learned, painfully, that asking him any type of question when he was not in the mood to answer, ended in painful punishment. Once, when I was eight, I was severely spanked for asking what kind of clouds were floating across the sky! It was impossible to tell when he was in the mood to receive questions and when he wasn't. I learned that it was safer not to ask about anything. Any thoughts I had about Dad and his way of dealing with me, I kept to myself.

When seventh grade let out for the summer, Dad sent me to summer camp for six weeks. During this time, I was not required to see Mother. After I returned, Dad decided I was too young to be left alone all day at home. So, he put me to work at the store. I knew his entire staff well and had fun relationships with many of them. All of them had taught me different aspects of my father's business, since I was about six-and-a-half years old. They taught me how to mount ski bindings, engrave skis, string tennis rackets, straighten and size garments on the racks, take inventory and check in and price merchandise.

Before this summer, when I was at the store I could do as I wanted. If I wanted to play, I played. If I wanted to work, I worked. This time it was different. I came to the store to work. My dad called one of his employees to the office. When the employee arrived, Dad laid down the law.

"Tracy, you do whatever this man tells you to do and when you are finished you ask him for another job. I have a store to run and I don't have time for any nonsense," Dad stated gruffly. "If you don't comply with his directives or don't do your job, you're going to be in big trouble with me, understand?" he added, sounding more irritated than before.

"Yes," I replied. I was embarrassed and did not understand why Dad came down so hard on me. I always did what I was told, afraid not to comply. As always, I kept my mouth shut about any thoughts or feelings that might contradict him.

I liked this employee. He was a nice man who was fun and playful with me. He seemed to be kind to everyone. When Dad was finished with his speech, we left the office and the man put me to work sweeping the floor.

This employee started a "tickle game" with me. Dad saw this and thought it was cute. He never did anything to stop it. The employee had increased the amount of tickling and then made it into a tickle tag-like game where we both tried to avoid being tickled by the other. Whoever gave the most tickles won the game. The game was ongoing and in the beginning, it was fun! It was a game played only between the employee and me. It was played in public, in front of the other employees, customers, my dad and, later, the man's wife. They all laughed and cheered us on. I was now working under this employee and reporting to him constantly. I had more contact with him and more tickle games. Then one day he took me into a storage area, under the office. "You need to take inventory of the merchandise in these boxes," the employee directed.

The office was up ten stairs and the area under it was a large space, a little over four feet high. There were many boxes and rows of long bars packed with hanging ski jackets that were stored there during the summer. There was no light, so with a flashlight, pen and clipboard I started my work with the boxes.

I became aware that the employee didn't leave me to my work as he had done previously. He stood behind me for a while and then, without a word, he pushed me down over the box and started fondling my breasts. I froze, afraid to breathe.

"Be quiet and don't make a sound!" he whispered. With the other hand he started fondling me through my shorts.

I tried to push his hands away. When he got tired of my futile efforts to push him off me, he put an end to it by grabbing both of my wrists tightly in one hand as he kept fondling with the other. I was thrashing around trying to get away.

He tightened his grip.

"It is useless to struggle and if you know what's good for you, you will be still," he whispered, breathing heavily.

I continued to struggle.

He shook me hard and squeezed my wrists painfully tighter as he hissed, "I told you to be quiet and still. Do you want me to hurt you?! No? Then you better do as I say!"

I was scared and complied.

Then he pulled my shorts and panties down and pulled my top over my head as he continued to fondle me. Someone came in the back calling for him. He stopped touching me.

"Don't you move a muscle until I come back. Wait for me, understand?" he hissed.

I nodded, obediently.

At first, I complied but he was gone for a long time. The longer he was gone the bolder I became. Finally, I dressed myself and went out to the sales floor. He caught me by the arm, spun me around.

"Why are you out here?" he asked. "I told you to wait for me."

"I'm here to work and you need to stop," I replied defiantly.

He released me, went to the switchboard and turned on the huge exhaust fan that blew out from the back of the store. Then he told me that he had an outside job for me cleaning up behind the store. I followed him outside. As we left, he locked the back door, grabbed me tightly by the wrist and pulled me behind the store in between the two buildings.

"What are you doing?!" I screamed. "Let go of me!"

He didn't reply.

There were a lot of huge old display cases and gondolas back there. The employee pulled me behind them so we were hidden from view. He turned me toward him and grabbed me tightly by the shoulders. He shook me like a little rag doll.

The employee was livid and I was petrified!

"I will do what I want with you -- when I want to do it! Your father told you to mind me, so you better keep your mouth shut and do as I say," he warned, angrily. "You obviously need to be taught a lesson. I won't bother your father with this. Since he put me in charge of you, I will handle *this* myself!"

Petrified by fear, I started to cry as he removed his belt and pushed me over a counter. He held my wrists tightly with one hand and bared my bottom with the other. He began whipping me with his belt.

"When I tell you to stay in a certain position and not move, I mean it. Don't *even* think about talking back to me again. Either you can make this easy on yourself by minding me or you can have some more time with the belt."

I cried and screamed out in pain, but the sound of the huge fan made it impossible for anyone to hear. Finally, he finished beating me.

"When you stop crying, you go right back under the office and prepare yourself as you were when I left you," he instructed. "Do you understand?"

I said nothing as I continued to cry.

"If you know what's good for you, you will do as you're told. If you ever disobey me again your punishment will be much more severe than it was today. You need to keep your mouth *shut* and never tell another soul or you will be *truly* sorry."

I didn't know what to do. I was scared stiff, so I did as I was told. My bottom was in terrible pain and my anxiety shot toward the stars. I was in a state of shock and could not think clearly. This man was muscular and strong. I thought he was my friend, but now I was confused. My father had put him in charge of me. I was afraid Dad would spank me if he knew I had made this man so angry.

When I stopped crying, I went back inside under the office

and prepared myself as I was told. I waited for the man, scared to death that I might be discovered every time somebody walked by.

He finally returned and held my wrists tightly with one hand and roughly explored my naked body with the other. He began to focus on my privates and warned me not to make a sound as he pushed his finger deep inside me, which was extremely painful.

When the man finished he said, "You can get dressed now. You need to do as I tell you, Tracy, and keep your mouth shut. If you do as I say, I will not tell your father about today. However, if you don't mind me, I will tell him and watch you get another spanking. Do you understand me?"

"Yes."

"I'm glad we have an understanding and you won't give me any reason to severely punish you. Now *finish* your inventory."

Fearfully, I did as I was told.

Day after day this animal molested me, repeatedly. If I didn't resist him, he was gentle, kind and almost loving with me. If I did resist him, his response was to painfully pinch my most sensitive areas. Then he asked me if I wanted another whipping.

I stopped resisting him. I soon learned that it was better just to comply.

He always had a job for me either under the office, up in the rafters, over the bathrooms, out behind the building or in any out-of-the-way place where we could be hidden from view. Sometimes he stripped me naked and then tied me up or bound my wrists and ankles. Other times he left me on my hands and knees or bent over boxes in various states of undress. Sometimes he left me for an hour or more. I was always fearful that someone would discover me.

That first summer this man fondled me, manipulated me and pushed his fingers deep inside of me. Throughout the day he would bring me to multiple orgasms. Nothing about this was pleasurable. I was terrified. I didn't know what was happening to me or why my body was reacting the way it was. The moment an orgasm came, he would clamp his hand over my mouth and restrict my movements like a huge snake as he hissed his warnings in my ear to be still and not utter a sound. It was torture all over again. Only this time it wasn't by my mother.

When the man took me up in the rafters, he would often strip me naked and tie me to the beams. The rafters were level with the window sill in the back of the office. The office had a long row of windows facing the sales floor and, on the opposite side, the same length of windows facing the rafters. The office was brightly lit and the rafters were dimly lit. The boxes in the rafters were arranged to hide my body from view of those windows. Most of the time I could easily see into the office from the spaces between the boxes or if the boxes were only arranged to hide me from my neck down. Just eight to ten feet away from where I was tied up, I watched Dad work at his desk. When I was being molested, I could often see my dad clearly.

Sometimes the man was called to the phone or sales floor. After he left, I would softly whisper, "Daddy just turn your head and look out the window" (but my dad kept working). "Daddy please turn around and look, I am right here," (but he didn't turn around). "Daddy please save me."

Dad never heard and he never saw. Through the office windows I watched employees come and go, while Dad was doing his office work. He would work in the office for most of the day and during this time I was tied up tightly in the rafters watching him. Most of the time, I was waiting for the man to return and molest me again. Dad often looked down at the sales floor but he never looked through the rear windows, by the rafters. I said many prayers and softly cried buckets of tears in those rafters as I watched my father work only feet away from my naked body.

I was powerless to stop this man and too frightened and ashamed to tell anyone what was happening to me. Dr. Gordon and I had ended some time ago, so I couldn't show or tell her what was going on. I didn't have anyone to talk with whom I felt I could trust or that even cared. I felt alone, abandoned and completely worthless. My happiness drained away and I became quiet again.

Every day that I was at the store, the sexual abuse continued. I knew that I truly didn't matter to anyone, anymore. I had been thrown out like trash. I was left feeling embarrassed, ashamed, helpless and unloved. I worked so hard to be a good kid and not let my past screw up who I was or wanted to become. I wondered, *How could all these bad things keep happening to me if I wasn't meant to be a terrible person needing constant punishment? Have I been cursed from the beginning?*

Instead of putting the blame on the molester, I put it squarely and heavily on myself.

As a preteen and teenager, I had no idea that what the man was doing to me was illegal. I had no idea he was a pedophile or even what that word meant. I didn't even know that there was even a name or term for adults who used children sexually. Why would I? I had no idea that some adults did this to kids. No adult had ever warned me about people like him. I just blamed myself. Hindsight is always 20/20. Sometimes, even now, I think if I had just told someone, if I had yelled to my dad and gotten his attention when I was tied in the rafters, if I had been smarter, better informed, stronger, braver, if, if, if.

Hindsight can be a terrible thing, because it makes a person think of all the options, knowledge or tools that they possess in the present moment. Most of these options would not have been available or even conceivable in the past. Abused children often blame themselves for everything that has gone wrong. The saddest part for me is that it has always been easier to forgive others than it has been for me to forgive myself. Unfortunately, hindsight feeds these feelings.

As the years passed, the man did other things to me, which included oral sex . He also forced me to bring him to an orgasm by hand, using my breasts or the lower parts of my body for the same purpose. He often took me with him when he ran errands -- or pretended to run errands. Then he would molest me in the car or take me to a wooded area, strip me naked, and molest me among the trees. When Dad, the employee and I went to lunch, we always sat at a booth and the employee would have me sit on the inside next to him. Dad would sit across from us. Under the table, the employee would have his hand on my privates, exploring and fingering me all through lunch. Dad never seemed to notice as he and the employee carried on a conversation and laughed as if nothing was happening.

I was this employee's fringe benefit. I was his little plaything, his little doll to do with whatever he wanted. Even though he sexually molested me, he never kissed me on the mouth or had vaginal intercourse with me. Later, he forced oral sex on me and forced me to do the same with him. I didn't realize, until the last edit of this book, that every time he forced me to perform oral sex with him, or he with me, or entered my body with his fingers -- he had raped me.

As an adult looking back, I realize there were similarities between the employee, Mother, Dad and me. The employee was torturing and traumatizing me, not unlike my mother did when I was a little girl. In both cases it was painful, awful and all a big secret. I was vulnerable, helpless and forced to do things against my will. The abuse had become routine and commonplace, just like it had with my mother. As it had been with her, I thought I had no way out of my situation. I felt abandoned again and empty inside. Dad's role was the same as it had been years ago: passive; in denial; hands-off; blindly thinking that I was safe and thus not watching over me, protecting me or stepping up to take a good look at the situation or saving me from the horrors I faced on a daily basis. I felt trapped like a little mouse in a cage. It was all the same, all over again.

As an adult, Dad told me that he had been sexually molested when he was six years old. He was an altar boy at church and was sexually molested in the bathroom by a priest. In light of Dad's experience, I was amazed that he wasn't more vigilant and protective of me. However, as the years went by, he became less protective.

Like many pedophiles, my dad's employee stalked his target -- me. I learned from my experience that these animals were looking for a certain type of child: one whose life had taught them to keep their mouth shut; one who had long suffered abuse or wasn't well looked after. I was just such a child: one who was alone, could be easily singled out and who didn't question authority figures. My life had made me a *perfect target* for a pedophile!

As the employee used me throughout the years, I swore that I would never put a child of mine in a position where they could be molested. I would be vigilant and would make sure they never suffered this or *any* abuse. I cursed my mother. If she were a normal mother, I would be at home with her and not at the store suffering.

Whenever I was at the store it wasn't long before that man's hands were all over me.

Needing a Guardian Angel
(Sexual Content)

When I was thirteen, I finally found the courage to talk with Dad about the employee who was molesting me. I was very nervous because I didn't know how he would react. I decided to tell him after he had finished watching the news, one night. I watched the news with him while thinking about what I was going to say. Then a story came on the news about a woman who had been raped. I listened to the story and looked at Dad, who was listening to it as well. She had been walking alone at 10 o'clock at night when a man jumped her and raped her.

"That woman probably deserved to be raped. She was probably asking for it!" Dad stated confidently.

I couldn't believe my ears!

"Women have no business walking alone at night," Dad continued, "She was probably skimpily dressed."

The news report didn't say anything about how she was dressed.

"In these situations women often set the man up and then yell 'rape!'" These women are *dirty* and deserve what they get. I am sure that most of them enjoy it," he grumbled.

I froze, as my anxiety sharply increased. Thoughts raced through my mind, *If my dad thinks this woman is dirty and deserves to be raped, then more than likely, he would think the same about me. He thinks women enjoy being raped. I wonder if he would think that I enjoy being felt up?!* I felt sick. I didn't know what to say or think for that matter. My brain just stopped working.

When the news was finished, Dad told me to pick a show. I couldn't think of a single one. I finally picked a show and halfway through I went to bed. With Dad's attitude toward rape victims, I knew there was no way I could tell him what was happening to me. I cried myself to sleep.

Between eighth grade and tenth grade, Dad dated more often. When he went on a late-night date, or traveled on business, he would leave me overnight in the care of his bookkeeper. There were times when she couldn't look after me, so, in an odd turn of events, my father asked the employee at the store (who was molesting me) if he and his wife would have me overnight. The answer was yes.

I liked the employee's wife and their pets. On the first overnight stay at their house, I felt safe and quite certain that the man would not touch me with his wife there. When I went to bed, I closed the door and went to sleep. I was jolted awake by a hand clamped down tightly over my mouth. My heart jumped out of my chest. The room was dark. For a moment I was disoriented and didn't know where I was or what was happening. Soon I realized it was the man. He had waited for his wife to fall asleep and then came to me.

"Be quiet!" he hissed.

I nodded.

He took his hand away from my mouth. Then he threw my nightgown up over my face and started molesting me with his hands and mouth. He kept going for about an hour, at times restraining me by holding both of my wrists in one of his hands.

"Don't utter a sound and keep your mouth shut about this," the man whispered in my ear.

I nodded fearfully.

When the man was finished with me, he went to the bathroom for a while and then went back to his bedroom.

While the employee was molesting me at the store, he

made a comment about how nice it was that I stayed overnight with them. I told him that he should have this kind of
sexual contact with his wife and *not* with me. The comment
was not well received and he took me out behind the building. As he started to remove his belt, I pleaded with him not
to whip me. He told me I needed to be punished and gave
me a hard spanking instead. He told me, repeatedly that it
was none of my business what he did with his wife and that I
was never to bring up that subject again. I cried in pain and
promised I wouldn't. After this punishment, I realized I was
trapped and did what I was told. I never again gave him another excuse to punish me.

Dad arranged for me to stay with them from time to time,
and every time the man came to me in the night.

At the store, I was not able to work as the man significantly
increased the amount of time he spent sexually abusing me.
The only time he would stop was when he was called to the
sales floor or to the phone. Then, as always, he ordered me to
stay where I was, until he returned. The minute he was finished
with whatever called him away, he would be back at me again.
Spending most of the day in the back of the store, I felt certain
that some of the other employees must have known what was
going on. If they did, they said nothing. One employee saw us,
but kept what he saw to himself. Dad spent his time in the office. He was ignorant about where I was or what was going on.

I was desperate for a safe adult I could confide in, but I had
no one. During the school year, I wrote a letter to Bobby Sherman explaining what was happening to me at the hands of my
dad's employee. He was always so good with advice; I thought
that maybe he could give some to me. I wrote the letter over
several times asking him what I should do. I explained that I
couldn't talk with my dad and why. Each time I read the letter I

tore it up and began again. With very little exception, the only adult advice I was getting was from Bobby Sherman's column in the monthly teen magazine. I thought that maybe he would keep my letter private and just write back advising me what to do. I knew I needed adult help, but had no one that I could trust. As I finished the last draft, my mind clouded with concerns about mailing it. I wondered what repercussions might come my way. Would Bobby ever really receive it? What position might that put him in, knowing this was happening to a girl he didn't know? How would he feel about it or me? Would it help or hurt my situation? After thinking about the content, I knew it would not be good to mail. I tore it up and threw it away.

Who Says Thirteen Is Unlucky?

In eighth grade, I turned thirteen. I had good friends, boy-friends, great classes and I attended every school dance, which I enjoyed immensely. I no longer pined for my old group of friends. I had moved on and so had they.

A friend of my dad's was a hunter and from time to time, he brought Dad ducks he had shot. Dad always sent me to the garage to *pluck* them, a job I absolutely despised. I thought of these beautiful birds flying freely without a care as I ripped their feathers out of their poor dead bodies. Tears of sadness rolled down my cheeks. The little downy feathers and dander made my breathing difficult as I coughed and choked.

One day I had had it! I didn't care what my dad would do to me. I decided I would never *pluck* another duck again! I walked into the house, holding a half plucked duck and found Dad snoozing in his easy chair. In mid-snore, I slammed the duck down on his side table. He jolted awake.

"Don't you *ever* tell me to pluck another duck again! I don't care what you do to me; I am done plucking ducks!" I declared in a loud booming voice.

The surprise on his face was obvious to see as he fumbled around for words. Finally, he shot back, "Then you will never eat another duck!"

My reply was twice as quick, "That will be just fine with me because I *hate* eating them, too!"

I left the half-plucked duck on his table and spun around on my heels to go shower off the feathery remains. I wondered how I was still alive after talking to my father that way. I never ate duck again and never plucked another one, either!

Over spring break, my father attempted to arrange a visit for me with my maternal grandparents. He called my mother's brother, my Uncle Ernie. He and his wife lived near my grandparents.

"Your Uncle Ernie is a good and honorable man. I have always liked him. He is your godfather, you know," Dad said as he dialed the phone.

Dad talked with Uncle Ernie for a while then he asked him if I could come for a visit. The only condition was that my mother not be told about the visit until after I returned to California. He told Uncle Ernie that he was concerned my mother would fly to Florida and attempt to gain custody of me while I was visiting. Uncle Ernie lived near my grandparents and said he would have to think about it. Three days later Uncle Ernie called to say he couldn't honor my father's conditions. He said he would be happy to have me visit, but he would have to inform my mother in advance. Because of this condition, I couldn't visit with them. Other than Uncle Les and Aunt Nita, my mother's family didn't seem to understand the scope of my mother's problems. Maybe they were in major denial, I don't know. They only seemed to know what my mother told them and wanted them to believe.

The school tested me and then put me in a pilot program with five other kids. To be eligible I had to be at least four grades behind in reading with an above average IQ. I met the criteria. The class was fun and I spent half of my school day there. The teacher worked with each student, one-on-one with reading and comprehension. We also spent time working on eye-and-hand coordination as well as physical coordination. This included trampoline, which I loved. The teacher identified that my reading problem was caused by the holes in my vision. Letters would literally appear and disappear as my eyes followed along, which was a result of Virus X. When the teacher started to break the word down to three or four letters then my eyes could concentrate on just that and my reading problem was solved! After that, I advanced quickly and by year-end my reading and comprehension tested at a college sophomore level. I caught up quickly in my other courses as well, and for the first time in my life, received all A's and B's on my report card.

Toward the end of eighth grade, I wrote another letter to Aunt Nita and Uncle Les. In seven years of writing to them asking for contact, there was never a reply.

For the first time I explained to my aunt and uncle how I felt about their decision to keep my cousins and me apart, how awful it had been not hearing from them for so many years. Bluntly, I told them that just because the adults have issues between them that did *not* give them the right to keep my cousins and me apart. I wrote that I felt there was no excuse for using or hurting children who were unfortunately stuck in the middle of all this. I added that if they didn't respond to my letter I would never write to them again.

I read the finished product to Dad.

"That is a strongly worded letter. Are you sure you want to send it?" Dad asked.

"Absolutely," I replied.

Since it was my last letter, I wanted them to know how I honestly felt. I sent it off with little hope of a reply.

A few days later, the phone rang. Dad answered it and to our surprise, it was my Uncle Les! I was amazed! I listened to my dad's side of the conversation and it was going really well. Then Aunt Nita talked with my dad. They had received my letter. After talking it over, they agreed with me that it was wrong to keep the kids apart. They arranged with Dad for us to visit with them for a week, after we returned from our trip to Canada. If all went well with that visit, I would stay with them, on my own, for an additional two weeks. After all these years, I could not believe I was finally going to see them again!

The vacation plans to visit my cousins in addition to our trip to Canada, took me away from the store for nine weeks during the summer months. I had been sexually abused for almost a year. It had almost become routine. I knew what to expect from the molester and suffered through it in silence. The molester usually treated me kindly, even lovingly. I didn't resist and there were no more punishments. I was thrilled that this vacation greatly limited my time with him. Visitation with Mother was also interrupted during vacation time. I missed ten visitations! Dad and I stopped at our friends, the Gibson's, on our way up to Canada. On the long drive to their house, I thought about talking to Jim Gibson about the employee at my dad's store. Jim was the Chief of Police of Arcata, California and I was certain he would know what to do. When we arrived at the Gibson's I felt good about my decision to talk with him. The question was when.

When Jim came home from work, he sat in his easy chair and watched TV. I sat on the couch across from him wondering when would be a good time to ask to talk with him in private. As the minutes ticked by, I started to lose confidence that this was a good idea. I wondered if he would understand. He was one of my dad's best friends. I began to worry that he might have the same opinions as my dad about certain women deserving to be raped. If he felt that way too, what would that mean for me? After a couple of days of thinking about it, and knowing how adults talked about all different kinds of issues about their kids, I realized I couldn't talk in confidence with Jim. If I were to share this situation with him, then he would definitely talk with my dad about it. I had to weigh which was worse: having to live with Dad and hear from him how I deserved this treatment that I was dirty and it was all my fault, or not saying anything and having to continue to deal with being sexually abused. Maybe, if I talked about it, Mother would somehow find out, and use it to gain custody of me. I decided that the consequences of talking with Jim would be too risky. Therefore, sadly, I decided again to keep my mouth shut.

After Dad and I returned from our trip to Canada, we went to see my Aunt Nita, Uncle Les and cousins. I was eager and a little anxious to see them. I couldn't wait to get there. The reunion with my cousins was wonderful. We all looked different because it had been seven years since we had seen each other; however, we also looked familiar. Emotions ran high as my aunt hugged me for the first time in seven years.

"Sometimes adults can be so *stupid*," she cried. "Please forgive us, Tracy."

"Of course I forgive you." I replied.

My cousins and I went into a room and got to know each

other again over laughter, telling stories about our lives and joking around. Dad, Aunt Nita and Uncle Les got along very well together, and we could hear their laughter drifting up the hallway. It was a happy and healing time. At the end of the week, Dad left me with them for another two weeks. We all had a great time together! After this visit, my cousins and I saw each other often.

When I returned from vacation, visitation with my mother resumed. I didn't tell her that I had reestablished contact with her brother's family. I knew she would most likely react badly and I didn't want her to cause them any problems. Shopping seemed to be the best activity during visitation. I needed things for school, which I had Mother buy for me. This way Dad didn't have to fork out the money. Mother didn't pay any child support and I believed strongly that she should pay for some of my needs. I thought it was unfair that Dad had to pay for everything; after all, I was *her kid too!* I would simply look disappointed if she didn't want to buy me something I needed, and told her not to worry that Dad would come back with me later and make the purchase. For some reason she couldn't stand the thought of this and always ended up buying the item for me. I never used this tactic for things I wanted, only things I needed. I also learned that it was easier to curb her "campaigns" if we were in stores with other people around. Once she caught on to my sudden interest in shopping, we spent less time in the stores.

In September, I started Lynbrook High School. Like junior high, I attended multiple classes each day and there were new students from other schools. Unfortunately, Mother's illness followed me into high school like a grim shadow.

The school assigned a counselor to each new student.

When I met with my counselor, it was not a positive first encounter.

"So you are the girl who was removed from her troubled mother and lives with her father. Poor dear, how does it feel to have a mentally ill mother?" the counselor asked condescendingly.

Without a word, I got up and left the counselor's office. I called Dad at work and told him what she had said.

"When are people going to drop these issues about my mother and accept me for myself, on my own merits, without associating me with her?" I asked sadly.

"People are often ignorant and don't know what to do or say. Therefore, they often say the wrong things when they shouldn't say anything at all. I'm leaving work now and will meet you at school. I will speak with your counselor and you won't have to worry, Tracy. There will be no more talk about how your mother's illness has affected you," Dad said confidently.

When Dad arrived, he and I walked into the counselor's office and he demanded an immediate meeting with the counselor and the principal. I sat outside as the three of them met. When I was called in, the counselor immediately apologized to me. She never mentioned the subject again.

After the first parent-teacher night, one of my teachers asked why I lived with my dad. Not wishing to get into it, I told him my mother had been gone since I was six. He looked uncomfortable and said he was sorry. I looked into his eyes and realized that he thought that my mother had passed away. I decided that this was how I would respond to new people's questions from now on. I was very pleased that I had found a response that stopped the questions, curiosity and unwanted conversations about Mother.

New Viewpoints and Interests

By the time I started high school, the hate I harbored towards Mother for most of my life had melted away and I began to feel sorry for her instead. I learned an interesting thing: you can't hate someone and feel sorry for that person at the same time! From time to time, Dad pointed out all the things in life that my mother's illness had prevented her from enjoying. When I was younger, I couldn't wrap my brain around this concept. However, as I matured I realized the wisdom of his words. I finally understood that holding on to hateful feelings or grudges against Mother was actually hurting me and served no useful purpose. As I truly began to feel sorry for Mother, I was able to look at her situation and our relationship differently.

When I was fourteen, Marine World opened, less than fifteen minutes away. I was lucky enough to talk Mother into going during Saturday visitations. While at Marine World, Mother became more interested in talking with the third person and began yet another campaign to win her sympathy. They talked so much that it encompassed the entire visitation. It bothered me that they seemed to be moving closer to a friendship, but I tried to ignore it. The good news was that she was talking to the third person and not to me!

Marine World was not very busy and I had some wonderful opportunities and experiences. I got to know the people who worked at the Dolphin Petting Pool and it wasn't long before they showed me what to do and put me to work helping them train the dolphins not to play or interact with people with their teeth. I was thrilled and eager to help. Marine World also had a tiger-breeding program. I got to hold and play with tiger cubs! We went every Saturday and I was in heaven. I learned a great deal about dolphins, whales and the tiger cubs that played like kittens. I met two marine biologists who were studying the intelligence and communication skills of whales and dolphins. Their hope was to "crack" the communication code of these fascinating mammals. This intrigued me and I was riveted to every word the marine biologists said. After months of thought, I decided that was what I wanted to do with my life. A curiosity inside of me had been awakened and I was engaged in a way that I never had been before.

As the weeks went by, the staff that I worked with was looking forward to seeing me every Saturday as much as I was looking forward to coming. I would think about it all week long. For the first time in my life, I felt alive and connected to something wonderful. I was overjoyed and honored to be involved. For the first time I had the twinkling of an understanding that there were bigger and better things out there. I felt I was a part of something very special and I was beginning to see the world in a larger and different way.

The months flew by and Mother still seemed quite happy to go to Marine World and spend the entire visitation talking with the third person. This left me free to follow my interests. She did her thing and I did mine. Finally, visitation was enjoyable!

One day Mother, the third person and I watched a training session with a killer whale. A beam extended out about fifteen feet from the edge of the show pool, high above and parallel to the water line. A male trainer walked to the end of this beam and held a fish out for the killer whale to take from him by jumping straight up and out of the water. On the first attempt, the whale didn't jump high enough and the trainer didn't give it the fish. The whale circled around and tried again. However, its body was at an angle, and again, it didn't receive its reward.

The whale tried again but the trainer wasn't happy that time either and pulled the fish away from the whale's mouth. The whale tried again, and again, received no reward. The whale dove down to the bottom of its deep show pool and started a circular speed run. Huge waves soon poured over the top of the pool.

I stood up and saw the whale swimming faster and faster. All of a sudden I knew exactly what the whale was planning to do! In an instant I realized that if the man stayed on the beam he could be killed.

"HEY! HEY YOU ON THE BEAM! GET OFF! *GET OFF THE BEAM, NOW!*" I hollered as loud as I could.

Mother looked up from her conversation with the third person and tried to get me to sit down and be quiet. I ignored her. I was completely focused on the man standing on the beam.

He looked over at me.

"WHAT?!" he yelled.

I yelled my warning again and frantically motioned for him to get off the beam. The man waved me off, disregarding my advice.

Mother grabbed me and was physically trying to force me to sit down.

"Not now, Mom," I said as I pulled away. "If that man doesn't get off the beam, he is going to die!"

Mother jumped to her feet and said, "What?! What are you talking about?!"

I yelled to the man again, but it was too late.

A split second later the whale abruptly turned on a dime at breakneck speed and leapt out of the water ramming the bottom of the beam, in between the upright support and where the man was standing. It was a purposeful act, seemingly driven by the whale's frustration and perhaps anger over not receiving its fish reward. The impact caused the beam to swing wildly back and forth in a huge semi-circle. It also was jerking up and down as it shook violently. The friction between the metal parts made loud high-pitched noises and metallic groans as they strained against each other under the enormous stress. I thought the whole apparatus was going to collapse and fall into the water. The man lost his footing and fell. On his way down he caught the beam with one hand and managed to swing his body up to the bottom of the beam. He wrapped his arms and legs around it and held on for dear life. His body clung tightly to the bottom of the beam. His back was to the water.

At the water surface, the whale waited for the man to fall with its mouth wide-open to receive him. The beam continued to flail violently and still made sounds like the structure was going to fail. The whale waited patiently. It ignored the efforts of the other trainers, as they slapped targets into the water, which was the command for the whale to come. With its jaws wide open the whale was only focused on one thing, the man clinging to the beam. The whale continued to wait for him to fall into its mouth. I wondered if this was an act of revenge.

I hoped and prayed that the man was strong enough to maintain his grip around the beam and that the structure would somehow hold together. Finally, the momentum decreased and the man managed to shimmy down the beam to the upright support and then climbed down the ladder to safety. With not even a ripple, the whale silently slid under the water. It started to swim around the pool slowly, almost thoughtfully. The other trainers opened a gate to a holding pool and the whale swam into it. The people in the stands were told to leave and were being ushered out. I stood there staring at the man, silently thanking God that he was okay. I passed him on the way out.

"I'm glad you're okay," I said relieved, "but next time you might want to listen."

We locked eyes.

He gave me a slight nod.

I turned and walked towards the exit.

"I think it is far too dangerous for you to work with these mammals," Mother announced. "From now on we will be doing something else with our time together. Say goodbye to everyone you know here; we will not be returning."

I never worked with the killer whales and attempted to reason with her, but her mind was made up.

Visitation went back to the way it was. Mother focused on her old campaign routine of getting me alone for her "little talks." When her efforts were unsuccessful to turn me against Dad, she told me what a disappointment I was to her.

The Pain of Not Meeting Father's Expectations

With all the emphasis to teach me to read over the years, math was allowed to fall by the wayside. When I was starting my sophomore year in high school, Dad suddenly thought it would be a great idea for me to take Algebra 1. He insisted on it, so I signed up for the class. I didn't understand it at all. The more trouble I had with the course, the more he insisted that I learn it. Dad told me it was a required course and that I had to pass with at least a "C." I was way behind in math and entered Algebra 1 completely unprepared. Dad started tutoring me, which was a disaster. Instead of being patient, he got angry and punitive with me when I didn't understand. He turned up the heat, pushing me to do better than I could.

Because I wanted to please Dad and make him proud of me, I began eating and sleeping Algebra. I went to school early for tutoring with my teacher. Other math teachers also tutored me during my lunch and after school. Then I went home and studied some more. I couldn't understand how letters and numbers worked together and I couldn't remember all the steps or understand their purpose. No teacher identified that I was lacking the Pre-Algebra building blocks, including: the skills to do complicated division, difficult multiplication and that I had never been taught fractions. Out of kindness, my teachers brought my grade up from an "F" to a "D." I was getting "A's" and "B's" in most of my other subjects. This wasn't good enough for Dad, and he continued to crank up the pressure by extending his lectures. He also called me names and labeled me as "dumb" or "stupid," just because I couldn't understand Algebra.

Dad lectured me for hours about how worthless I was and how I wasn't trying hard enough. Trying to explain my difficulties with the subject was viewed as "weakness," "cop outs" and "excuses," which only served to enrage him. When I said I was sorry he became livid and yelled that only *losers* and sympathy seekers say they're *sorry*. He told me being sorry was pitiful and disgusting and that I was never to say that again. He made it clear that I had better improve my grade and stop "screwing around."

The relationship between my dad and me had hit a wall and was falling apart rapidly. Of course, I believed it was entirely my fault because I was dumb and could not do math. Somehow, I had to do better. Soon there was nothing else in my life but Algebra and I had grown to hate it! Not only did I lack the needed skills, but I was also having trouble remembering all the many different steps for solving the different problems. With every failed attempt and every hostile lecture from Dad, I was quickly developing math phobia. The more I tried, the more

Dad tore me down and let me know how disappointed he was in me as a person. In response, I would try harder. It became a vicious cycle.

My world revolved around Algebra. It was hard enough to deal with forced visitation and the continually increasing sexual molestation, but now on top of that Dad was turning on me. At fifteen, my life was becoming more than a living hell.

Then, there was a ray of hope. I learned that Algebra 1 was not required by the school! I was hopeful I could drop the class. However, when I told Dad about this, I was shocked that he didn't care. Now Algebra was *required by him!* He equated my failure with the subject as failure as a person and he let me know how he felt about me every day. When I reminded him how well I did in my other subjects, he just shook his head.

"Tracy, you are just a *flash in the pan,* you *always* have been and *always* will be. You are a day late and a dollar shy and a *great* disappointment to me," he grumbled.

I heard this from him on many occasions throughout my teen and young adult years. It all started with his obsession with Algebra.

I was quickly becoming depressed, putting in four hours of homework every day on top of all the tutoring and class time. Every math teacher in school took a shot at tutoring me with no success. All of this work equaled an "A+" for effort and an "F-" for results.

One day, I came into class and my teacher had a wooden puzzle. When put together properly it formed a perfect cube. The teacher said it was all about math and anyone that could put the puzzle together would do well in the subject. A couple of the top students in my class tried but couldn't put it together. The teacher made a game out of it and we were all having a good time watching him put it together in a few seconds while everyone else struggled. When the interest in the puzzle had died down, I asked if I could try. The teacher handed it to me with a laugh. I looked at the parts, then put it together in about fifteen seconds and handed him a perfect cube. No one in class said a word. The teacher just stared at me in disbelief and then congratulated me. I was excited that I was able to put the cube together and told Dad about it that evening. His response made me wish that I hadn't.

"Tracy, that puzzle is a toy, nothing more and nothing less. It means absolutely *nothing*. I am not impressed that your teacher brings toys to his class when he should be teaching. You better stop screwing around and get down to business. If you are so good at math then I want to see some good grades. I don't want to hear anymore stupid stories like this." Dad went on and on.

When he was finished with me, I felt stupid and ashamed. My excitement over my small accomplishment vanished completely.

Dad noticed I was depressed and called Dr. Gordon to talk about it. Looking back, I think it's interesting that he seemed unaware of the reasons for my sadness. She had a teenage group that was led by two psychologists, one male and one female. Dr. Gordon suggested I join. When I started attending the group, they were discussing the different thought processes of children versus teenagers and the causes of teenage rebellion. I wasn't rebellious but found the comparisons interesting as it helped me to understand why some of the kids I knew were rebellious with their parents. After the group ended for the evening, we all waited in the parking lot for our parents to come and pick us up. Some of the kids were selling drugs and smoking pot. They offered me a free sample, which I refused. As we got to know each other, the kids pushed me harder to try drugs. I still declined and kept my mouth shut.

On the way to my fifth group meeting, Dad told me I needed to leave fifteen minutes early. We were going to meet an important business acquaintance of his for a late dinner. As I left the car, he reminded me to meet him in the parking lot and not to be late. I went in and when it was my turn to talk I mentioned that I needed to leave fifteen minutes early. The male psychologist told me I couldn't leave.

"No one is allowed to leave early because it is a huge distraction to the group as a whole."

I sat there wondering what to do. When the time came to go, I got up to leave. "I'm sorry, but I have to go," I mumbled. "My dad is waiting for me."

"Sit down," ordered the male psychologist in a loud stern voice.

"You don't understand," I pleaded. "My father is going to be very angry if I don't meet him on time."

"Your *father* doesn't run this group or make the rules for it, now SIT DOWN!"

I sat down and the group picked up where they had left off.

My anxiety grew as minutes went by. I glanced at the clock; I was five minutes late and I knew my father was fuming. A few more minutes had passed when the door to the building opened and then slammed shut. I heard my father's heavy footfalls as he quickly walked down the hall.

The door flew open and there stood Dad. His bright crimson face contorted in anger as he pointed at me.

"YOU OUT, *NOW!*"

"They wouldn't let me leave. I tried, but they wouldn't let me." I replied fearfully.

"WHO SAID YOU COULDN'T LEAVE?"

"I did," the male psychologist piped up. "It's disruptive to the group," he explained as he stood up, "we have a rule that no one leaves early."

"When I tell my daughter to be somewhere at a certain time, then *she better bloody well be there! Who the hell do you think you are?"* Dad demanded.

It felt like adrenaline started squirting out my ears. I had seen him like this before and knew all hell was about to break loose.

"I want to meet with you to discuss your daughter," the male psychologist replied, as he tried to maintain his calm demeanor.

"I'm *busy,* you can call me," Dad spat back.

"I don't communicate well on the phone; I want to talk with you in person."

Dad saw an opportunity to humiliate the man.

"You're supposed to be a psychologist and you can't even communicate over the phone? You must *not* be very good at what you do." He went on verbally tearing the psychologist apart.

My dad was a big man and so was the psychologist. No one else in the room made a sound, including the female psychologist.

I felt sorry for the male psychologist. I thought to myself, *He probably doesn't communicate well over the phone because he has a thick accent.* I was completely embarrassed because of Dad's behavior and wished that I could disappear. The psychologist was now becoming angry as well. They kept going back and forth. The psychologist finally lost his temper.

"I now understand your daughter a lot better," the male psychologist fumed. *"YOU* ARE THE REASON YOUR DAUGHTER IS HAVING PROBLEMS! *YOU* ENJOY TEARING PEOPLE APART AND *YOU* ARE EXPLOSIVE!"

Then he calmed himself and added, "For the sake of *your* daughter *you* need to sit down with me and talk about these issues *face-to-face.*"

Dad glared at me and yelled, "GET IN THE CAR, *NOW!*"

I got up and ran past the psychologists and Dad.

"When you get over your issues and learn to talk on the phone, give me a call," Dad demanded, on his way out.

It would have been a lot less disruptive to the group and everyone else if they had just let me leave in the first place!

After we left, all I heard about that night was Dad's anger towards the male psychologist. I was grateful the anger wasn't directed towards me! Dad seemed to understand my predicament about leaving. I knew that he wouldn't let that whole scene with the psychologist go or even give the man a second chance.

A day or two went by and Dad told me the psychologist had phoned him at work to set up a meeting. "I have nothing to say to that man and he has nothing I want to listen to either. I hung up on him," Dad grumbled.

I knew the argument between them would never end. I enjoyed the group, but didn't feel comfortable with the kids trying to sell me drugs and was embarrassed about Dad's behavior with the psychologist. All of this left me thinking that I needed to quit. I knew Dad would never let me go back if I told him about the drugs, so I did. That put an end to the group meetings, but it wasn't the end of my problems at home.

One day Dad came into my room while I was studying and told me to take a break. He showed me a knife that he had purchased. I had never seen one like it.

"This is a Hara-kiri knife. The Japanese use it to commit suicide when they have been shamed or lost face in some way." Then he went on to explain exactly how it was used.

"I am giving it to you and want you to keep it on your desk

where you can see it every day." With that, he turned around and walked out leaving the knife in my hand.

I put it on my desk and didn't think about it further.

Each quarter my dad made me retake Algebra 1. Some adults in my life, including teachers and some of Dad's employees, saw how depressed I was becoming over math. They tried to help me out. Even the man who was sexually molesting me tried to tutor me. This was all done without Dad's knowledge. It had been so long since any of them studied Algebra, they had forgotten most of the steps needed to solve the problems. What they did remember only confused me more.

In the middle of all this, Dad told me we would go fishing together every Sunday. I was excited and looked forward to the fishing trips. When Sunday came, he changed his mind and decided to clean the garage instead. He told me we would go fishing the following Sunday. I was disappointed, but offered to help him clean the garage. The middle of the next week he started telling me about the fish we would catch and how much fun we would have. I was so excited and could hardly wait until Sunday.

However, when Sunday morning arrived, Dad changed his mind and decided to watch a game on TV instead. I was crushed. Going fishing was the only thing I had to look forward to and at the last moment, it was snatched away from me, again.

My dad had always told his friends, "If you promise a kid something, you need to follow through, even if it's inconvenient for you." Then he would give examples of how he did that for me. "One of the worst things you can do to a kid is tell them you are going to do something fun, let them get all excited about it and then cancel it -- killing their joy. I'll never do that to my kid." All Dad's great advice went out the window with his weekly unfulfilled promises to go fishing.

The cancelled fishing trips continued, week after week. The constant disapointment, combined with the other negative issues, was taking a toll on me and I started to feel sad all the time. I knew Dad and I were not going fishing even though he said that we would. Then, one day when he told me we were going the next Sunday, I didn't get excited.

"If you're not going to get excited about fishing then I guess we won't go," Dad said indifferently.

"Okay," I replied.

Dad never again said we were going fishing on Sundays.

About halfway through the year, my grades in my other subjects started to decline. I felt broken and became more depressed. I was convinced Dad was right about me -- I was a disappointment and a complete failure! I started to hate my life and myself again, feeling that I was definitely the problem. I was beginning my fourth quarter of Algebra 1. Alone at home I was sitting at my desk halfway through my four hours of pointless Algebra homework, when I looked up and saw the knife. I stared at it for some time, thinking about what Dad said about Hara-kiri and why people committed suicide that way. I remembered his instructions, picked up the knife, and took it from its sheath. As I looked at it, I thought about how Algebra had become my life, which Dad had made into a living hell due to his fixation on the subject. I knew he felt I was a worthless person. As far as he was concerned, I was a complete failure and waste of time. I also knew that he *despised* me. This continual negativity directed at me and about me continued to deflate any self-esteem I previously had.

I wasn't old enough to understand that my dad had done something evil by giving me this knife, the formal instructions to commit Hara-kiri and the reasons to do it in the first place. However, I didn't realize all this until I was well into adulthood.

Not until then did I finally understand how this, too, fit into the big picture of my family's abuse and dysfunction.

I decided to use the knife to end my suffering, thus relieving Dad of his shame of having me for a daughter. I felt the knife's blade and it was sharp. I thought about it and how final it would all be. I thought about writing a note and then, frustrated by the thought, decided against it. I thought that committing suicide was the only way out. I vividly saw myself kneeling on the floor with my shirt off, the point of the knife pushed into the skin of the lower left side of my abdomen. I knew what to do and was certain I could carry it through.

Minutes passed as the train wreck that had been my life raced before my eyes. Then, feeling overcome with sadness about my decision, a thought came out of nowhere, *If I kill myself now, I will never know what tomorrow might bring.* I thought about that for a moment. It made sense. I had always lived my life with the thought that it would get better, if I just kept riding out the storm. I always felt that I had the ability to outlast any horror, by holding on to the hope that better times would come. I thought to myself, *If I end it all now, I'll never know how my life would have turned out.* I was a fighter and at fifteen, a survivor too! This I knew about myself. I looked at the knife, put it back in its sheath and threw it in the bottom drawer of my desk, slamming it shut.

"I am a survivor and I will continue to follow that path," I stated confidently, emerging stronger. "Things will get better, they just have to!"

My determination in my darkest hour empowered and inspired me. After all, it was just one course! I became determined to find another way out of my dilemma. I spent the rest of my homework time thinking about how I could accomplish this.

On trash pick up day, I threw that knife in the bottom of the garbage can, disposing of it permanently. I didn't care what Dad might say about the matter, if he ever found out. What nasty thing could he say that he hadn't said already? Besides, he couldn't think any worse of me than he already did! Immediately, I began to feel better. Ridding myself of that knife empowered me. It is interesting that Dad never asked me what happened to the knife.

A few days later, I sat down to talk with my math teacher. He was a nice man who wasn't much older than I was. I decided to trust him, probably because I felt I had no choice. Leaving out the part about the knife, I told him in detail about what was happening at home over Algebra 1. I explained to him that my father wanted me to receive a "C." If I did, then he would be satisfied and would not require me to take any more Algebra or any other math classes. My teacher's response was supportive and his words helped me feel better about myself. I left the meeting with a weight removed from my shoulders. I was happier than I had been in months. Although he didn't assure me that I was going to receive a "C," I felt sure that under the circumstances I would -- and I did!

Slowly Dad's attitude towards me improved and the Algebra issues were dropped as if they had never existed. I never took another math class in high school and my report card returned to the good grades that I had previously received. As an adult, I went on to study higher math and received excellent grades.

One day, toward the end of my sophomore year, Dad told me that he planned to pick me up after school, because he had a surprise for me. I went through the day wondering, half excited about it and half dreading it, not knowing what kind of surprise he had in mind. I wondered if this would go the way of Sunday fishing -- promises never realized. Part of me was doubtful that he would show up at all, but after school he was there to pick me up.

Dad told me that his aunt, his father's sister, had died in England. She was never married and my grandfather was going to England to help settle her estate. I sat and listened to all this as I silently wondered what it had to do with me. Dad went on to tell me that she had owned a lot of the family furniture, which was close to 100 years old. Her siblings wanted to sell it. My dad had asked his father to represent him in buying some of the family furniture. Dad told me that this furniture wasn't any ordinary furniture, but was carved especially for our family back in the 1800s. It was ornate and some pieces were massive. He explained that our house wasn't big enough for the furniture. So the surprise was that we were going house hunting. Shocked, I didn't know how I felt about moving.

Dad wanted an English Tudor style home in the Los Gatos or Saratoga Hills, about five to ten miles from our home in San Jose.

Driving, Dad glanced over at me and said, "After all Tracy, the house doesn't hold any fond memories for either of us, does it?"

"No," I sighed.

I wasn't thinking about the house but of leaving the Knudson family. While I hadn't set foot in their house for four years, I was friends with the three youngest sons, especially Brian. He and I had a lot of fun together. Although younger than I was, Brian was far older and wiser than his years and always had been. I didn't want to lose him! I was too young to drive and depending on where we moved, Brian might not be able to bike the distance to visit. I was also worried that I might have to change schools. I really didn't want to move, but didn't let Dad see my concerns. Nothing was going to happen right away. As time passed, the decision to move seemed to hinge on whether or not we were going to get the furniture.

A Difficult Man to Understand

As a teenager, Dad was nice to me when I met his expectations, but he turned into my worst enemy when I fell short. What defined the latter was something he often kept to himself. I walked in emotional minefields, never knowing when one might blow up in my face. In addition, there was that other issue: I was beginning to look more and more like a woman. He didn't like that at all! To make matters worse he would become angry when I unconsciously used some of my mother's mannerisms, which he despised.

When it came to women, my dad loved them to an extent. However, he also harbored a strong dislike and distrust of them. He had mixed feelings. Dad told me that he was just six years old when his parents divorced, and his mother became very cruel to him. Dad often told me that she would beat him for no reason. He told me that when she wasn't beating him, she was ignoring him or not speaking to him. This treatment went on for months at a time, throughout his growing up years. When he was eight, his father moved to Hawaii leaving him to grow up without a dad. When he married my mother, she verbally and physically abused him as well. The two women in the world who should have loved him the most treated him horribly. As a result, Dad developed a misogynistic viewpoint.

The more I developed into a woman, the more I felt Dad was confused about his feelings towards me. At times, I wondered how he truly felt about me. I knew that he loved me dearly, but there was also that other part of him that didn't. Often I felt that I had betrayed him as I was moving into womanhood, perhaps because he treated me that way. Instead of using the physical violence his mother had used on him, he was verbally and emotionally abusive to me, which at times, wounded me deeply. I don't think he made a conscious decision to do this, but it hurt just the same. Living with him during my teenage years was often very difficult and even scary. He could turn hostile in a heartbeat.

Dad and I never watched reruns of *I Love Lucy* because he said that Lucy reminded him of my mother. As I matured, he became more vocal about his animosity toward women in general. Whenever Dad perceived femininity or saw my mother reflected in my looks or actions, he acted as if he detested me too.

There were certain physical features women possessed that Dad didn't like. He often told me that women's knees were ugly. In his opinion, men's bodies were always cleaner than women's bodies. In addition, he couldn't stand the higher pitch of women's voices. He often told me to "lower my pitch," which trained me, over the years to have a lower voice than was natural for me. He also reminded me that certain aspects of my body were not appealing, like my knobby knees and he always disapproved of the way I walked. There was nothing wrong with either, he simply disapproved.

If I made an offbeat comment about women or ran them down in some way, Dad would be very pleased. Unless I constantly did things that were spectacular in his eyes he, more often than not, considered me a disappointment. Smaller achievements, like solving the cube puzzle, were ignored or turned into failures. He was far from perfect himself. He often stated that he couldn't stand people who claimed to be perfectionists. Anyone making the comment that they were a "recovering perfectionist" would enrage and disgust him.

My dad was a hard man for most people to understand. Sometimes he said and did things that were very hurtful and impossible to understand. He was complex and sometimes unpredictable. When I was little, he would do anything and everything in his power to help me. He loved me dearly and was consistent with me. At times, when I was a teenager he was angry, suspicious, mistrustful and verbally abusive. His willingness to do things with and for me waned, as did his interest in me.

There were times where Dad stood up for me during high school. If he thought I was in the right, he would take on teachers and the principal. Once, when I was unjustly given detention, he went to the principal demanding it be dropped by saying he would serve detention for me and have the story written up in the local paper. Another time he stood up for me when a teacher falsely accused me of taking some missing Betty Crocker coupons. This was done in front of the whole class. I had no idea what Betty Crocker coupons were, as I didn't bake.

He also went out of his way to surprise me on one occasion.

One Monday morning I was in Spanish class when my teacher told me to go to the office. She said my dad was there waiting for me. I wondered why he was at school. He should have been at the store working. I was scared that I had forgotten something and he had come to school to be angry with me. As I walked to the office, my mind raced to try to figure out why he was there. I knew whatever the reason, it couldn't be good and prepared myself for the worst. I walked into the office. Dad turned around and looked at me. I was shocked to see that he was smiling!

"Are you ready?" he asked.

"Ready for what?" I replied completely confused.

"Ready to go fishing, of course! I have the car all packed," jerking his thumb in the direction of the car parked outside the office.

I looked past him, out the window and saw fishing rods propped up in the backseat.

"I am taking you out of school for a week," he continued. "We are going fishing at Owen's River Ranch in the Sierras. I have rented a cabin for us by the river."

"What about my clothes and the things I'll need?"

"Everything you'll need is packed," Dad replied reassuringly.

Wow! What a wonderful surprise, I thought, *No school for a week and we are finally going fishing!*

Before I could express my joy, the school secretary, who had been listening to our conversation frowned, as she glared at my dad over the top of her reading glasses.

"You can't take her out of school for a week to go fishing! She will fall behind in all her subjects!"

I panicked, fearful Dad might change his mind.

"I am not concerned. She'll catch up," Dad replied, giving me a wink. "Let's go!"

We had a great week together. Dad was fun to be with and interacted with me more the way he used to when I was much younger. However, when we returned home, he slowly changed back to the way he had interacted with me, prior to our fishing trip. When he was verbally and emotionally abusive to me, it made my life miserable. He seemed to run in cycles. Sometimes, I could not identify his triggers.

As I grew into womanhood, Dad became more abusive, often when I least expected it. Anything he perceived as weakness, procrastination, femininity or any hint of a fear of failure would be enough to set him off. As an adult, I began to wonder if some of my mother's mental problems were worsened by my dad's interactions with her. Later, I was certain that he had a negative effect upon her. He didn't cause her mental illness, but he certainly was not part of any solution to help her.

Sometimes when Dad would see a group of teen-age girls he would point them out to me and say, "I can't help but wonder, Tracy, how many of them will grow into women who will make men's lives miserable."

I knew Dad loved me. He would have given his life, if it would have saved mine. However, as I grew into womanhood it became harder for him to reconcile the negative feelings he held toward women, with how he truly felt about me. The dysfunctional relationships he had with his mother and his wife, I believe, shaped his thoughts and feelings about women and left him very conflicted.

Grains of Salt

One Saturday, at visitation, Mother thought it would be a good idea to go to the salt ponds in Redwood City. The third person remained in the car reading her book, as Mother and I walked the grounds toward the base of the huge salt hill. It was a gray cloudy day, sprinkling on and off. Her topic of conversation made the day even gloomier.

"I am not happy with the person you're turning into," Mother complained. "Your father has ruined you! You're a tomboy, wearing pants all the time."

I did not respond to her.

"You are such a disappointment to me and *it is all your father's fault!*" she rambled on. "He is responsible for you turning out the way you have. It just makes me sick when I think of you living with him, listening to his lies about the past. It just makes me *sick*, Tracy."

Mother kept on attacking Dad and then me, repeatedly.

I said nothing. For years I had listened to my mother tearing my father down at every opportunity, but this was the first time that she really attacked me as a person. I had listened to enough of this at home. Underneath my calm exterior a volcano was about to erupt.

Finally, I reached my limit and was fed up!

"Mother, I can't stand to listen to you for another second!"

With that statement, I scrambled straight up the salt hill, which was about ten stories high. I had to use my hands and feet to make headway at the steepest parts. I was amazed at how hard and firm the large salt crystals were which provided good traction as I continued my climb.

"TRACY! COME DOWN HERE THIS MINUTE!" Mother screamed.

As I reached the top, my hands were sore and a bit dried out. I sat down and looked around. I could see everything from up there! What a nice view on such a rotten day! My mother was becoming hysterical which, on some level, gave me great satisfaction. She was acting as if my life was in terrible danger. She continued to yell for me to come down.

"I will be happy to come down when visitation is over and not a moment before!" I yelled down to her.

Then she started to threaten me.

"If you don't come down here right now, I'm going to come up and get you and it will not be pretty or nice for you when I do!"

"Why don't you come up here then?" I asked sarcastically. I knew there was no way she possibly could. She was dressed in a dress and high heels, which I thought was odd for the outing she had planned.

"When you come down here, I am going to slap the heck out of you!"

"Well that's great motivation, Mother. I'll just stay up here then!"

This infuriated her even more. Mother tried to climb up

but couldn't get more than a couple feet off the ground. She screamed and screamed her threats and warnings, but I ignored her. Occasionally I reminded her I would come down when visitation was over.

When Mother realized she was getting nowhere, she went back to the car and talked with the third person who came out and tried to coax me down, but I still refused. I told her the same thing that I had told my mother -- I would come down when visitation was over. It was the first time I felt empowered at visitation. I realized that I was in no danger. The plant was not running and no one was there except the three of us. I stopped listening to the words Mother and the third person were hollering at me and enjoyed the view! Soon the third person gave up and went back to the car. Mother remained at the base of the hill.

Being on top of the salt hill was the most fun I'd had in a long time. I felt free, a feeling I had never experienced at visitation before. I had time alone on my own terms and I had time to think about things. I thought about how both of my parents were now saying that I was a disappointment to them. Instead of feeling sad, it struck me as humorous. After all this time, they *finally* agreed about something! I laughed aloud at my private thoughts. My mother thought I was laughing at her.

"Wait until you get down here, I'll give you something to laugh about!" Mother yelled.

I stopped laughing and tried to trick myself into not really caring, but was aware of my anger and resentment over her threat.

Between my two parents, I wondered if I would be better off by myself. I was still too young to leave home and live on my own. Even as a teenager I knew I couldn't run away from my problems. I had learned this lesson from my dad a long time ago, "problems, like shadows, follow you wherever you go." No, there would be no running away from my problems. My little vacation on top of the salt hill was good enough for now. It started raining and Mother joined the third person in the car. Thankfully, the shower didn't last for long.

After I was up there for about an hour and a half, Mother came to the base of the hill and announced the time and that visitation was almost over.

"I don't even know if I can get you back in time, so you better come down, *now*."

I scrambled down the hill and jumped off the last five feet, landing on the ground right in front of her.

Mother raised her hand to strike me and, quick as a wink, I reached out and grabbed her offending hand by the wrist. In a split second, I realized I was stronger than she was. I locked eyes with her.

"If you ever try to hit or hurt me again I *will* defend myself and I guarantee *you* will end up in intensive care! *Do you understand me, Mother?*"

She was shocked and stared at me for a moment in disbelief. She finally said, "Yes," as her arm went limp.

I let go of her wrist and we walked to the car in silence. Now she knew I was physically stronger than she was and this was a game changer.

On the drive back, Mother lectured about how badly I behaved. She was putting on a real show for the third person, but was careful not to attack me personally. She made no mention about what had just transpired at the bottom of the salt hill. At first, sitting in the back seat I just ignored her. Then she accused me of saying things that I hadn't and I became angry. I told her to stop lying and showing off for the third person. She got so angry and distracted, yammering at me over her shoulder that the car started swerving all over the road. The third person said nothing.

When we returned to the third person's house, my mother told her that she would call later so they could "talk." I said nothing and went into the house. After Mother left, the third person entered the house.

"Tracy, you shouldn't have disobeyed your mother. Climbing up to the top of the salt hill was not a safe thing to do. I hope you're happy, because you have upset your mother terribly and there is no excuse for that!" the third person scolded.

I said nothing.

The third person was no longer a "neutral person." I was angry about what she said to me and I couldn't wait to leave. When Dad showed up at the front door, I pushed past him without a word as I walked towards the car.

"What's wrong?" he asked.

"Adolescence," the third person replied.

Dad followed me and got in the car.

"What happened?"

"Nothing, let's go."

We obviously were not leaving.

"I really want to understand what happened today and I would like to hear it from you," Dad said patiently.

So, I told him everything and was amazed he listened without interrupting or judging me. When I finished and finally looked at him, I was shocked to see his reaction. Instead of the anger, irritation and disappointment I had seen in his face for months, I saw kindness and compassion.

"Stay in the car, I'm going back into the house to talk with Mrs._____ [the third person]."

Dad was in the house for about twenty minutes. Then he

followed the third person back to the car. She came to my side of the car and asked me to get out. I was shocked to see she was crying. She hugged me snuggly, rubbed my back and said she was so sorry. She told me it was wrong of her to be judgmental and she wouldn't be doing that anymore. Then she asked if I would forgive her.

"Yes, but you don't understand. There are things between my mother and me that you don't know about. Don't be sad, of course I forgive you." I replied.

She smiled as she softly touched my cheek with her hand. Then, without another word, she went back into her house. By this time, Dad was in the car.

"What *did* you say to her?" I asked astonished.

"I helped her to understand that your interactions with your mother were not a case of 'adolescence.'"

After this visit, Mother rarely discussed my dad and dropped most of her campaigns. She seemed to spend more time talking with the third person about her life and current events, which I zoned out. We never had visitation at the salt hill or ponds again.

A New Friend That Was Heaven Sent

When the school year ended, we towed our boat to Shasta Lake in northern California for a two-week fishing and water-skiing vacation. Through his store, Dad had met Dr. Richard Spademan, an orthopedic surgeon who had invented a unique ski binding. Dad liked the doctor, and his ski binding. He was so impressed that he bought 100+ for the store's ski rental department. Dad invited the doctor to vacation with us. During the drive to Shasta Lake, my father instructed me to be sure to call him "Dr. Spademan." We had never taken another adult along on vacation and I was concerned because I didn't know him. Dad assured me he was a nice guy and that we would get along just fine.

After we picked up Dr. Spademan at the airport, Dad asked what he would like to eat for lunch.

The doctor looked over his shoulder at me sitting in the backseat.

"We have a *teenager* with us, so I guess we'll have *no choice* but to have hamburgers." Dr. Spademan smiled.

I smiled back but thought to myself, *Great; I'm stuck for two weeks with a guy who doesn't like kids!* I had no idea how wrong I was.

Dr. Spademan asked me a couple questions and then made it quite clear to both my dad and me that I was to call him by his first name.

Richard brought some medical books with him to read. He was studying for an exam to renew his surgical certification. I was curious and I asked if I could look through the books.

"You can read them, but don't look at any of the pictures. They'll give you nightmares!" Richard replied with a smile.

The books were big and heavy. Richard looked over his shoulder at me, as I flipped through the pages.

"You're not looking at the pictures are you? I'll have to take the books away if you are; I don't want to be responsible for you having bad dreams!" Richard teased with a laugh.

I laughed as I assured him I wasn't looking at the pictures, which of course I was.

Over lunch, I got to know Richard a little and soon the hamburger comment was forgotten. He was bright, comfortable to be around and easy to talk with. He also had a great sense of humor.

The days were so hot that Dad only wanted to go out on

the boat in the early mornings and at dusk. The place we stayed was on a huge lakeshore property. We were at the resort only a few days when a man working there started showing interest in me. He tried to talk to me or get my attention when Dad and Richard weren't around. I told him I wasn't interested, but that didn't stop his advances. I told Dad about the man and that I felt uneasy about his persistence.

"Ignore him, Tracy," Dad instructed.

"I tried that and it doesn't work," I explained.

"Figure it out for yourself, Tracy; I don't want to hear any more about it," Dad snapped.

One day during lunch, I went to the women's room and the man cornered me on my way out.

In a thick Mexican accent he said, "I work here for the summer because I go to high school. I get off at 2:00, my room number is___, meet me there and we will have some fun!" He was obviously in his early to mid-twenties.

"I'm not interested. Leave me alone," I replied as I pushed past him.

Feeling unprotected and painfully aware that this was going nowhere good, I went back to our table. It seemed every time I turned around this man was there looking at me. I was so uncomfortable that I didn't want to go anywhere by myself.

One day Dad and I were in our room watching TV. It was well over 100° outside and I silently wished I could go swimming, but didn't want to go by myself. I was half watching TV and half bored.

"Why don't you put your swim suit on and go to the pool?" Dad asked.

"Would you be willing to go with me?"

"*Why?*" he blurted out.

"I am afraid to go alone because of the man," I replied. "What if he sees me and decides to go swimming too? I did what you said, I tried to ignore him, but he won't leave me alone. I know you said you didn't want to hear any more about it, but Dad, I'm afraid of him."

To my surprise, Dad became enraged.

"If you don't put your swimsuit on right now and go to the pool, I will give you a belting you will never forget!"

I was shocked! The look on Dad's face told me that he immediately regretted his threat. I waited to see if he would take it back, but he didn't. Shooting him a look of betrayal, I went into the bathroom and quickly changed into my swimsuit, grabbed a towel and left for the pool.

The only people swimming were getting ready to leave. I didn't know what to do, but I knew that I couldn't go back to the room or be in the pool area alone. Then I thought about Richard. He had his own room a few buildings down the hill from us. At lunch he mentioned that he was going to study for a while and then take a nap. I went to his door and knocked softly. There was no answer. I said his name and knocked softly again, but there was still no answer. I thought he was probably asleep and didn't want to wake him. Sitting on the chair outside his room, I decided to wait for him to wake up. I felt somewhat safe. If the man came along all I had to do was pound on the door and wake Richard.

Richard walked up to his room about an hour later. He had been out hiking. So much for feeling safe! He was surprised to see me and asked me if I was going swimming.

"I was but I was worried about going by myself because of that guy I told you and my dad about. He got angry with me when I said I was afraid to go swimming by myself. He told me to go anyway. I was hoping you might want to go for a swim or study by the pool, so I could feel safe," I quickly explained.

I felt bad about asking Richard. After all, I barely knew him. I felt even worse when I asked him to keep this between us and not tell my dad.

Richard looked at me for a moment and said, "I haven't had a chance to study today, I'll grab my books and we'll go." He winked and smiled. I was instantly relieved.

I was enjoying my swim and looked up occasionally to see Richard sitting in the shade reading his book. It wasn't long before the man entered the pool area. He was at the shallow end and I was at the deep end. Richard had dozed off and was about five feet away from me. The man made a shallow dive and was cruising towards me under the water. I quickly jumped out of the pool and woke Richard. I pointed to the man who was still gliding underwater. Richard jumped up and went over to the edge of the pool. I'm sure the man was surprised when he surfaced to find Richard standing over the top of him. Richard had gotten up so quickly that he had forgotten to put his book down.

"What do you want here?" Richard asked the man.

"I want to talk to the girl," the man replied.

"Well, she doesn't want to talk with you, so I suggest you leave."

"This is none of your business. I'm here for the girl," the man insisted.

"I'm making it my business," Richard replied. "The girl is not here for you, so leave."

"What is she to you?" Then, looking at the book in Richard's hand the man asked, "What are you some kind of doctor?"

Richard looked at his book and said, "Yeah, I'm an orthopedic surgeon. I know how to fix bones and I know how to break them. This girl is here on vacation, she is *not* here to be bothered by you.

She has asked you multiple times to leave her alone and you have ignored her wishes. Now I'm *telling* you to leave her alone."

The man said something in Spanish and then stated, "This is a free country and I will do what I want."

"That's fine. But if this girl even sees you again during her stay here, your own mother won't recognize you when I'm finished! Am I making myself clear?"

The man nodded, swam to the shallow end and left the pool area.

I couldn't believe what I had just witnessed.

Richard came back to where I was standing.

"That man won't bother you anymore," he said in a calming voice. "While we are on vacation together, I will watch out for you. If you want to go swimming, or do anything else, just let me know and I'll go with you."

"Thank you so much, Richard, but what about your studies?!" I asked.

He laughed and told me not to worry; he would have plenty of time for that.

I was deeply grateful and felt as if a 100 pound weight had been taken from my shoulders.

As Richard walked me back to my building, he said, "Tracy, I don't want you to worry about anything, including your father."

During the hot daytime hours, Dad stayed in his air-conditioned room watching TV while Richard and I went everywhere together. He was right, I never saw that man again. We found common interests in ski bindings. I was curious about the toeless one he had invented and he was interested that I had been mounting bindings since I was six years old. I knew a great deal about the latest testing equipment and the functional differences between most ski bindings available on the market. He asked me many questions and seemed truly interested in my answers. After that, we found other common interests, which included hiking and nature. I enjoyed listening to him. He talked and interacted with me differently than most adults I had ever known. The main differences were that he didn't speak down to me; he respected me and valued my opinions. We always had something interesting to talk about. I finally relaxed as I became more comfortable with him. He made me feel safe in a way that I hadn't for a very long time. We were fast becoming friends as the days progressed. My father, who thought I had finally resolved my fear, was delighted to see me spending my days outside of the hotel room, he assumed, by myself. It was a win-win situation all around!

When the vacation ended, I felt a bit sad. I had been having such a wonderful time that I never thought about going home.

"When will I see you again?" I asked Richard anxiously.

"I have some free time on Saturday afternoons and I would like to come by the store and have you show me how the ski binding testing equipment works and, if it's okay with your dad, perhaps you can help me run some comparisons," Richard said confidently. "Also, your father has invited me to your house for dinner in a couple of weeks. After all, I've gotten used to looking after you! Just because our vacation is over doesn't mean that I won't look in on you from time to time." Richard laughed.

After Saturday morning visitations with Mother, I would spend the rest of the day working at the store. Richard started-ed coming most Saturday afternoons. Richard had arranged with Dad for me to work with him when he was at the store. After he learned how to use the testing equipment, he made test comparisons between his binding and the others, and I assisted him. Since we sold almost every ski binding available, he had a great many to compare. The more I was around

Richard, the more interested and involved I became with his ski binding and the less available I was for the child molester.

Before Richard, no one had ever stood up for me against a man who had inappropriate sexual intentions. I was unprotected, isolated and, quite frankly, made to be an easy target. There was no trusted, solid adult that I could confide in who wouldn't go straight to my father upon learning about the molester.

About a year after Richard and I became friends, I started to realize he might be my ticket to freedom from the child molester.

All a child needs in this situation is one solid adult who will stand up for the child without being judgmental. I was certain that Richard would not judge me. He believed in me, supported and protected me. Richard had proven himself a solid, safe and trustworthy adult -- just what I needed in my life.

Finally, I built up enough courage to broach the subject with the child molester. He had been sexually abusing me for many years. I informed him that I had an adult in my life *that* would protect me against men like him. He laughed and thought it was a joke until I told him who the person was and then he knew that I was serious. I had told the molester the story about the man I had encountered on vacation and how Richard stood up for me. I told the molester if he ever touched me again that I would tell Richard and I was certain he would know what to do about it. I locked eyes with the man and saw the fear in his. I was no longer the frightened, isolated child that he could control at will. I had just taken my power back; the power the man had held over me, all those years. He never touched me again. Several months later, the man gave my father notice and left. Little did I know my friendship with Richard would stop the child molester in his tracks!

As a result of being molested, I felt deeply ashamed, embarrassed, traumatized, victimized, guilty and dehumanized.

These feelings stayed locked away inside of me for decades, as I was too ashamed to tell anyone, until well into my mid to late thirties. During this time, no one knew what I had suffered.

A child molester is almost certain that the child will keep the secret because of humiliation, guilt, and all the other negative feelings associated with being molested. Also, the molester's position of trust within the child's family nearly always ensures, for multiple reasons, that the child will keep his or her mouth shut. Fear and control can play a role, as it did with me.

Almost, without fail, children are molested by a trusted family member or others who are entrusted by the family. Very rarely do strangers molest children. If a stranger was spending time with a child, of course this would jump out as a red flag and be noticed. The family's trusted inner circle, though, is *not* under scrutiny. As the molester builds trust with the parents, they are also building trust with the *target child.*

Before the employee started molesting me, he started "the tickle game." I trusted him because I knew him, he was nice to me, played with me and Dad liked him. This game was a precursor to molesting me. No adults who witnessed the tickle game had any concerns about it, including my dad, the man's wife, nor other employees or other adults who watched.

Heads up! Today's statistics state that **90% of child molesters are known and trusted by the parents. Only 10% of child molesters are strangers.** *Please don't live in denial. Protect your children, and all children!*

Life Changes

Dad and I found our new home in the Saratoga foothills. It was a large English Tudor house on a little more than an acre of flat ground -- just what he had wanted. The circular driveway was lined with 40-year-old orange trees. The pool and bathhouse were on the right side of the driveway. The pool had a slide and a diving board. The bathhouse had a covered patio, changing rooms and a bathroom. A sailboat builder had built the older part of the house with decorative mahogany and teak throughout. Upstairs were four good-sized bedrooms and the master. The house had five bathrooms. What a change from our three-bedroom ranch house! The property also had a shed, a long grape arbor with concord grapes, an orchard, a rose garden with a fishpond, a large redwood lathe house and another larger structure that was like a barn with a cement floor. The barn was the same square footage as the San Jose house.

Brian came over often and my fears of losing contact with him, because of the move, vanished. He helped with the yard and house. Brian also started working at my dad's store. Our friendship deepened and we spent a lot of time together. My dad was much happier in the new house. As he relaxed, he started to have fun again and more resembled the dad I used to know.

My new bedroom was the only one in the house that faced the backyard. Dad had just painted my room pink and we were still in the process of picking out drapes and settling into the new house. One night I was sleeping on my side facing the wall when I woke suddenly to yellow and orange flickers of light covering the wall. Then I heard a loud, explosive BOOM from the backyard, flipped around and looked out the window.

The shed was on fire! I ran down the hall to Dad's room and flew through the door. He was awake and fully dressed with the lights on. He jumped up and grabbed me by the shoulders.

"THE SHED IS ON FIRE! THE SHED IS ON FIRE!" I yelled.

"Wake *up*, Tracy! You're having a nightmare! Everything is fine, now go back to bed and go to sleep," Dad ordered.

I tried to convince him but he was pushing me back towards the hall. I knew I had better think of some other way to prove it wasn't a nightmare, and fast. All of his bedroom windows faced out to the front of the house except a skinny, long frosted bathroom window that faced out toward the backyard. I looked at it and it was bright orange!

"If I'm having a nightmare, why is that window bright orange?!" I asked frantically.

The fire was progressing toward the house.

My father froze in his tracks.

"Oh my God, what should I do?" he gasped.

"Call the fire department," I instructed.

He wasn't moving, he was just staring at the orange window as if in a trance.

I shook him hard and yelled, "CALL THE FIRE DEPARTMENT *NOW!*"

Dad snapped out of it, ran to the phone and I watched him make the call. His digital clock was next to him and I noted the time. It was exactly 1:03 AM.

While Dad was on the phone, I ran downstairs and out the side door. I was almost hit by a car flying down the side driveway without its lights on. It kept going into the street and then vanished. The fire had spread from the shed to the redwood lathe house. It was burning about ten feet from the house! The flames were fed by the gasoline powered garden tools and extra fuel we kept in the shed. The flames from the shed were about fifty feet tall!

Our property had very strong water pressure, so I grabbed the hose and started soaking down the wooden shingles on the back of the house. Dad came out and took over for me and I told him about the car, which turned out to be a concerned neighbor.

When the firefighters arrived, they couldn't get the hydrants to work. Dad told them to pump the water out of the pool, but they refused. They went to another hydrant down the street that was working. Thankfully, they put the fire out before it burned the house.

The Fire Chief talked with me during the investigation. Because I knew the exact time that Dad called the fire department, he told Dad it was very possible I had set the shed on fire! Dad told him it was impossible because he knew for a fact I was in bed asleep, as he had checked on me a few minutes before I alerted him to the fire. A few days later, the fire department discovered that the actual cause of the fire was combustion. They also found an electrical problem almost in the same spot the fire had started. They seemed uncertain as to which event had actually caused the fire, but they were now certain that I didn't cause it!

Although Mother never knew about the fire, she seemed to know about the new house almost immediately. I was questioned at visitation, but gave very little in the way of answers. I had learned many years ago that the less she knew about my life, the better off I was. In between changing the subject and using other distractions, I became quite skilled at evading her landmines and arrows. Even though her campaigns to brainwash me and alienate me from Dad were abandoned after the salt hill incident, she would occasionally drop a nasty comment about him. Mother could tell it had no effect on me. No matter what she had said to me over the years, she was never successful at turning me against my dad. Since the day at the salt hill, Mother never again tried to physically hurt me.

As time went on, Dad gave dinner parties. One of these

parties included a couple around Dad's age who were also in the sporting goods business. The husband was drinking heavily and, to my shock and surprise, started coming up to me and kissing me on the mouth! I asked my dad if he would say something to stop the man.

"He's drunk. Just put up with it, Tracy," Dad replied casually.

I couldn't believe my ears! I wondered if this was how most fathers would react? "Just put up with it?" I decided that most fathers would protect their daughters.

I looked at the man's wife with pleading eyes as he grabbed me and kissed me again. She simply turned and walked away. I managed to break free of him and ran upstairs, worried he might follow me. I slammed my door shut, moved some furniture against it to block it from opening and waited for them to leave. Dad and I never spoke about it again.

After I passed my driver's license test, I always picked Brian up at the Knudson's for work or to come visit, but I always waited in the car. Now that I was driving, we went fun places together. Some weekends we went to the Sierras to ski.

I was well into my seventeenth year before I went inside the Knudson's house again. After so many years it felt odd to be back in their home. Mary Jane was happy to see me and interested in catching up with me. At first, I felt very awkward, but after several visits, Mary Jane and I slowly became close again. After a while, I looked forward to our visits and long talks, which often ran into the wee hours. I started to come over more often and slowly felt more a part of the family again. Our relationship goes deeper than just friendship. We have a shared history and a special kinship that makes us family.

When I was in high school, the legal age to become an adult was reduced from twenty-one to eighteen. I couldn't have been happier, because the new law would end visitation with Mother three years earlier. On my eighteenth birthday I would be free of her! It felt like I had just received parole from an unjust sentence that seemed to go on forever.

During my senior year of high school, I was accepted to Humboldt State University in northern California. They had a marine biology department and arrangements were made for me to stay with our friends, the Gibsons, who lived relatively close to the university. Finally, the feeling of control over my destiny was *almost* within my reach!

As I approached graduation from high school, I began to see my mother less often. Sometimes I would call her on a Thursday and tell her that I wouldn't be available for the next two Saturdays. I believed that there wasn't much she could do about it because I was now seventeen-and-a-half years old. I saw her two weeks before graduating from high school. At that visit, I handed her an invitation and she said that she would come. It was Dad's idea to invite Mother to my graduation, saying it was the right thing to do, although he felt she wouldn't show up. He was right, she didn't. I convinced myself that my mother's absence would have no effect on me, although from time to time I noticed I was scanning the crowd in the stands to find her face. The next day I phoned to ask why she didn't come, just to see what she would say. She told me an amazingly elaborate story of how she had car trouble on the way to the ceremony, but that she had really wanted to be there. She asked if she could see me during the summer and I told her I would be too busy. I told her that I thought we should stop visitation at this point and I wished her well. She told me to have a good summer before she said goodbye. Just like that, visitation ended.

I never intended to see my mother or talk with her again.

My plans for university changed when Dad came to me and practically begged me not to go. I was seventeen and he convinced me that he could not run the store without me. I was young and gullible! He promised me it would only be for one year and then I could go to Humboldt State University, as planned. I felt torn and gave it a great deal of thought. I weighed what I wanted to do with my life against the debt I felt I owed my dad. I knew he had sacrificed a great deal to fight for custody of me and to raise me on his own. As a result, I was very loyal to him. The feeling was internal; he didn't constantly remind me or "guilt" me into staying. I told myself that it was only for one year, then I could start university and work toward the things I wanted to accomplish in life. I started to take courses at the junior college. The decision to stay on to help Dad changed the course of my life.

Fourteen years old with Dad.

Sixteen years old with Dad at his store.

Seventeen years old.

4

Beyond Survival and Healing

Turning Eighteen

As a child, I never thought I would survive to become an adult. I felt certain that my mother would kill me long before then. I was amazed and delighted when I finally turned eighteen! A couple of days before my birthday, I received a card from my maternal grandpa. He wrote that he was in his 98th year and would very much like to see me while he was "still in this earthly life." He added his hopes that "one day there would be some form of reconciliation in your family, so that you could come with your mother to visit us."

As I looked at Grandpa's card I thought, *Now that I'm an adult I can go see them without worrying about Mother or the courts.* For a few weeks Dad had been asking me what I wanted for my eighteenth birthday. Up to the time I received Grandpa's card, I had no idea. I showed Dad the card and said I would like to see my grandparents in Florida. He read the card, nodded and choked back tears while saying he would be happy to arrange for the trip.

I phoned my grandparents and told them I was coming for a visit. Grandpa was delighted, but Grandma was not. She told me I could come with my mother if I wanted to visit. In her gruff Hungarian accent she told me if I showed up without my mother she would not let me in the house! My heart sunk as I told Dad what she had said. He suggested I take my picture album that contained pictures from my last visit with them when I was little. He thought that that might give us a place to start and a smoother beginning, if she decided to let me in the door! He also gave me $800.00 and told me if my grandmother refused my visit to catch the next flight to Orlando and go to Disney World for a week. If I needed more money he would wire it to me. Regardless of my grandmother's feelings, the plans were made. Two days later, I was on a red-eye flight to Florida.

After landing in Tampa, I took a cab to see where my grandparents lived. On the way, I told the cab driver the reason for my visit and that I would need to find a small motel somewhere near my grandparents' house. He knew a family that ran a motel and dropped me there. I took a nap and then a shower. Later that day I called the same cabbie and with my picture album tucked under my arm was driven to my grandparents' house. The cabbie said he would wait for me to be sure that my grandmother would let me in. He wanted to be certain that all was well before he left. Tightly clutching the photo album, I walked up to the door and knocked.

"Yes?" Grandma said, as she opened the door.

"My name is Tracy Cable. I'm your granddaughter," I replied confidently.

She looked at me for an uncomfortable moment. I wasn't certain whether she was going to invite me in or not.

"Come in," Grandma finally said.

I walked in and hugged her and Grandpa.

After we talked for a while, they seemed happy to see me and I was soon comfortable in their home. I showed them my pictures from the last visit and shared what I could remember.

Grandma pointed to some indentations on her wooden coffee table. She told me that during my last visit I was playing with a little nut cracker and had hit her brand-new coffee table several times. She told me of the many times she had run her fingers over the little indentations I had made.

"I could never bring myself to replace the coffee table because it was the only physical thing I had left of you," Grandma said emotionally.

Grandma was always so gruff with me that this tender comment caught me off guard. I quickly swallowed back a tear.

The visit was going well. After a few days, my grandparents began to pick me up at the motel in the early morning and return me at night. Grandpa was still driving at ninety-eight years old! Every morning around seven, I received a call from the woman in the lobby.

"Your most darling little ol' grandparents are here," she said in her lovely, thick southern drawl. "Hurry up now and don't keep them waiting, ya hear?!"

"Yes ma'am," I replied and I hurried out the door.

My grandparents took me to a great place for breakfast. They were amazed that my mother never taught me any Hungarian and proceeded to teach me six words: yes, no, please, thank you, grandmother and grandfather. I enjoyed every minute I spent with them. For their age, they were amazingly active and didn't tire easily. By the third day of my visit, *I* was getting tired, but they kept on going with lots of energy to spare!

One day, Grandpa was showing me what part of Hungary

he and Grandma came from, on a globe they had by the front
door.

Grandpa started in his thick Hungarian accent. Phoneti-
cally it sounded like: *"Vell, you see dah-link* (darling) *yer grand-
mudder is frum outside Vudapest* (Budapest) *vhich is right here,"*
he said pointing at the globe. *I em frum dis ah-rea over here,"* he
continued, pointing at Romania. (Okay. No more attempts at
mimicking his accent!) He saw my confusion and continued,
"Well, when I was born, this area was part of Hungary, but
don't worry dear, *we will get it back someday!"*

"Old man!" Grandma abruptly interrupted.

Grandpa and I looked up at her with the "deer in head-
lights look" on our faces.

"The young girl does not want to hear your old stories! Go
away *old man!"* she ordered.

"Where shall I go, old woman?" he asked confused and
bewildered.

"Go down to the gas station, old man. Tell the boys at the
gas station your *old stories, old man!"*

I looked at Grandpa who seemed a bit flustered.

"All right, old woman, I am going!" he said shaking his
head as he walked towards the door.

I was wondering if they were as angry as they seemed. Their
interaction was quite funny to watch and I had a hard time
not laughing aloud. When Grandpa left, Grandma burst into
laughter hugging me and saying, "What can you do with an *old
man* like that, darling?!"

A couple of days before I was to leave, Grandma wanted to
go shoe shopping. We went to a large department store and she
started trying on shoes.

"I have just received a letter from your mother," Grandma
said.

I thought, *oh great – now what!*

Before I could say anything, Grandma started to cry. She opened her purse and handed me the letter, which was written in Hungarian.

I looked at Grandma, who was still in tears and said, "I can't read Hungarian."

My mother had sent the letter unaware that I was visiting. I felt it would only bring my grandparents grief if Mother were told about the trip. I also didn't want her to fly in on her broomstick and ruin our visit. Grandma took the letter and started to translate it for me.

Mother wrote that she had no idea of my whereabouts, where I lived or even my phone number. She said I didn't know how to bathe or dress myself properly and that I wore dirty clothes all the time. She went on to write that I was backwards and couldn't write or speak very well. Mother stated, in her letter, that she didn't know what to do.

"How can this be?" Grandma asked. "I have been with you for a week now. You are well dressed, well spoken and intelligent. You are not anything at all like my daughter describes."

Grandma was crying again. I felt sad for her.

"My mother has problems, Grandma. She has had them for a very long time," I said softly.

Grandma looked confused as she asked, "Why? Why would she write such things about you that are obviously not true?"

"Uncle Les tried to tell you many years ago that my mother had problems," I replied gently. "You didn't believe him, but he was telling you the truth. My mother is mentally ill and has been for a very long time, Grandma. She sees things and hears things that other people can't and she has other challenges with reality. My mother's behavior can be quite unpredictable."

"She is my daughter!" Grandma replied gruffly. "How

could I not have seen this? How could I have not known this?" she demanded.

"It would be hard for you to see the truth of my mother's illness because she is very good at deception and she can be very convincing," I replied kindly. "I would imagine it's also hard to believe this would happen to your own child. You weren't there to see what was happening first-hand and only believed what she told you. You took her word to be the truth, but it's not." I felt very sorry for Grandma. I never thought I would be the one to tell her that her daughter was mentally ill and that she had been deceived for so many years.

Slowly Grandma began to pull herself together and we left without buying anything. She never again asked any more questions about my mother.

The next day my grandparents took me to a souvenir shop. Grandma noticed a rack of postcards on the front counter.

"Tracy, please send a postcard to your mother telling her your address and phone number."

I was amazed. It was as if Grandma did not understand anything I told her the day before.

"My mother already knows my address and phone number. She has *always* known it."

"Please dear, make an old woman happy. Send a card to your mother to let her know how to contact you."

"Grandma, you have no idea what Pandora's box you're asking me to open. If my mother finds out I've been here to visit with you and that you shared her letter with me, this is going to cause you and Grandpa problems you can't begin to imagine," I explained. "You don't understand. I have to protect you and Grandpa! You don't know what my mother is capable of when she's angry. She will be livid if I send her a card, because she will know I have been here visiting with you."

Grandma started crying and pleading with me to send my mother a postcard, regardless. People were beginning to stare at us. I tried to calm and reason with her, but she wouldn't listen.

"Please dear, make an old woman happy," she begged -- for what felt like the hundredth time.

I finally caved. Against my better judgment, I asked Grandma to help me choose a postcard. We chose one with an alligator on the front saying "Greetings from Tampa Florida" across its open mouth. I wrote, "Mother, My address is... my phone number is... as you well know. Tracy." I gave it to Grandma and asked if this would make her happy.

She was ecstatic. She took the card and asked the woman at the front counter for a stamp so we could mail it right away. Then she handed it to me to mail.

"I won't mail this for you, Grandma. Please hold onto it for a while and think about what I have told you. I hope you will decide not to send it."

Grandma shook her head and then put it in the mailbox.

I was having a good time, so I extended my stay a couple of days longer. I figured it would take about five days for my mother to get the postcard and I wanted to be back in California before she received it.

A few days after I returned home, Grandpa called. He sounded sad and exhausted as he said, "Your mother was just here. After she received your postcard, she boarded a flight to Tampa. We didn't know she was coming. Our front door flew open and she walked in and angrily declared 'my daughter has stayed in this house.' I was shocked. I started to tell her that you had stayed in a motel, but before I could finish she slapped your postcard down on the table and screamed that I was a 'liar.' Then she yelled, *You're all a bunch of liars! I will never talk to you or have any contact with anyone in the family ever again!'*

Then she turned on her heels, stormed out of the house and slammed the door behind her."

As I listened to the sadness in Grandpa's voice, I heard Grandma sobbing in the background. I was filled with sadness and afraid that something like this might happen. Again, I explained to Grandpa that this was the reason I didn't want to send the postcard.

"My mother is mentally ill, and this makes her very unpredictable. I am very sorry that this has happened." I felt completely and utterly responsible. I believed none of this would have happened if I had flat out refused to write the postcard in the first place.

I was heartbroken for my grandparents. This whole experience had popped their bubble of denial in regards to my mother's illness.

Soon after, the family felt the repercussions. When family members called, Mother would hang up on them. When they wrote, she returned their cards and letters, unopened. Feeling horribly responsible for this turn of events, I never visited my grandparents again.

I was carrying eight units at the junior college and working for Dad thirty-six hours a week. School was going very well for me and I ended up on the Dean's List. I was living at home and had planned to do so until I went to Humboldt State University the following year.

Things at home took a turn for the worse, when Dad created some very odd rules. Perhaps it was his need for control, but I really don't know. Dad told me that I couldn't listen to music for more than half an hour, because I would "wear out the stereo." One day when I was sitting on the sofa reading, he came into the room and declared, "From now on you will sit on the floor. The furniture is for guests."

When I made friends in college and went out in the evenings with them, Dad demanded to know where I was at all times. My friends and I would often meet for coffee and talk. If we decided to do something else, Dad insisted that I phone to tell him where I was going and with whom. He also wanted their addresses and phone numbers. It became a real problem when we would go to several places in an evening. My friends didn't understand. I was embarrassed and very uncomfortable as no one else had to do this, but me. With the new restrictions and Dad's lack of flexibility, it wasn't long before life at home became intolerable.

One day I asked Brian what he thought about the situation.

"If I was eighteen and my parents treated me like that, I would move out," Brian replied.

It was good advice.

Then one night, while I was sleeping, Dad barged into my room and flipped on the light. He was dressed in only his briefs and was yelling at me. I couldn't make out a lot of what he was saying at first, because I was groggy. My adrenaline kicked in when I finally realized what he was talking about.

"...Do you have any idea how hard it is for me to sleep knowing that you are just down the hall from me?" Dad demanded.

I locked eyes with him and said nothing.

"A man has *urges*. Do you understand that, Tracy?"

I understood only too well! I wondered if Dad was seriously thinking of raping me and became nauseous. I immediately realized I was no longer safe. All of a sudden the house felt cold and dangerous. "Our home" was history. Now it was only my father's house. I continued eye contact with him, but said nothing. He became furious and yelled something about how stupid women were as he slammed the door on his way out.

My bedroom door didn't have a lock, so I tiptoed downstairs to get a chair and wedged it snugly under the doorknob. I didn't sleep for the rest of the night. I had to leave, and soon.

The next day I started hunting for an apartment. I only made minimum wage, which was $2.00 per hour! This made it difficult to find an apartment in a safe neighborhood that I could afford. I spoke with a family friend who owned some local apartment buildings. He rented a one-bedroom apartment to me at a reduced rate. Even with that, I could barely afford it.

Other than the cost, the apartment was perfect! It was close enough to ride my bike to work. My new neighbors were friendly and close to my age. Most attended Stanford University.

I told Dad that I had found an apartment and felt it best to be out on my own.

Dad acted very hurt by my leaving and only said one word, "Fine." He was certain that I couldn't afford to live on my own, and told his bookkeeper about his concerns. He didn't speak to me the day I moved out. When I said goodbye he just grunted something I could not understand. On my day off I rented a carpet cleaner and cleaned the carpet in my old bedroom at the house. Dad wasn't home. I left a fan on to help dry the carpet and a note for him, before I left. Dad did not speak to me for six weeks. At the store he used employees as go-betweens. When I said good morning or goodbye to him, he ignored me. I recognized that Dad had learned the silent treatment from his mother. He was doing to me, what she had done to him when she was angry with him. Because I knew this, his silence didn't upset me as much as it might have.

After settling into my apartment, I realized I was finally free! Free of Mother, Dad and my past. I was happier than I could ever remember. I still worked for Dad -- but, at that time, I didn't work directly with him. I was on the sales floor with other employees, while he worked primarily up in the office. Slowly, Dad started to talk with me again. It took at least six months for us to have a regular conversation.

Although I had no extra money, I enjoyed playing my guitar, fishing, hiking and other free activities. I ate low-cost foods which included: bread, popcorn, hot dogs, candy, rice, spaghetti, soup and the fish I caught. I ate over at the Knudson's from time to time, which helped me, both nutritionally and financially.

I honestly felt that I owed my soul to Dad, which was a terrible thing. I continued working at the store attempting to please him and to repay him for the personal sacrifices he had made to raise me.

A year after I moved out of Dad's house, I could no longer afford to attend junior college. After a couple of years of working for him, I realized that I would never be able to follow my dream of becoming a marine biologist or to enjoy the lifestyle this profession would have provided me. I never attended Humboldt State University, or any other. I worked for my dad's store more than full time, six days a week. He never paid me more than minimum wage. I ended up working for him for eighteen years. After the first eight years, Dad told me that he was going to start turning the business over to me, eventually giving me the store. This was the main reason I stayed on so long. Ten years later, this promise was still unfulfilled.

I decided I didn't want to be like either of my parents and I didn't want my past to dictate what kind of person I would become. It was very important to me to make sure that I never became labeled, pigeonholed or stereotyped because of my past. I read many books and believed that I could truly break the link of abuse and dysfunction in my family's chain. I also read about people who had suffered child abuse and how their unresolved issues negatively affected their lives. I became even more determined that the cycle of abuse in my family would stop with me! I worked on myself diligently and privately. I tried to disable the toxic inner tapes from my childhood. It felt like an impossible task. Many of these inner tapes contained my parents' negative views and judgments of me. I was finally an adult and didn't want that negativity to control me or hurt my chances for a happy life. Trying to erase my parents' hurtful words was difficult and took many years of hard work. I realized, as a young adult, that it was my own personal responsibility to rise above those inner tapes and my horrible childhood experiences.

Meeting with the Judge and Indian Joe

When I was about twenty years old, Dad thought I should visit Judge Riley. He thought I might be able to help other kids of divorce by thanking the judge for granting my dad custody. The last thing I felt like doing was thanking the man responsible for sentencing me to twelve years of forced visitations with my mother. However, I told my dad I would think about it.

The last time I had met with Judge Riley I was eight years old. I had practically pleaded with him not to force me to have contact with my mother, let alone live with her. Now here I was twenty years old and, no matter how hard I tried, I could not visualize myself voluntarily sitting in the same room with this man. How could I warmly greet him and thank him for allowing Dad to raise me, while trying to ignore the pain he had caused by forcing me to see Mother for so many years?

I decided to work at extending myself to a point where I

could finally think of being in the same room with the judge. I visualized a visit with him in my mind over and over again, until I could see myself doing it with ease. That didn't happen overnight! Although it would be easy to thank him for giving Dad custody, it would be almost unbearable not to mention Mother or the horrible visitations he had forced me to endure year after year. I thought that if I even mentioned her that I might as well not see him at all. I realized complaining about his visitation order or saying anything even slightly negative about Mother would ruin my chance to help other kids, because it would put the judge on the defensive. Dad agreed. Helping children in similar situations would be my only purpose for visiting the judge. I decided that no matter how difficult it would be for me to see this man again, it would be well worth the effort to help someone else. I resolved to do it.

I ran through different scenarios in my mind and concluded the judge would think I was there to complain. Therefore, my "thank you" would have an even greater effect on him. Determined to give it my best effort, I made an appointment to meet with him.

When the day came, I found myself sitting on a hard wooden bench outside Judge Riley's chambers, waiting for him. I had rehearsed this meeting repeatedly. I knew exactly what I was going to say. With kindness in my voice, I would extend a warm heartfelt "thank you" to this man. If he brought up my mother, I would answer politely and redirect the discussion back to the purpose of my visit. Like an actress, I was ready to deliver my lines and give a great performance. Despite my issues with his visitation order, I was truly grateful that the judge had granted my father custody -- and have been grateful throughout my entire life.

Judge Riley walked past me without uttering a word.

Surprisingly, he didn't look that much older. I followed him into his chambers. He walked behind his desk and our eyes locked. I thought to myself, *I'll just wait for him to speak first.* His words reflected his guarded feelings about seeing me again.

"Why are you here?" he asked stiffly. There was no smile and no greeting.

I smiled warmly and said, "I have come to thank you for granting my father custody of me so many years ago. I felt it was a difficult decision for you to make, given the attitudes of the time and I wanted to personally let you know I deeply appreciate you going out on a limb for me. I'm an adult now, Judge Riley, and I felt a responsibility to come and tell you this in person."

He couldn't have looked more shocked if I had doused him with a bucket of ice water! He immediately warmed up, smiled at me and asked me to sit. He went on about my parents' trial and what a difficult decision it was for him to grant my father custody of me.

Wishing I could get up and leave, I sat there smiling and nodding, acting as understanding and supportive of his situation as I possibly could.

When the judge was done talking, I got up to leave thanking him again for all he had done for me. I shook his hand and left his office, realizing that I had made his day. As I walked to my car, I hoped these efforts would help other children to be placed appropriately for their best welfare.

When I turned twenty-one years old, Indian Joe called and said he wanted to take me to lunch. I hadn't seen him for many years and had never seen him without Dad. I wondered, with some anxiety, if he might want to talk about the past, which he did. I met with him and was relieved that he wanted to carry the conversation.

Indian Joe told me he would never forget the first time we met and how I tugged on his shirtsleeve asking him to help us. He said, "You touched my heart. After that, I couldn't turn away from the case."

Laughing aloud, I told him I remembered it well.

Indian Joe's face turned serious as he said, "You're old enough to know a few things now that I'm sure your father hasn't told you. Because you know how much he loves you and the sacrifices he made for you when you were a child, I think it's safe to tell you that he didn't know at first whether he wanted to have custody of you or not. As time went by, he realized that he didn't want to make the same mistake with you that his father made with him by leaving him in the hands of his mother. I've known your dad since childhood. When he was a boy, his mother was cruel to him. He felt abandoned and unloved by his father when he moved to Hawaii. After some soul-searching your dad decided he didn't want the same thing for you."

Indian Joe talked about Dr. Gordon, saying that she gave excellent testimony and was the best expert witness he had ever seen in his entire career. "When the judge chose not to believe a part of her testimony, he took over the cross-examination from your mother's attorney. [When I was writing this book, I read the testimony on this incident. Mother's attorney was trying to use a hypothetical scenario with a non-existent child and tried to apply that scenario to me. Dr. Gordon explained why that would not be a realistic comparison. The judge was not convinced and took over her cross-examination. Despite the pressure, Dr. Gordon never wavered from her position.] Most psychiatrists make terrible expert witnesses because they tend to be very vague. This was not the case with Dr. Gordon, who made every point specifically clear."

Indian Joe told me about the many hurdles he and Dad faced throughout the custody hearing. He told me that the solid evidence, which he had produced regarding Mother's inability to parent me, including things she was doing to me during visitation: drugging me, hitting me, trying to brainwash me, etc., were completely disregarded by the court. The judge had ordered that neither Indian Joe nor Dad were allowed to question me about anything to do with Mother, including my relationship with her before she went to Agnews State Hospital. If I brought up the subject, then all they were allowed to do was listen and not comment or question me. I remember that silence, when I was a child, which felt like Dad was disapproving of me and what I was saying. Indian Joe told me how he fought to keep me from testifying in open court. He said that putting me on the witness stand was something that my mother and her attorneys desperately wanted so that they would have an opportunity to cross-examine me.

Toward the end of the custody hearing, Indian Joe felt certain Mother was going to be granted custody. He said that Dad refused to give me up, no matter the outcome or the consequences. Dad had an attorney friend who obtained two passports under falsified names. Indian Joe said that if the court had given custody to Mother that Dad would have about two weeks to turn me over to her. During that time, Dad and I would simply disappear. He planned to take two small suitcases and leave the store, the house and everyone we ever knew behind. He felt certain that the authorities would look for him in Canada and England as he had relatives there. Dad knew no one in Australia and that was where he planned to take me. Each month he took a small amount of cash and put it aside for this purpose, but other than this he would leave his bank accounts untouched. Indian Joe said my father planned to start from scratch in a new country under

BEYOND SURVIVAL AND HEALING

a false name and that we could never again have contact with the people we knew or loved. The plane tickets were purchased before the court handed down its decision. My dad was willing to go to this extent to protect me. This was the first time I had ever heard about this plan.

When Indian Joe and I were finished with lunch, I gave him a hug goodbye and thanked him for everything that he had done for my dad and me. I never saw him again.

Later, I asked Dad about his plan to move us to Australia. He told me that he had put enough money aside to buy a small piece of land where we would live as farmers and raise sheep.

"Dad, you would have risked losing everything?" I asked.

"If I had not done everything I humanly could do to save you from your mother, the cost would have been my very soul."

Surviving Abuse

Victims of abuse can suffer lifelong effects, which include: depression, low self-esteem, anxiety, attachment disorders, PTSD, Borderline Personality Disorder (BPD), eating disorders, sleep disorders, disassociation, addictions and more. Despite the common misconception, most abused children do not grow up to become abusers. Even though they rarely pass abuse on to others, they are at great risk of passing the abuse inward instead, leading to self-hatred and self-injury. In an attempt to alleviate the pain that they have suffered, they may turn to alcoholism, drugs or other addictions and self-destructive behaviors. I did *not* want this to happen to me.

Children and adult survivors of abuse can recover and live happy, productive lives. Help and support are available. Despite this, some continue to suffer by denying their situation or reliving their tortures over and over again. Many go through life without seeking assistance. They may not know help exists nor where to turn. The physical wounds from abuse may have healed long ago, but the mental and emotional wounds will not heal without first identifying they exist. The person must have the courage, determination and will to recover.

I was a survivor of all four categories of child abuse: physical, emotional, sexual and neglect. I had not received any professional help since I had last seen Dr. Gordon when I was a child. Dr. Gordon never knew about the sexual abuse or some of the other things I endured during my childhood and teenage years. I was unsettled about this, thinking that these things were left unresolved and that I wasn't self-aware enough to realize how they may have been affecting me. I was still uneasy with people learning about or knowing about my mother's mental illness. I felt they would judge me based on her problems. I had experienced this growing up. As a young adult, I didn't talk about Mother with new acquaintances or friends. However, I always told my boyfriends about Mother and much of the abuse I endured at her hands -- at some point during our relationship. I was aware, during my young adulthood, that this was the age when schizophrenia often showed up. At the age of nineteen and again at twenty-seven, I was tested for this and other psychological abnormalities. Except for a heightened vigilance, all my test scores fell within the normal range. I had dodged the psychosis bullet and I was relieved!

Working for Dad brought on a completely new set of issues as well. As time went on, his misogynistic viewpoint caused our relationship to take a turn for the worse. No matter how hard I worked, I was never good enough. I was often treated like a second-class citizen simply because I was a woman! It took me some time to figure this out. At one point he had me convinced that I couldn't possibly hold a job anywhere else. He would tell me that if I wasn't his daughter, he would've fired me. The reasons were unspecified and I never knew what prompted his outbursts. Some of his comments were not obvious, they were almost like hints or innuendos. At first they were inferred but not solidly stated. Later, he yelled them in my face. These, along with the challenges I had already faced, sometimes made working for Dad unbearable and again brought up the issues from childhood about my self-worth. As the years went by, I came to the understanding that part of Dad loved me dearly, but the misogynistic part of him hated me. At twenty-seven, I did work with a psychologist to help resolve some personal issues and to help me cope with the unhealthy aspects of working for Dad.

As a young adult I was still having night terrors, was blindly obedient and trying desperately to please everyone in authority. I was still scared to death of doctors and potentially painful medical or dental procedures. I was also hyper-alert. Every time someone raised his or her voice or argued with another person, my anxiety sharply increased. I had a strong distrust of others, although I tried never to let this show. I knew that the abuse I had suffered as a child at the hands of my mother had greatly altered me from the person I would have been. I wasn't very in touch with my feelings, motivations or who I really was as a person. By the time I turned eighteen, I had already started my journey. I read books to improve my self-esteem and self-confidence. I wanted to recover from the trauma I had endured. I also did a lot of self-reflection.

Meanwhile, I continued to read. I spent endless hours in the self-help section of my local bookstore searching for answers and information that would assist me. Some of the books that I found helpful included: *Coping with Difficult People; Celebrate Yourself; Feeling Good about Feelings; Letting Go of Stress; People of the Lie; Enjoy Yourself;* and *The Gentle Art Of Verbal Defense.* I don't know if any of these are still in print. As the years went by I found other helpful books including: *How to Survive the Loss of a Love; The Art and Practice of Compassion and Empathy; Emotional Intelligence; Life after Trauma; Care of the Soul; How to Go on Living When Someone You Love Dies;* and *The Creative Journal.*

I made lists of things I wanted to do to better myself and put it on my refrigerator, where I saw it every day. I wanted to strengthen myself against the damaging effects of being an adult survivor of child abuse. I made a list of personality traits that I liked and didn't like in my parents. My goal was to be a happy, balanced and well-rounded individual. I wanted to feel safe, be productive and to improve my ability to trust others. I wanted to be good to others and become my own person. I also had a strong desire to protect children and animals. A strong need was within me to make up for my mother's atrocities. One way I felt I could do this was, if given the opportunity to become a mother, I would work hard to learn everything I could to be the best I could be. I did not want anyone to fear leaving a child in my care. I realized that any changes I needed or wanted to make would be my responsibility, and mine alone. As we venture into adulthood, we have the opportunity and responsibility to decide how we want to live our life. It's completely up to each of us, individually. I never wanted to use the negative things that happened to me as an excuse not to thrive.

One of the first lessons I had to learn on my personal journey to surviving child abuse was to begin feeling sorry for my mother and to put an end to hating her. I had identified the positive effects of this practice since I was a young teenager. I knew that if I continued to hate Mother, then I would only hurt *myself*. I had been hurt enough in my life without adding more pain. When I thought of all the wonderful opportunities and experiences that Mother had lost over the years, I could no longer hate her. However, more time and inner work was needed before I could find compassion and empathy for Mother. I believe that mastering the ability to feel sorry for her was the first step in this process. About the time I started to feel sorry for my mother, I also tried to learn *not* to feel sorry for myself. This was deeply significant because I could not begin to take responsibility for my own life's path, if living as a victim.

As a child I often felt sorry for myself because I didn't have a loving mother. This feeling was reinforced every time I witnessed the warm and loving relationship that other girls had with their mothers. I saw them everywhere I went. It was *so* very painful to watch. Other girls' mothers were attentive to them and the daughters were always better dressed than I was and acted more feminine. This made me feel even worse about myself and my situation during my childhood. Their moms fussed over them and I could tell they were deeply cared for. I would watch them and wish with all my heart and soul that one day my mother could be that way toward me. I was young and felt at fault because Mother was incapable of having this type of relationship with me. As a child I was sure this had to be my fault and that there was something defective about me. As I grew up, I eventually realized that this was not the case.

Dad was very helpful in teaching me not to feel sorry for myself. He would tell me from time to time, "Tracy, you have a lot to be thankful for. Don't ever feel sorry for yourself because there is always somebody who is worse off than you are." Sometimes he would say, "Tracy, if you feel sorry for yourself, you will only hurt yourself in the long run." I heard different versions of this advice as I grew up. It was always said to me with a great deal of kindness and compassion. By the time I was ten or eleven, I began to understand the wisdom in those words. In my mid-teens I realized that feeling sorry for myself dug me deeper into a hole; although, at times, it seemed completely unavoidable.

Mary Jane had been a substitute mother when I was younger, but that had ended abruptly. I had no mother figure whatsoever during my tween through teen years. Those motherless years were terrible for me. I had no female role model to teach me what a girl needed to know including: my period, wearing pantyhose, shaving my legs and underarms, how to fix my hair, apply makeup, dress, cook, gesture, communicate, move and behave like a woman, etc. I was still learning about these things, mostly by trial and error, in my twenties, thirties and even forties.

When I decided that digging deeper into a state of sadness and despair over my lost childhood made no sense and was counterproductive to my progress -- I started to recover from that loss. As a young adult, I had no idea that the sexual abuse had affected me and didn't give it any thought. It wasn't until later in life that I learned about the affects it had on me and had an opportunity to work on the issues. I did know that following a path of self-pity or acting like a victim was *not* going to give me the strength I needed to heal and the opportunity to have a good life. I also knew that "self-medicating" myself through alcohol or drugs to dull my pain, playing games, sinking into the depths of denial, becoming a drama queen or taking any other negative paths would not do anything to improve my situation or help me to reach my personal goals. I watched others take this path and knew it wasn't right for me. Why would I want to do anything that would make it harder to heal?

As I was figuring out how to do feminine things, like apply makeup, I was also working hard at figuring out how to make my life better. I wondered what would be the best course to take as I settled into my adult years. I wrote things down that I wanted to change and ideas that might help. Certain books were helpful, workbooks were helpful. Mary Jane and I had long talks together and that was helpful. I paid attention to certain family members and friends and decided what I liked and didn't like about their ideas, attitudes and outlook on life. I took new ideas for a "test drive" to see if they would work for me or not. Since childhood, I had a strong will to survive -- no matter what! I knew I was resilient because I always had the ability to bounce back from the horrors of my life. I don't know if this was genetic, environmental, a learned behavior or a combination. As for me, I think it was mostly a learned response; if I was going to survive in that moment of severe abuse I had to bounce back and make internal repairs. I had to learn what worked to calm Mother down and what didn't. Figuring this out quickly was important to my survival. I knew I could not do that if I was busy feeling sorry for myself. As an adult, I was proactive and still maintained a strong will to survive. I was also driven to thrive and become my own person.

Throughout my life I have been blessed with many things. These included my dad who fought in court to keep me safe, people who believed in me and true friends who loved and supported me. Plus, I knew how to be a good and true friend to others. I was nurturing, outgoing and, no matter how Dad tried to dissuade me, I was generous and liked many different kinds of people. Despite the abuses in my childhood and teenage years, I was generally a happy person who enjoyed having fun. I was also fun to be around and others enjoyed my company. I was able to keep and maintain lifelong friendships. The friends I sought were kind and genuine people. I had good relationships with boyfriends and many turned out to be life-long friends. Yes, despite everything I have gone through, I have been truly blessed.

To help offset the horrors of my past, I went out of my way to help others and practiced random acts of kindness towards to-tal strangers. When I saw children who were abused, lost or hurt, I got involved and stood up for them by taking the appropriate action, as I wished somebody had done for me. When children or teenagers had personal problems and sought me out for advice or help, I took them under my wing and did all I could to help them. I excelled and felt gifted at being able to get between two warring factions, calm everyone down and help find a mutually agreeable solution. When someone was grieving, I always came to his or her aid with a tissue and an offer of help. I learned to become an excellent advocate for terminally ill or infirmed pa-tients. Some of these patients were friends and family, and some were complete strangers. In memory of Cinders and her kittens, I also volunteered at the local animal shelter to comfort, care and help adopt stray animals out to good homes. As the years went by, I joined multiple organizations to help children and their families. These actions represented the perfect antidote to many of the negative things that had happened to me. I felt that if I worked on being a kind person and helpful toward others then, perhaps, I could heal some of my hurtful past, while making a positive difference for someone else.

During my twenties and early thirties, I made life-changing decisions from years of observing my family's interactions. The terrors of my childhood gave me other insights, too. I knew my parents were very dysfunctional and I knew the abuse I had grown up with was not a normal situation. As a child, I had witnessed how one parent grating upon the other could turn violent. Their interactions were horrifying to witness; I knew I didn't want to grow up to be like them! I didn't want the tragedy of my childhood to negatively affect my life. As a young adult, I started to take immediate steps to ensure that my life would take a better, healthier and happier path. I saw my family as a chain of dysfunction, violence and abuse. Every family member I knew functioned as a link in this chain and, of course, I functioned as a link as well. I decided to modify my link and break from this chain. I knew I was onto something special with this idea. The idea became a decision, which helped me heal and become my own person. I became very aware of everything I said, how it felt internally and how it affected others. I became aware of my thought patterns and the old tapes of my parents that played in my mind when I was up against life's challenges. The more I thought about this and worked on it, the more convinced I became that this would be the right path for me to follow.

I tried to convince other family members to follow this path as well. I knew this path would require time, personal work, reflection, courage and commitment. Others felt it was a worthwhile pursuit, but they didn't want to make the commitment to change. Sometimes when people get comfortable in a bad situation, it is often easier for them to remain in that situation than to strike out into unknown and unfamiliar territory. It is along the same lines as the old saying: "Better the devil ye know than the devil ye know not." I felt badly for them as my life started to improve and theirs stagnated or declined. I learned that everyone must find their own path and direction in their own time. Some people never find it. It didn't take me long to realize that I was alone in my quest to better my life and myself.

Up to this point in my life, I still felt guilty and somewhat responsible for my parents' actions. It took a long time to learn that I did not cause any of this nor have any responsibility whatsoever for their actions or the actions of other people. Learning this is one thing; internalizing it is another. It was a long and lonely path to grow as a person. Through reflection and a strong personal commitment to succeed, I was able to change and improve upon myself. When I couldn't bring about change on my own, I read books, talked with other survivors of child abuse or found professional help.

When I finally broke away from my family's chain of dysfunction and abuse, some family members began opening up about the abuse that they had experienced as a child. With the amount of improvement I made in my life, I unknowingly challenged them to look at their lives. After I learned the skills that I needed to successfully survive and thrive, I helped my family and some of my friends by raising their awareness of the effects of child abuse and the truth that there is hope to heal from it. I told them about the insights I had learned from reading books, seeking professional help and how this had helped me. It is a personal choice either to remain shackled to past abuses or to work hard to heal and move on.

Certain family members began seeking my opinions about how to deal with the child abuse that they had suffered. I helped them with ideas to deal with the abuse and "games" that they were still being bombarded with as adults. I have helped relatives recognize other choices to escape from the chain of family abuse and dysfunction. I talked with them about the benefits of establishing boundaries with certain family members. Some of my suggestions have been used and some not. It did bring a new way of thinking to others who were stuck in an old mindset.

Other family members, who were the abusers, sought me out to try to convince me that the abuse they had done had never really happened. I knew that game well! I had survived years of my mother's attempts to change the facts. I had witnessed some of their abuses. Changing what I had witnessed was simply not going to happen! When they realized that they could not alter my memories, I noticed a momentary fear in their eyes. Perhaps they were successful at convincing others and feared that I would remind them of what had actually taken place.

Journeying through adulthood I focused on taking personal responsibility for my life decisions. I didn't blame other people for my faults, problems or actions. Throughout my life I had been used as a scapegoat. I was quick to identify people attempting to do that with me and I certainly did not want to do that with others. I disliked people who blamed others for everything under the sun that was wrong with their own lives. I also broke with the notion that I was responsible for other people's actions and would no longer allow people to blame me for problems of their own creation.

I have spent a lifetime working to be the best person I could be and I am still working on it! I did this for myself as well as everyone else in my life. I convinced myself that I would do my best to be a good person and practice kindness toward others, no matter how many bad things had happened to me. No matter how much abuse had come my way, I did my best not to pass it forward. I have heard it said that if you can't pass abuse back to the abuser, then you are somewhat doomed to pass it forward. I made a decision that this was not going to happen with me.

Advancing into adulthood, I learned that I didn't have to please everyone and that the happiness of others depended not on me, but on their ability to maintain positive emotions for themselves. I also learned that everyone is solely responsible for his or her own feelings. I could make myself happy, but I didn't have the ability to make others happy on a long-term basis. We can never make another person feel one way or another; we simply don't have that power over others! I learned that when a person's words and actions conflict, *always* believe their actions! The actions hold truth. Conflicting words are often riddled with lies. I learned to verbalize my needs directly and to set and keep healthy boundaries in relationships. This helped me feel safer interacting with dysfunctional family members and others. Setting boundaries was very important for certain family members and certain friends. If a person forgot or disregarded those boundaries and brought unnecessary drama or pain into my life, I would remind them why I had boundaries in the first place and why I needed to have them respected. If they felt that was unimportant to them and continued disrespecting my limits, then I would become unavailable to them. Later I might re-open the door for contact to see if things had changed for the better. If not, I would regretfully back out of the relationship altogether.

Another thing I learned, which was most helpful, was to live in the present moment. At first, this was very difficult for me to do because I had to focus completely on the present moment and not think about anything else. I taught myself this skill by focusing on the new leaves that came out in springtime. I looked at all of the different leaves and focused on the different shades of green -- thinking of nothing else. I was vigilant as to when the first extraneous thought came into my mind. At first, it was a stretch to do it for just five seconds. However, as I worked on it my skill improved. I thought I was doing marvelously when I reached five minutes! Now I can go all day. It has been a blessing to me as this skill has brought me peace and has helped with many of life's challenges.

I did survive my childhood and lived to thrive without the use of alcohol or drugs to self-medicate the pain. (However, chocolate has always been good!) I put the responsibility for my destiny squarely on my own shoulders and made it my personal responsibility to become a well-adjusted person.

Over the years I have learned a lot about myself, both positive and negative. The abuse, trials and challenges of my youth have given me a strong will to survive, along with the resilience and determination to do so. I also have a strong belief in God and the power of prayer. In times of despair, this had comforted me. Instead of focusing on the abuse I had suffered, I focused on the person I wanted to become. If I failed at something or didn't advance the way that I felt I should, I picked myself up, dusted myself off and carried on down my path. Instead of constantly taking inventory of my scars, I reached higher. I did, and still do, expect more from myself. I found that doing all of the aforementioned, along with learning and using good life skills helped me to heal. I am very comfortable with myself and like the person I have become. My determination and effort at finding my true self was the real journey and worth every step! Now, I enjoy myself and the life I have created.

Reaching Out for Professional Help

There were times, especially when I was working for Dad, when reading books and others' advice were not enough and I realized I needed professional counseling to get over certain hurdles. I went through a couple of psychologists before finding my way to one that would be a good fit for me. I learned that going to a psychologist is not like going to any other type of doctor. With most doctors, you walk in and tell him or her what's wrong and the doctor goes to work to bring about an improvement or a cure. With a psychologist, the patient is the one who has to work to get any benefit from it. "Bitch sessions" go nowhere, are unproductive and a waste of everyone's time. I wasn't much into complaining or wallowing in a pity-pool feeling sorry for myself. I was into working to bring about positive changes in my life. Working through trauma and abuse can be painful. When I worked with a psychologist it was the *hardest* work I had ever done, but it was also the *best* work I had ever done.

Finding a good psychologist takes some interviewing. Most psychologists are not used to this approach, and I have met a few who have had major problems with being interviewed. During the process, I would ignore this and continue interviewing the therapist to see if they were just uncomfortable or if it was a control issue. If it was the latter, he or she was not for me! I interviewed one doctor who became hostile and impatient with my questions. I interviewed another who became extremely suspicious of my questions, and another who opened up and told me her life story, leaving me feeling more like the psychologist than the patient! I did not work with any of these. Most of the other therapists fell somewhere in the acceptable zone. Interviewing psychologists was very important to me. Before I made a commitment to work with one, I wanted to know how the therapist worked and a little about him or her. I wanted to know why the therapist pursued psychology as a career, what he or she liked about being a psychologist and the types of patient issues the therapist had worked with previously. I wanted to make sure I could work with the therapist. Most importantly, I wanted someone I could trust and entrust with my mental health.

During the interview process I would sort out whether the psychologist was supportive or punitive, the average length of time he or she worked with patients and to get a sense of the therapist's personality -- to feel confident that it would jibe with mine. I would try to get the psychologist to talk with me about his or her interest, what method of psychology the therapist used and his or her background in the field. By listening to the therapist, I could usually decide whether he or she would be a good fit for me. I had to feel comfortable with and be able to make a connection with the person. If I could not have those things, then how could I ever trust the therapist enough to work with him or her? I also tried to find psychologists who were *very* experienced. The complexity of my situation and the issues I brought to the table were more complicated than most. I knew I needed a psychologist with experience and education in the areas of my concerns, who was comfortable with different methodologies.

After I found a good fit, working well with a therapist was the most important thing. I would start by identifying what was bothering me and why. Sometimes this was easy to do and sometimes it was a challenge. If I could find the causes for the issues I was experiencing or the memory attached to it, then that was a bonus -- a jump-start out of the gate. The more pieces of the puzzle that I was able to put on the table, the faster the therapy progressed. This saved time and money. When I worked with a therapist, I tried to only bring out relevant information. It bogs the process down if too much non-relevant information is offered.

It is important not to hide things because of embarrassment or guilt. It is also important to answer all questions honestly, no matter how badly it hurts. I guess this is why psychologists are referred to as "shrinks," because looking at the past pains and traumas can hurt as memories unfold. That's why *courage* is so important in therapy.

Over the years, I had to be very courageous to find solutions to my problems. Often when I started to work through an issue, it felt like I was completely lost in the dark. I stumbled around and no matter what I did, I couldn't find my way out. After all, if it were easy to figure out, I wouldn't have needed help! When I was in a situation like this, I realized that this was when a psychologist was most helpful.

Although the patient does most of the work, the psychologist brings a flashlight and a roadmap to the darkness to help the patient find their way. The therapist takes the journey with the patient, but the patient does the internal work with the therapist's guidance to move forward.

Therapy really doesn't make a person feel like they are shrinking: it expands the person's horizons instead! By challenging patients to step outside of their comfort zone -- personal growth, understanding and acceptance happens. Psychologists accompany you on your journey from the darkness into the light. Along the journey the therapist offers new tools, skills, ideas and different ways of looking at the situation. All of it is done in a safe place with baby steps. The therapist is the guide, but the patient has to do the work.

We all have to find our own path and in our own good time. Nobody can tell you what the best choices are for your life or what you should or shouldn't do. It's your life and only you can live it! How you choose to live it is entirely up to you. Just as it was for me.

When people give me suggestions or advice, I have to see whether it is a good fit. I might take it for a spin on a trial basis. If it works, I make it a part of me. When a person I trust gives me advice, they could be giving me a diamond to make my life sparkle, something worthy of consideration.

BEYOND SURVIVAL AND HEALING

Gain and Loss

For many years, I had no contact with Mother. My phone number was never listed because I didn't want to hear from her or have her show up at my front door. Occasionally I would see her around town. Once, while waiting for a stop light to turn green, I was surprised to see her driving the vehicle next to me! She never noticed me. Another time, when I was going out to dinner with my boyfriend, Cary, she was sitting across the room from us. I pointed her out and he immediately suggested we leave. She looked over and gave a little wave. I waved back as she continued her conversation with the man she was with. Cary and I had already ordered our food; she didn't show any interest in coming over to talk with me, so I told Cary that I didn't need to leave. That was her only acknowledgment of me. When my mother and her friend finished their meal, they left without saying a word. Years later, I was in a Mayday Parade that went right past her apartment building. She was out front talking to a woman. I walked in front of her waving the sign I was carrying. It caught her attention and she looked right at me, but she didn't recognize me.

One day in my early thirties, Dad suggested I initiate some contact with my mother by sending her birthday and holiday cards.

"Why would I want to do that?" I asked.

"The reason I went over to my mother's and made her meals for years, was not out of any great love I felt for her, but for the sole purpose of not feeling guilty when she died," Dad said mechanically. "I think you should send your mother cards so you won't feel guilty when she passes away," he added.

I almost started laughing as I assured him not to worry. I would never feel even a little guilty after my mother passed away, cards or no cards!

He was not convinced of this and asked me if I would think about it.

I told him I would, but I didn't give it another thought.

He never brought the subject up again.

The years flew by and I still had no contact with my mother. In the latter 1980s, Dad wanted to retire. I returned to help him sell off the merchandise and close the store. During our going-out-of-business sale, the employee who had molested me as a child stopped by the store. He was walking up the main aisle and I was walking down towards him.

"Hi Tracy!" he said in a friendly manner.

"Hello," I replied coldly.

"You don't remember me, do you?" the man asked, looking a little surprised.

"I know *who* you are, and exactly *what* you are," I spat back.

Our eyes locked.

"Well, I'll just go up to the office and say hi to your dad, then." He mumbled, looking down at the floor.

The molester started to walk past me, but I quickly side stepped to block his path.

"That's a great idea!" I said with mock enthusiasm. "I'll go up to the office with you. We can talk about old times with my dad; tell him all about the things you did to me when I was a child during all those years when you couldn't keep your hands off me!" I finished sarcastically.

He said nothing as he quickly turned and walked towards the front door to leave.

"That's a better idea," I said loudly. "Leave! Get the hell out of here and never return."

The molester ran out the front door.

"Tracy, was that guy bothering you? Are you okay?!"

I turned to see one of our employees standing behind me frowning.

"I wasn't before, but I think I'll be okay now," I answered, half thinking out loud. I looked into his concerned face and wondered how long he had been standing there.

He just kept looking back and forth, first at me and then at the front door. He looked like he was getting angry and I thought for a moment that he might go after the molester.

"Hey! I'm okay. Come on, let's help some of these customers!" I said with a reassuring smile.

He nodded and we went back to work.

I never saw the molester again. I learned many years later that he had passed away.

After the store closed, I became an optician. Nine years later I married Trevor, a Canadian, and moved to Canada to live with him. My mother was not invited to our wedding.

Trevor and I were interested in the possibility of adopting a Canadian child and started to learn about the process. We were horrified and deeply saddened to learn that most children in foster care, available for adoption, had been babies of alcoholic or drug-addicted mothers, or both. The children were born with Fetal Alcohol Syndrome (FAS), or Neonatal Abstinence Syndrome (NAS) and sometimes both. The effect upon the unborn child is horrible. The brain does not develop properly and the baby can be addicted when it's born. With NAS, the newborn has to go through withdrawal and later in life can be easily addicted again. It was heartbreaking to learn that addicted mothers, who knew the consequences, knowingly harmed their children before they were even born! Our hearts broke for these children who had come into the world so damaged. Because of this, attachment disorders or other emotional challenges, children in care were considered "special-needs children." As we learned more through seminars, meetings and assigned readings, I realized how lucky I had been.

Throughout my life, Dad told me that my mother's greatest gift to me was the care she took while she was carrying me. He said my mother had read every book and article available about having a healthy baby. She immediately stopped smoking and made my dad stop too. She stopped having an occasional drink and started taking vitamins. The more I learned about the children in foster care, the more I felt I owed my mother a special thank you for looking out for my best interest, before I was even born. After giving it a lot of thought, I decided to write to her.

I rented a post office box so I didn't have to be concerned about Mother knowing my whereabouts. My letter to her was short and politely written. I thanked her for the things she did to ensure that I had a healthy start in life. There were no questions or anything that would prompt her to reply. I mailed it off to the only address I knew, her old Palo Alto address. I hadn't had contact with my mother for twenty-four years. After visiting with my grandparents, Mother had stopped all contact with family members. I sent my letter fully aware that it might be refused or that she might not reply. I thought her curiosity might get the best of her and at least she would read it. Three weeks later the letter was returned, stamped: "unknown person, no forwarding address." The thought crossed my mind that she might have died. It was a weird feeling to think that she might be dead. I went online to find her and learned that she was still alive, but had moved to Florida. I mailed my letter to the Florida address.

About two weeks later, there was a letter from Mother in my post office box. Holding the envelope while looking at her handwriting brought back terrible memories and feelings from the past. I actually felt a little sick, wondering if opening the letter would expose me to something toxic or hurtful. I asked Trevor to open it for me and watched him silently scan over her words. When he knew the content was okay, he offered to read it aloud. The letter was intelligently written. It was informative and interesting. There was no mention of the past. She indicated that she would like to continue contact with me through letters. I felt apprehensive about this idea, as I had not planned to have regular contact with her. The old anxieties settled in at the very thought.

Trevor and I talked about the pros and cons of continuing contact with my mother. I wondered if her mental condition had improved and what it would mean for me if it hadn't. I was also worried about Trevor and our life together. What if there was a knock on the door one day and she was standing there, on our front porch?! I thought about the stories Aunt Nita and Uncle Les had told me about Mother walking into their house unannounced, undetected and unwanted. My anxiety grew and some of the old nightmares returned.

One day, Trevor and I were talking about the pros and cons of contact with my mother, when he said, "If you want to try corresponding with your mother and it doesn't work out, we could simply close the PO Box."

His suggestion gave me the confidence to try. A couple of weeks had passed when I decided to write back to Mother. My letter to her opened the door to communication. Mother and I wrote back and forth fairly consistently.

Then one day, I received a letter from Mother in which she mentioned the past. Mother stated that the reason she went to Agnews State Hospital was to receive help with her menopause. I didn't want to go into the past with her and told her so. Then a few months later another letter stated that she knew how scared I was, when I was little and had found the knife under her pillow. I knew I had to make a clear boundary with her. I wrote back stating I would keep in contact with her only if her correspondence did not mention the past. After that, her letters always remained the same; informative, light, interesting, fun and upbeat. One day, I got a letter from her promising me that she wouldn't show up on my front porch, if I wanted to use my real address and discontinue the PO Box. I didn't respond to her suggestion, but months later, I did give her my home address. The past was left behind. Through correspondence Mother and I began a new relationship as acquaintances. We wrote to each other regularly. For every letter I wrote, she often wrote two. Within a year, I was actually looking forward to her letters!

I told Dad that I had been in contact with Mother and what had prompted me to write to her. He had once suggested that I send her cards, so I was quite stunned and baffled at his response. He became angry, demanding to know why I would write to her and became even more agitated when I reminded him about his suggestion.

"If you insist on having contact with your mother, I will have to change my will. I will *not* have one dime of my money given to her," Dad exploded.

"Why in the world do you think that I would give *your* money to *my* mother?" I asked bewildered.

"I *know* if she asks you for money you'll send it to her!" Dad accused.

Dad's statements were bizarre and I wondered why he thought that way.

"Dad, I would *never* give my mother any of your money. I would think that you would know this. Why are you getting so upset?" I asked.

Dad fumbled around for an answer but couldn't really come up with one.

I became concerned that something wasn't right with him.

I reminded him that it was his idea for me to have contact with my mother in the first place.

"I KNOW IT WAS!" Dad yelled, completely flustered and not knowing what to say next.

I assured him that I would not get too close to my mother and encouraged him to do whatever he felt was best in regards to his will. He finally calmed down. Looking back, I now realize that this was the beginning of Dad's mental decline. He never did change his will.

As time went by, Mother and I continued writing to each other. The letters remained upbeat and interesting. She was still active, playing tennis and jogging. She required no medication. She enjoyed volunteering at the local library several times a week and still enjoyed reading. Her letters often contained current events and her views about them. Some of her letters included comic strips that she had cut out of her local paper. She had a good sense of humor. In one letter she enclosed a recent snapshot; she looked about sixty years old even though she was eighty-seven!

Dad was showing obvious signs of mild dementia symptoms, which steadily worsened. He became increasingly suspicious about me and started to confuse me with my mother. Some of his past interactions with her were projected onto me. Some of the things she had said to him a long time ago, he now thought that I had said them to him just recently. He was confusing me and my actions with my mother and her actions of long ago.

When Dad's valuable R. Lalique mermaid platter went missing, he blamed me and accused me of taking it or perhaps breaking it and throwing it away. It was simply untrue. I was 1000 miles away in Canada, but that didn't seem to matter. He started telling his friends about his suspicions of me. His friends believed him, which made my interactions with them quite miserable. I was concerned about the cleaning people and their friends who came in and out of his house sometimes without his knowledge. More than once, when Dad left the house, the gardener had caught them trying to enter his home through the doggie door. I pointed this out to Dad, but he felt the cleaning people and their friends were above suspicion. However, I was not!

On top of Dad's dementia issues, it was determined that he needed a heart valve replacement. In his youth and young adulthood he had always been slender. Now he was a *big* man. He weighed over four hundred pounds when he went under the knife. His surgeon was supposed to be very good. However, he had never worked on such a large person before. A couple of days after the surgery, he had to have pacemaker surgery. A day later, the pacemaker had moved and he had to have another surgery to correct its position. Dad was never the same again. Physically it took a very long time for him to heal. He declined mentally and could no longer take care of himself. The dementia had increased in severity. He became angry and unpredictable so in-home care was not an option. He needed to be placed in a nursing home. It was hard to find one that would accept a person of his size.

It was a very difficult time for me knowing that Dad was so unwell and trying to balance time in between living in Canada and being down in California for him. Every time I was in one place, I felt I should be in the other, causing me to feel very torn. Dad's friends no longer liked me or trusted me. Dad's dementia made him think that things were true, which were not. Yet his friends believed everything he was saying and they didn't give me the benefit of the doubt. His friends became hostile towards me and protective of him. A couple of them told me that I was "a thief," "a disgrace" and "a terrible daughter." They told me that they felt they had known me, but after listening to my father, they realized they had never known me at all. It was terrible. The more I tried to correct the situation with my father's friends, the worse it got. I was very alone and no one understood what I was going through.

Things with Dad took a turn for the worse. Physically he was not well and his dementia was quickly becoming more severe. Sometimes, there comes a point when life is no longer good to live. Dad was definitely at this point, and there was no way to turn the clock back or make things better for him. I felt *so* badly for him and *so* horribly alone with this sadness. I lived in Canada, but spent every minute I could with him. If I was at home, I phoned several times a day. Every time I phoned, he pleaded with me to get him out of the nursing home.

"If you love me, you'll get me out of this place!" Dad demanded.

Dad repeated this over and over so quickly that I could rarely get a word in edgewise. Since part of his brain was no longer functioning, he could not be reasoned with. He no longer understood explanations.

At the end of the phone call he would say, "Tracy, I love you, I love you, I love you -- and I *will* always love you -- and I have always loved you."

I had only seconds to tell Dad that I loved him too, before he hung up.

I loved Dad dearly, but there was nothing else I could do to make his situation better. I cried buckets of tears. I have witnessed many horrible things in my life, but one of the worst was watching dementia take Dad's mind away, one day at a time and knowing there was nothing anyone could do to stop it.

From the age of six, Dad had been both a mother and father to me. He was my only parent and often times my rock. Our relationship issues improved immensely after I stopped working for him and we closed the store. Since then we had been close for many years. He used to call me at least once every day to catch up and just shoot the breeze. When I was an optician, most days off were spent at his house helping him or just talking. Sometimes it was stressful, but most of the time it was very nice. Sadly, I realized that those days were now gone forever as his physical, mental and emotional decline swiftly overtook him.

A very wise psychologist once told me, "Nobody will ever be as interested in you as your parents. Parents are interested in every detail of your life, in a way that no other loved one can ever touch." He was right.

In early June 2002, Dad became more unpredictable and very violent. This forced the nursing home to strip his room down to only a mattress, a pillow and bedding, because everything else he would angrily throw at people when they walked through the door.

Then one night in early July, Dad went into the empty dining room and started smashing glass tables and throwing chairs through plate glass windows. A man that worked there tried to stop him and Dad decked him. Another man came and tried to restrain Dad, and he knocked him out. It took five men to restrain him and Dad was in a wheelchair! They took him to the hospital and kept him there for several days. When Dad returned to the nursing home, his health took a sharp decline.

A few days later, I got the call that Dad's organs had started to shut down. Dad's doctor, who had just returned from a long vacation, called me wanting to transport Dad to the emergency room to save his life. I had a very tough decision to make; his doctor's phone call didn't help.

The doctor said *he* could bring my father back.

Knowing this decision was mine alone I asked, "Bring him back to what?"

"Get his organs working again, of course! Once we get him in the emergency room we can start working on him," the doctor stated impatiently, not answering my question.

The doctor was anxious to get going and I was slowing things down.

"I don't think my dad would want that."

Now, the doctor started to get angry with me and told me that I was wasting precious time.

"If you get his organs working again, all you will have accomplished is to trap him in a body that is forcing him to stay in a life he *hates*," I explained. "You may be able to bring his body back, but you cannot bring his mind back. It's all about quality of life and my dad has none of that anymore. I think we should just keep him comfortable and let nature take its course."

The doctor exploded, telling me that I was "*murdering*" my father by stopping his efforts to save him. The doctor's monologue was long and *intense*.

Trevor was listening to the conversation and was also completely shocked by the doctor's comments.

I finally told the doctor that I had to take another call, would call him right back, and hung up.

I was very upset but I knew I couldn't let that get in the way of making this important decision. I thought about my dad and the many talks we had about this subject and his wishes, over the years. I also thought about myself and what I would want if I were in the same situation. I knew that living without some quality of life would be something neither of us would want. Trevor and I talked about it and he agreed with me. Then I called Dad's lawyer and ran it past him. Dad had known this man since he was five years old and was good friends with his family. The lawyer agreed with my decision. I called Mary Jane and she agreed. I called the doctor back and told him to keep my dad in his room and as comfortable as possible -- not to transport him to the hospital.

"My dad is dying and I don't want him to be in a frightening, loud, unfamiliar place with bright lights glaring at him and a lot of strangers poking at him and hurting him during the process," I instructed.

"You will have to live the rest of your life with the knowledge that you killed your dad," the doctor accused. "Your dad will only live for about five days, so if you want to say goodbye you better get down here."

I realized how out of touch the doctor was from being away on vacation for so long.

"I don't think my dad has *five hours*, let alone *five days!* I am leaving for California immediately."

Trevor and I packed and left. Six hours after I hung up with the doctor, Dad passed away in his sleep. I could not get there in time to say goodbye. First, the dementia took away Dad's mind; then death took the rest of him away. And just like that, Dad was gone.

Mother became very supportive. She sent flowers and cards. Often, the cards were humorous, but always in good taste. I started looking forward to the mail and her daily cards, as they were one of the few things that boosted my spirits during that difficult time. She continued sending them every day for a couple of months.

One day, I received a phone call. As the conversation progressed, I thought I was talking with my cousin Gwen, but then I caught a very slight southern sound in some of her words. I knew it couldn't be Gwen. I asked who was calling, and was shocked to hear it was my mother! Neither of us had ever written about expanding our contact. Unexpectedly hearing Mother's voice over the phone for the first time in twenty-nine years was nothing short of a bloodcurdling shock! It was *not* something I was prepared for, it was very eerie and unsettling. I didn't want to share my feelings with her, so I hid them. The content of our conversation was upbeat and interesting. The call lasted over an hour but the unsettling effect lingered for days. However, as time went on, the phone calls became more frequent than the letters. She left the past in the past, respecting my boundaries. As time went on, it became easier to talk with her.

I suggested to Mother to put a claim in for Dad's spousal Social Security. I knew she was eligible for this benefit and that it would help her financially. I had no problem telling her about this as the money belonged to the government, not to Dad.

A year after Dad's death, Trevor and I were divorcing and I moved back to California. Several years later, Mother started dropping hints about coming to Florida to visit with her. At first, I was very hesitant. Then, slowly, I would warm up to the idea, until old memories returned. Then I would decide completely against it. It was like touching a hot stove and then remembering the pain when going to touch it again, even if it was no longer hot. I spoke with friends and family about the possibility of going. Most of my family members were wary of the idea and were ultimately against it. Gwen was very concerned for my well-being and offered to go with me. However, Linda was for me going and also offered to accompany me. Some of my friends were cautious and thought it wasn't a good idea. Mary Jane, however, was for me visiting with my mother. Except for my serious boyfriends, none of my friends or family had any idea the scope of abuse I had endured as a child. For the most part, I was still *keeping Mother's secrets*.

Finding Forgiveness?

When I was younger, I studied the faces of older women and wondered about their life stories. Sometimes I wondered what I would look like when I was their age. Some looked very happy but others looked so bitter, as if they had carried so much anger and resentment throughout their lives that it was forced out and permanently etched into their faces. The expression on these women's faces made them look unapproachable, unfriendly and old beyond their years. I *never* wanted that to happen to me! I also knew that if I couldn't heal my past I could very well end up looking like that. This gave me extra incentive to travel the path of healing, which included forgiveness.

I believe the antidote to resentment and bitterness is forgiveness; but how could I ever forgive my mother and the horrible things she did to me? She had beaten, burned, tortured, drugged, tormented, neglected and abandoned me. She had used me sexually, attempted to brainwash me and alienate me from my dad. She hurt and terrorized the people I loved, tried to destroy my mental health and later attempted to destroy it again, for no other purpose but to get back at my dad. She had made my childhood years into a living hell and even tried to kill me. She *never* admitted to this or said she was sorry for any of it! At times, even thinking of forgiving her was impossible to consider.

When a person holds tight to resentment and bitterness they give their old painful memories power over them. I realized that if I gave my painful memories power they would only hurt me. I would be forcing myself to live in a private hell of my own creation! I would become a prisoner by reliving negative memories and wallowing in negative feelings. Mother was no longer hurting me, why would I want to let her negative old memories do the hurting for her?!

Holding onto bitterness and resentment is corrosive to our very soul. For me, it is the worst form of self-torture because it becomes toxic and seeps into other relationships, including the most important – my relationship with myself. The antidote is forgiveness. I have discovered that forgiving another is a personal choice and, at times, may be very difficult. From my own experience I can tell you that forgiveness is a gift; not for the other person, but for yourself. So it was for me.

I learned that if I had forgiveness in my heart for a person who had wronged me, then I could not possibly harbor resentment and bitterness against that person. The negative feelings held against a person will stop forgiveness from developing, because those feelings are diametrically opposed to the process of forgiveness. As long as I held on to negative feelings toward my mother, I would never find peace. If I chose not to forgive her, then I would be giving her past actions power to continue haunting and hurting me -- even though she had not physically been in my life for many years.

I was never counseled about the path to forgiveness. Over the years, I was given suggestions or exercises for releasing anger and resentment. These included: writing a letter that you never intend to send, popping balloons with the person's name on them, burning a picture of the person or buying inexpensive plates, glasses, bowls, etc. for the purpose of breaking and smashing out my anger. However, none of those things worked for me. I felt frustrated during and after writing a letter I knew I wouldn't be sending; I felt irritated after popping balloons; I felt upset and hollow after breaking things; and I wouldn't suggest burning a picture of *anyone*. I was looking for long-term solutions not short-term "fixes." Maybe these work for some people, but they didn't work for me. How can any of these exercises make anyone feel better in the long run? None of these exercises got to the core of the matter. Recovering and healing requires processing, and that doesn't happen overnight.

Long-term exercises like writing in a journal, or even better, drawing my feelings worked the best for me. The latter was the most time efficient. I have never taken an art class, but the colors and what the drawing was about spoke volumes. The therapist didn't have to read pages of journaling, which saved time and money. All the therapist had to do was look at the drawing and he or she could quickly decipher exactly how I was feeling and what the drawing was about. The therapist would then ask questions about my drawing and my answers helped the therapist to better understand and assist me. Another avenue that worked well for me was thinking about what I really wanted for myself, how I wanted to feel and what I needed to do to achieve this. In some instances, role-playing was also very effective. Visualization was another useful tool.

I began to look at my negative thoughts and the emotions they produced. I visualized my negative thoughts as a floating rope all tangled in decaying garbage and debris. I visualized myself in a motorboat gliding along the calm water's surface. The vessel represented my life and the motor represented my thought process that propelled me forward. I visualized that this entangled, smelly mess fouled my propeller to the point where my motor stopped and would not function. Just like the feelings of betrayal and resentment that stop us from healing and moving forward in life, I was a prisoner, caught in the rotten garbage that was my past. The massive tangle seemed impossible to remove. However, little by little I made headway as I cut the foul mess off the propeller. When it finally came free, I had a choice: haul the horrid mess into my boat or cast it off and be done with it. I decided to cast it off. I watched for a few minutes as it slowly drifted with the tide, then sank into oblivion. I was free to go on my way. That is what forgiveness produced for me: freedom. The freedom from negative feelings, resentment and past pain – all thrown out like yesterday's trash, because that is what they were: trash! Holding onto them is toxic. I still have the memories of what happened, but I no longer have the harmful feelings that go with them, because I chose to forgive.

Some people say it is better to forgive and forget. While I don't believe in harboring or reliving painful feelings and memories, I don't believe in totally forgetting about them either. It was healthy for me to forgive and let go of negative feelings, but not to forget why I had them in the first place. As a child, I had worked diligently to maintain my memories as they were under fire by my mother. As an adult, I set boundaries with her to protect myself. I needed to remember what she had done to me, so I could protect myself from any future pain. What I *didn't do* was hang onto the hurtful emotional responses from those atrocious events. For me, this is the healthiest way to forgive.

As the old negative feelings faded, other feelings replaced them like: confidence, empowerment, courage, self-esteem, self-love, hope, empathy, kindness, acceptance and then finally, forgiveness. As you can see, this is a positive list and it is a happier and healthier way for me to live my life!

Forgiveness takes time. It is a process that cannot be hurried or rushed. It does not come easily and requires dedication to the process. If you try to force forgiveness too quickly it will not be complete or sustainable. As painful memories come up, forgiveness fades or pulls thin like a rubber band stretched to its limit. As memories fade or are processed, the rubber band eases and gives an opportunity for forgiveness to fill the void. Forgiveness is a process of healing and freeing yourself from the emotional wounds you have suffered at the hands of another. To say that I have completely forgiven my mother would be a true statement. However, with some memories, the rubber band still stretches a bit!

Some people are buried so deep in their anger, resentment and bitterness toward others who have inflicted past hurts upon them that forgiveness seems impossible. My Aunt Nita and Uncle Les would agree with this statement. Several years ago, I phoned Uncle Les to talk with him about my mother. Their parents and siblings had all passed on and they were the only ones left. Mother was eager to receive a card from my uncle, if he was interested in contact with her. Given their past, she didn't feel it was appropriate for her to write first. I shared this with him and how healing it had been to write to my mother. I told him that my hope was that he could find some peace by having this kind of communication with her. I assured him that most of her mental issues had improved. I suggested that maybe it was time to leave the past in the past where it belongs.

At first, Uncle Les was very apprehensive about the idea. He began to warm up to it as I spoke about the benefits that forgiveness had brought to me. I reminded him that my mother was a very old woman and she couldn't hurt him anymore. I offered that this was an opportunity to find some peace and, perhaps, closure. I asked him what he would have to lose by just writing a card? He felt it was probably safe and that the idea had merit. I suggested that if he didn't like her response it would be easy enough to discontinue contact. I told him that I thought it would be positive for both he and my mother to heal and that time was running out. I added that I thought that it would make God smile. As I spoke, he became more comfortable and favorable with the idea.

Unknown to me, Aunt Nita was on the extension, and she

didn't like what she was hearing one bit! She took over the conversation and explained to me all the reasons why they should hold resentment toward my mother. I realized that all the good advice I had just given my uncle was going right out the window. I started to talk with my aunt and tried to soften her position. I asked her what would be accomplished by holding resentment and bitterness? Was there some sort of benefit I was missing? She justified her position by telling me about all the hurt my mother had brought to them, back in the early 1960s, almost fifty years ago! As I listened, I heard the resentment, hate and fear building in her words. I tried to soothe and calm her. I tried to circumvent these feelings to get her to look at them in a healing light. I offered her the benefits that forgiveness would bring to their entire family. The best I could do was get my aunt to say she would think about it, which I realized would go nowhere. Although it wasn't her choice to make, she was often the one who decided things for the two of them.

Uncle Les never wrote to my mother. A year-and-a-half later, he passed away. Mother cried and cried when I told her. She sent flowers; it was all she could do. I was sad that Mother and Uncle Les had lost the opportunity to heal their relationship. The next year my Aunt Nita also passed away.

Others may think that forgiving someone is a sign of weakness. I see it as the opposite. Forgiveness can only come from inner strength. There is nothing about the process that is weak. It doesn't mean you have to be friendly with the person, like them, have contact with them or *ever* trust that person again. Forgiving others is a practice of self-love, we do it for ourselves. It was the greatest gift I could have ever given myself, because it healed the negative feelings I held for my mother. Forgiveness helped me to find peace and healing. It is one of the best ways to turn a survivor into a thriver.

Turning Point

In 2010, Mother was ninety-six years old. She still had full mental capacity and was in good health. How long this would last was the question. She wanted to see me. I didn't know how I felt about the idea. However, I knew time was running out. If I was going to visit her, it needed to happen soon. There were many unanswered questions as to whether visiting was a good idea or not. I had many concerns, which I needed to process. I had to work internally to find answers and calm my anxieties. Even though I had forgiven her, I wondered if I could ever really be in the same room with her again. Could I look into her eyes and naturally be pleasant when visiting with her? I wondered how big a toll it would take on me just to be in the same room with her again. In my mind, I visualized being with her and wondered how I would feel and if I could really do it? The visualizations were not going well because I would become anxious at the mere thought of seeing her again, let alone being in the same room with her for an extended period. The old tapes played in my mind warning me that it was unsafe. I wondered if I could visit her without feeling internally or externally forced or coerced. If I visited her, would I go because I actually wanted to see her? There were many questions about visiting with her, the most pressing was whether this would be a healthy thing for me, or not.

It had been over three decades since I had last visited with Mother. I had to constantly remind myself that she seemed greatly improved mentally, which was hard to remember as my mind floated back to the last interactions we had in person. Now she was an old woman in her mid-nineties. She couldn't hurt me anymore, or could she? Of course, physically she would not be able to, but perhaps mentally she still could. If I went to see her, I would have to be constantly on guard. Despite all my concerns, I was moving towards the idea of making the visit; I was not there yet, but closer. A month or two went by during this process.

Then I thought about what it would feel like if I never saw Mother again. I realized that this would be a great loss and didn't like the way that felt. Now I knew I had to visit her. I had to see who she really was in person. I did have many years of mostly positive interactions with her through letters and phone calls. These interactions definitely helped me to feel more comfortable with my decision. Even though I still had concerns, I felt that visiting my mother would ultimately be a good thing for me.

Although I was asking family and friends their opinions about this, I had already pretty much made up my mind. Friends and family came forward with offers to accompany me. It was a tricky task to pick the person to go with me. For many reasons I felt family might not be the best choice. They, too, had a history with my mother and had been affected by her actions. Janie Knudson offered to go with me. She had very little history or experience with my mother and was the best choice.

I became cautiously optimistic about the trip. For most of my life I had sworn I would *never* see my mother again. Now I had reevaluated that and the reasons behind it. Mother and I enjoyed exchanging letters and phone calls. I wondered if seeing her would diminish that relationship. I was concerned about losing this positive aspect of our relationship. I finally concluded that it was worth the risk. When I phoned Mother to tell her, she was overjoyed. We spoke several times before the trip and often she would be in tears telling me how happy she was that I was coming to visit her.

During one of our conversations, Mother became very serious.

"How can you ever forgive me enough to even *stand* to be in the same room with me again?" Mother asked. It was a pivotal question.

"I have forgiven you, Mother, some time ago. I wouldn't be able to visit you if I hadn't," I replied.

She broke down and cried tears of relief.

The trip was planned months in advance. As the departure date neared, my anxiety grew. My feelings of apprehension about being in the same room with Mother were with me constantly. I hadn't thought how it would feel to *walk* into her space on my own free will for the first time ever. When this thought came to me, I worried about it. I had never set foot into her residence. Fear had *always* kept me from doing so. Here I was an adult, and just the *thought* of entering her room set off alarms for my safety.

Thoughts and memories crowded my mind with the life and experiences Mother and I had together, long ago. I began having nightmares and seriously considered canceling the trip on several occasions. The triggers that accompanied these thoughts came from my fear of the unknown. When these thoughts came up, I would gently remind myself of her age and that she could not hurt me anymore. Physically I knew this was true, but emotionally I remained unconvinced.

I had kept my mother's secrets. Because of this, I couldn't share my anxieties, thoughts or feelings with others in my life. When I tried, they would dismiss my concerns by telling me, "That is all in your past. Now you should concentrate on visiting with your mother." Without the background, they truly couldn't understand my concerns or feelings. I realized this was *not* the time to educate them!

A Visit after Thirty-Six Years

A beautiful spring day with bright blue skies accompanied Janie and me to the airport. The day held the promise of a smooth flight and a good start on the trip to Florida. As we boarded the plane, I said a silent prayer asking God to keep me well during the trip, protect me from emotional harm and to help us have a good visit together. I felt God was listening. With tears running down my face, I thought of Dad as I continued to pray that he would forgive me for going on this trip. It had been eight years since he passed away and I was certain he would have been very concerned for my safety and well-being. I thought of my childhood loyalties to Dad and almost laughed out loud realizing that they were still there to a certain degree. The plane roared down the runway. As I stared out the window, the San Francisco Bay Area, where I was born and raised, slowly vanished from view. No turning back now, I was on my way.

In the shadows of my mind lay the uncertainties of the days ahead. My mind turned to past memories with Mother. Thoughts opened and closed like doors leading to another time and place. I realized I was searching for any good time or memory that I had of my mother during our many years of visitation. Sadly, I only recalled one. As the memory unfolded, the sounds of the plane and my surroundings faded into the background. I sat back and let the old black and white movie play in my mind. I was transported back to one visitation when I was fourteen years old. Mother, the third person and I went window-shopping at the local mall. Mother was being wonderful, fun, upbeat and witty. She played no mind games and said nothing bad about my dad or me. She did not mention the past. She made this one visitation joyful for both of us.

I searched my mind to find another good memory from my teenage years and came up empty.

My mind wandered back to the present. I had survived my childhood and was genuinely thriving as an adult. Gratefully, I thought to myself, *I am a genuinely happy person! I feel comfortable and happy with the person I have turned out to be. How can you ask for more than that?* I remember what Mary Jane always said, "You have to live with yourself, *first.*" There is a lot of wisdom in that statement.

I looked out the window as my mind wandered back to my childhood memories. I looked down at my hands remembering the many times she held them over a lit candle or stove burner for what seemed to be an eternity. I looked at Janie sitting in the seat next to me. We were six days apart and had known each other since we were eighteen months old, when my parents purchased the house two doors down from her family. When we were little, Janie and I were best friends. We went separate ways as teens and young adults and now were like sisters again. I had kept my mother's darkest secrets, even from her. Janie, along with most of the other people in my life, had no idea of the horrors I had endured as a child. Although she knew enough to feel I should not see my mother alone and she wanted to be there to help me, if necessary. At some point during the flight I said, "Janie, you should thank God that you weren't born two doors down!"

Janie agreed.

Our hotel room had a great view of the Gulf. Janie and I enjoyed a long walk on the beach. The next morning I was going to see my mother. That night was restless and plagued with vague nightmares. In the morning, I woke with a mild migraine and felt exhausted. Not a great start to the day, but I was not going to let that deter me.

Several times Mother had mentioned that I should wear a suit to visit with her. When I told her I didn't own a suit, she made a big deal about what I should wear. It took some time to get ready, as I changed my outfit several times. The issues and uncertainties of the day loomed over me and, at times, the anxiety was causing my heart to skip and my hands to shake. I took breaks to calm myself by sitting on the balcony looking at the beach and the blue waters of the Gulf. I enjoyed watching the stingrays glide in the shallow water. Janie wanted to get going, but my feet felt like I was slogging through mud. It seemed I couldn't do anything quickly.

New concerns were crowding my mind. I wondered if the visit with Mother would somehow alter me and if the happiness that I had worked so hard to gain and maintain, would somehow diminish or fade away. Would I be the same person after visiting my mother as I was when I woke up this morning? I finally shook off the doubts and worries as I reminded myself that I was in control of the visit and could leave at any time.

Arriving at the nursing home, I became even more anxious. I tried to hide it as Janie and I went up and down the halls looking for my mother, who was not in her room. Finally, we found her sitting alone in a wheelchair. I felt numb and mechanical. I was polite, pleasant and nice to her, as she was to me. I was struck by her beautiful deep blue eyes. Over the years I had assumed her eyes were green like mine, as my dad's were blue. I'd forgotten that Mother had blue eyes and wondered how I could forget such a thing. Then I remembered that I didn't look into her eyes very often. I was too busy watching what her hands were doing. Also, most of my memories, although vivid, were fairly devoid of color.

There were lots of smiles and laughter about little things. Mother was sharp and witty. Her humor broke the tension at times and made the visit easier. During the visit, she continued to honor my boundaries, and the past was never brought up. We enjoyed some delicious homemade peach ice cream, which Mother adored. Later we had lunch with her and went to her room. The visit went fairly well, even though I was on edge most of the time and felt uncomfortable with the multitude of thoughts and feelings running through me. Many things I had forgotten became familiar to me again and I could feel old circuits in my mind and thought processes somehow being re-connected. Every connection seemed to have feelings attached to it. It is hard to explain, but the internal experience was ex-traordinarily exhausting. The first day passed slowly.

One day Janie, Mother and I went to the mall, across the street from the nursing home and did some shopping. My moth-er wanted to try on bras and Janie was in a dressing room *physi-cally* helping her with that. When I popped into the dressing room and saw this, I immediately became *very* uncomfortable. It brought back memories of being forced to touch her there. I couldn't stay in the room and asked Janie to tell her what to do, instead of physically doing it for her. We had a delicious lunch and enjoyable time at a Greek restaurant. We talked about things lighthearted in nature. We joked, laughed and had fun. It was very relaxing. Mother was up on current events and we spoke about them. After lunch, on the way back, we enjoyed the nurs-ing home grounds, which were beautiful with ponds and foun-tains. We spent time outside every day enjoying the grounds.

As the days passed, I noticed things about Mother that I hadn't thought of in years, including her laugh and the way she was always impeccably dressed to look her best. I also noticed the way her head rhythmically shook from time to time. Her hands, even though they were very old, still looked similar to the way I remembered them. I also recognized some of the things that I wished I hadn't. Mother's paranoia was still intact and she told me, throughout the visit, that people were listening to our conversations in or through the walls or on the unused telephone.

Once, when we were alone, Mother said, "It's better if you whisper, because there are people listening."

There were times that she said the government was listening to us as well.

"Mother, we don't have anything interesting enough to say for somebody to go to all that trouble to listen to us. We aren't celebrities or with the government; we're just average people visiting together. No one is interested in what we have to say except us," I replied, on several occasions to disarm her fears.

Mother just smiled and looked at me as if I didn't understand at all.

At times Mother thought the government had even gone so far as to record our conversations! She told me that some of the eavesdroppers could even make themselves invisible and, at times, were standing in the room listening to our conversations. There were people she could see, but I couldn't. Sometimes these comments were made in front of Janie -- and later, Brian.

Not long into the visit, I realized that I had another challenge. The social worker, at the home, didn't like me one bit! I had prepared myself that certain people might think poorly of me for not visiting my mother previously. I knew that some people at the home would make up their minds about me, before they ever met me. I was surprised and grateful it was not more widespread. The staff seemed to have no knowledge of my mother's past or of our history together.

Mother had sold her condominium and bought into the

independent living to end-of-life plan at the nursing home. At first, she had denied my existence to the staff, even though we had been writing and talking on the phone for years. However, in the last year or two, my existence was made known to the staff at the home. Since then, I had been involved with the home, on several occasions, advocating for my mother and helping with decisions for her benefit. I had been her Power of Attorney and designated Health Care Surrogate for years. I was becoming more involved with her medical decisions and was now the "go-to person" when it came to matters regarding Mother's finances, health and welfare. Mother was still mentally sharp and could make her own decisions, but wanted my opinions and was turning more of that responiblity over to me.

On the third or fourth day, staff at the nursing home wanted a meeting with me. I was happy to go to the meeting, which my mother did not attend. As I sat down, the social worker handed me some papers.

"Well, it's nice of you to *finally* come and visit your mother. When she passes away you won't have to feel guilty," the social worker said coldly, in front of others as we were settling down for the meeting.

I decided to make a comment as well. When everyone sat down and introductions were made, I said:

My mother has a good size family and you would think that there would be so many visitors -- it would be like a revolving door. Yet, only one relative, besides me, has ever visited her. There are reasons for this. Although my mother has been sweet and kind during her stay in the nursing section of the home, she has not always been this way. I hope her kindness towards others continues. Other employees here at the independent living section of the home have had the opposite experience with my mother and she has been very negative towards some of them. This other side of her is the reason why relatives don't come to visit. She hasn't always been sweet and kind.

I looked at the social worker and noticed that her face had softened significantly. Each department: nursing, physical therapy, nutrition, etc., gave a report on my mother. We had our meeting and I thanked each one for taking good care of her.

On the fourth or fifth day of the visit, I realized I wasn't very happy. Something was wrong, but I couldn't put my finger on it. I was upset, but didn't know why. I was worried that something like this might happen during the visit. Mother was pushing a button that I could not immediately identify. I finally realized that she was saying things like, "I could just hit you," or "I want to box your ears off," or other remarks expressing her intentions to do physical harm to me. It slipped under the radar because I was often distracted by her quick comments immediately followed by laughing them into a joke. Then she immediately changed the subject. These comments came unexpectedly and were not connected to anything we were discussing. When I realized what was happening, I became very upset and told Janie on the way back to the hotel that if she does it again I will end the visit. Janie wasn't aware that my mother was doing this and said she would listen for it when we were together again.

The next day we were outside when my mother said to me, "Oh, I could just spank you until you're black and blue." I immediately turned to say something to Mother about it and saw in an instant that she realized I was unhappy with her. Before I could say a word, Mother made it into a joke, laughed and started a conversation with a woman who was passing by. It was all lightning quick. These events happened so fast that they were almost simultaneous. By the time the woman had moved on, so had my opportunity to discuss her comment. During the remainder of the visit, she never made another comment like it.

A lady took care of Mother's bills and tax returns. I had an opportunity to meet alone with her and immediately liked her. She told me that sometimes her children come along and she leaves them unattended with my mother for short periods; I became very concerned for her children's safety.

"I hope you will stay in the room with my mother when your children are present and not leave them alone with her." It was obvious she was curious, so I continued, "In the past my mother has not been very good with children. She could be just fine and predictable one minute, but the opposite the next. Please stay in the room and don't leave your children unattended with her."

The lady thought for a moment and offered, "I help people in the nursing home by paying their bills, doing their taxes and running errands for them. I've been doing this for twenty years and I always choose the people with whom I work. I was introduced to your mother while she was being transferred to the skilled nursing center. As you know, she came from the independent living section. I was warned that she was difficult to deal with and I almost didn't take her on. I decided to, on a trial basis. Since she has been in the skilled nursing center, she has changed into the sweetest person you could ever hope to meet. It has been a joy to work with her. I will keep in mind not to leave my children alone with her."

"Thank you," I replied, "and thank you for not asking a bunch of questions about her past."

"Your mother goes to church every Sunday," the lady said, "she never talks about her past. But one day, unexpectedly, she said, 'It will take ten lifetimes of forgiveness to make up for the things I have done in this lifetime.' I was shocked by the statement and tried to get more information from her, but she avoided my questions, so I dropped it."

Another lady, who worked with Mother, when she was in independent living, did not have good experiences with her. She told me that my mother disliked her and didn't trust her.

"Your mother doesn't like me and has accused me of stealing her money," the lady said sadly. "However, we can't give her cash because she loses it, and sometimes she gets confused and doesn't remember we gave it to her. If you want me to give her the cash, I will. However, I hold cash for many of the patients in the nursing center and in all the years of working here, there has never been a problem."

I told her I was sorry for the suspicions and the problems she was experiencing with my mother. I asked her to please continue holding cash for my mother and I reassured her that I felt she was an honest person. I promised her I would talk with my mother about the situation.

Later, when I broached the subject, Mother became very unhappy and agitated.

"I don't trust that woman. *She steals!*" Mother ranted.

"No Mother, she is doing you a favor by holding your money," I explained. "She is not stealing anything! She showed me all of the records. I believe she's a very honest person and has been very hurt by the way you have interacted with her and accused her. I think you should try to be nicer to her. She doesn't have to hold your money for you. It would be much harder if you had to make a withdrawal from the bank every time you want to go shopping." No matter what I said or how I explained the reality of the situation to Mother, I could not change her viewpoint.

It was a full and busy week. On Saturday, Brian flew in and joined Janie and me. Brian and I were going to start a vacation in Florida, after the visit with my mother was over. Janie was going to fly home.

On Mother's Day morning, Janie, Brian and I went to the Crystal River to swim with the manatees. My mind was on the events to come later that day when we planned to visit my mother. I hadn't spent a Mother's Day with her since I was five years old, forty-eight years ago. I was anxious and couldn't relax. Although my mother had never really been a true mother to me, I was planning to make *this* Mother's Day great for her with a nice card, flowers, cake and balloons. I was a little worried about pulling it off with sincerity. I was searching for any kind of sign that, somehow, it would be all right.

Crystal River was a very cool place. The river was lined with willow trees and ran along the backyards of neighborhood homes. Most of it was green and lush. The first place we stopped, a manatee surfaced and looked up at us in the boat. Then she dove down and disappeared. When she resurfaced, her baby was balancing on her head, neck and back. It was obvious that she was showing us her "pride and joy," a little Mother's Day treat! It was a good sign. After that, I knew spending Mother's Day with my mother would be just fine.

With all the trimmings, Brian, Janie and I arrived at the nursing home in the early afternoon. Mother was put out that we hadn't been there in the morning, but she soon calmed down. She was happy with the card and enjoyed her piece of cake. She didn't say much about it, but I think she appreciated it. Janie asked my mother if she would like to go through her clothes, so Janie could sew any items that needed mending. I thought it was very kind of her to offer. She and my mother found a few items and Janie worked on them while we visited. Later, we spent the rest of the afternoon outside enjoying the grounds. Then we had dinner together in the dining room.

The next day Janie would fly home and Brian and I would start our vacation.

Overall, it was a pretty good visit. At times, I was extremely busy with meetings at the nursing home, reviewing tax returns, setting up accounts, trying to make sense out of some of her paperwork, making adjustments to better meet her needs and discussing her last wishes. Talking with Mother about her last wishes was not easy, as she was very evasive. I let the subject go and she finally came to me with what she wanted.

The visit was, at times, very stressful. Sometimes, I felt I was on a treadmill racing around to get things done. At times, I didn't know how I felt about being with her again. When the visit was over, I was exhausted, stressed and on edge. I had no idea that I was so emotionally spent. There was no downtime to process, recover, recoup and settle before Brian and I started our vacation. Looking back, it would have been a good idea for me to have had a week alone between the visit and the vacation.

On Monday morning, before we left town, Brian and I went to say goodbye to Mother. She had just finished physical therapy when I told her that Brian and I were leaving.

"Where are you going?" Mother asked.

"We are going to drive through the Everglades and then down to Key West," I replied. "I'll call you in a day or two."

Mother didn't react one way or the other about our visit coming to an end. She acted as if I was just going to run an errand and would be right back. Yet, she fully understood I was leaving and would most likely not be back. It was similar to the lack of attachment she demonstrated at our first visitation, when I was seven years old and she hadn't seen me for more than a year.

I had arranged for my cousin Linda, Mother's niece, to visit with her for a week. Linda was due to arrive in a few hours. She had told me some time ago that she would like one more opportunity to see my mother. She hadn't seen her for many decades. We thought it would be a good idea for her to visit directly after Brian and I left. I thought Linda's visit would help ease my mother's feelings, if she were upset by my leaving.

As it turned out, Mother was not upset in the slightest. She didn't ask when I would be back or whether she would ever see me again. The finality sunk in as I stood in front of her. I was certain this would be the last time I would see her.

"Goodbye, Mother, and take care," I said with mixed feelings.

"Goodbye," she replied with no emotion.

Walking to the car, I stopped several times to look back at the windows to Mother's bedroom. I was torn about leaving. Did I forget about anything I was planning to do for her while I was here? Searching my mind, I came up with nothing. She was so old and frail, but she was happy living here and that comforted me. The facility was the best I'd ever seen and the staff was fantastic. I took a few more steps toward the car and then looked back again. Brian said nothing and patiently looked on, waiting for me. I realized how sad I felt about leaving. I thought about all the quality time and mother-daughter moments that were stolen from us by her illness. Again, I searched my mind, but there was nothing more that needed to be said or done. With a heavy heart, I got in the passenger seat.

Brian looked at me thoughtfully and said softly, "I know this is hard. If you want to stay longer, we can."

I thought about that for a moment and replied, "No, it's time to leave. Linda will be here soon and it's time for us to start our vacation."

Brian nodded, started the car and we drove away.

Twenty-nine years old

With dogs Kona and Harley

Janie, Tracy, Brian and Mother

Epilogue

On our vacation, Brian and I visited the Hemingway House in Key West, Florida. Walking the lush grounds and gardens, I realized what a wonderful place it would be to write. There was a feeling of serenity that was very inviting. In a way, it felt like time stood still. At the gate, I asked if people came here to write and was told that they did. In fact, many popular books had been written on this property, but the staff was not allowed to give the titles. In the gift shop, I found a fridge magnet, which I liked. I bought it and took it home to my fridge. The words inspired me.

Soon after Brian and I returned from Florida, I sat down and wrote the beginning of the first chapter. The words flowed easily. Afterwards, I sat back and wondered where this was going and why I would want to write about my life. I put it away for a while to think and pray. It wasn't long before I had my answer: *Because I had survived and was thriving, I had a responsibility to share my story for the greater good.* I believed my story could enlighten readers, while supporting others. I believed it to be a worthwhile endeavor and decided to take the journey.

I had no personal need to revisit the horrors of my childhood, as that was all settled inside me and resolved a long time ago. If sharing my story could help others, it would be worth the effort. I continued to write.

Up to the time I visited with Mother, I would often phone her and share what I had been writing. She was interested and often asked me to read it to her. I hadn't offered to share any of my writing since returning home and working on my story, although Mother and I spoke often. One day, Mother called.

"Have you been writing lately?" Mother asked.

"Yes."

"You haven't been sharing your writing with me. Could that be because you are writing about *us?*"

The moment of truth and the talk I had been dreading was at hand. I confidently stated, "Yes Mother, I have been."

"Why?"

I took a deep breath.

"Because I think that our past and our journey is worth sharing. It is an important story. I am thriving and our relationship has mended. I feel a strong responsibility to share our story to enlighten and help others," I explained, preparing myself for a negative response.

She had always been so secretive when I was a child and she threatened me to get me to keep those secrets. When I visited with her, she was paranoid about invisible people listening to our conversations. It was only a couple years back that she had stopped denying my existence to others.

Therefore, I was completely *amazed* when Mother replied, "I think your heart is in the right place and I think you should write the book for the reasons you have stated. But, I *never* want you to read any part of it to me and I *never* want to read it."

I told her I would respect her wishes.

Mother's response demonstrated to me how far she had come and how much she had healed. I was very proud of her.

A little over a year later, Mother started showing signs of mild dementia. She knew she was starting to deteriorate mentally and shared her fears with me. I listened and supported her while talking together as often as possible. She had enjoyed such a brilliant mind that it was sad to see her decline, as she lost her cognitive abilities. Unlike Dad going the way of anger and violence, she maintained her sweet and kind side in interactions with others. As time went on, her dementia worsened.

Mother is now over 100 years old. For the last three years, I have made all her care decisions and attended all nursing home meetings by phone. Her dementia has advanced and she has been unable to recognize me for the past two years.

I'm not sure that Mother and I ever truly found a mother-daughter relationship. However, we certainly built a *special* and wonderfully supportive relationship over the years, through our phone conversations and letters. She never tried to tell me what to do with my life or give me much in the way of "motherly advice." Looking back, I think she realized I didn't need it, or maybe she felt that that opportunity had long since passed. She was interested in my life, and supported me in the things I wanted to do or wanted to accomplish. She never criticized or tore me down, as she had done when I was younger. In fact, it was quite the opposite; in my adult years she encouraged me. Once, when I was going through a difficult time she said, "Tracy, you are my only chick and I am behind you all the way!" She was especially supportive and enthusiastic about my writing, creativity and music. Sometimes we would talk on the phone for hours and, at times, she would ask me to play something on the piano or flute for her. I am certainly glad I made contact with her and have the multitude of letters she wrote to me over the years. She signed them off saying things like, "God bless you and watch after you, my lovely child. Remember, I'm as near as your phone. Much love, Mother" or "I love and pray for you, God bless! Mother" or simply, "Love, Mother."

Throughout my childhood, Dad had always said, "Tracy, your mother loves you dearly. Her illness gets in the way of her ability to show it and express it to you. But, have no doubts, your mother has always loved you."

Finally, I know in my heart that Dad was right.

Resources for Support and Assistance

National Child Abuse Hotline or Child Help USA (also serving Canada):

- Crisis hotline for the prevention of child abuse. Professional crisis counselors are available **24 hours a day, 7 days a week.** Interpreters are also available to assist in 170 languages. They serve the United States, its territories, and Canada. All calls are confidential and **anonymous.** They offer many programs and services including residential treatment services, children's advocacy centers; therapeutic foster care; group homes; child abuse prevention and education and training.
- Phone: 1-800-422-4453
- www.childhelp-usa.com

Child Abuse Prevention Association:

- Website: www.childabuseprevention.org
- Services offered include: education, family support and counseling.

Child Molestation Research and Prevention:
- Offers resources, help and information.
- Website: www.childmolestationandprevention.org

Stop It Now:
- Child sexual abuse prevention help.
- Website: www.stopitnow.org
- Helpline (Monday -- Friday, 9AM -- 5PM EST): 1-888-PREVENT.
  » This is a confidential helpline for adults who are at risk of sexually abusing a child and for friends and family of sexual abusers as well as for victims, and for parents of children with sexual behavior problems. This helpline is available. Resources offered include: answering questions about child sexual abuse, specialized information, guidance and support.

National Suicide Prevention Lifeline:
- Phone: 1-800-273-8255 (TALK) anytime, 24/7.
- Website: www.suicidepreventionlifeline.org

Parental Alienation Awareness Organization:
- Website: www.paawareness.org

<u>Child Abuse Hotlines in other Counties:</u>

United Kingdom:
- Website: www.help@nspcc.org.uk
- The phone hotline is open 24/7. They offer services and will accept anonymous callers. Phone: 0808 800 5000 or Tex: 88858.

UK and Ireland -- Stop it Now:
- Child *sexual* abuse prevention helpline.
- Website: www.stopitnow.org.uk
- Helpline, toll free, (9AM -- 9PM Mondays -- Thursdays or 9AM -- 5PM Fridays): 0808 1000 900
- Email: help@stopitnow.org.uk

Australia:
- Website: www.childabuseprevention.com.au
- Phone (9AM -- 5PM, Monday -- Friday, closed on public holidays): 1800 688 009. Toll free from anywhere in Australia. Services include: resources, family support, group support, support playgroups and parent training.

New Zealand:
- Website: www.familyworks.org.nz
- Phone (9AM -- 11PM, 7 days a week): 0800 456 450

Contact the Author

If you have questions, comments
or wish to contact the author,
please write to the following address:

Tracy May
1111 W. El Camino Real, unit 109 -- 229
Sunnyvale, CA 94087
USA

Website:
keepingmotherssecrets.com